KU

Please return/renew this item by the last date shown

**Herefordshire
Libraries**

**Herefordshire
Council**

'An extraordinary book' Cory Doctorow

D1330125

7700000 87 1

PERMANENT RECORD

Edward Snowden was born in Elizabeth City, North Carolina, and grew up in the shadow of Fort Meade. A systems engineer by training, he served as an officer of the Central Intelligence Agency, and worked as a contractor for the National Security Agency. He has received numerous awards for his public service, including the Right Livelihood Award, the German Whistleblower Prize, the Ridenhour Prize for Truth-Telling, and the Carl von Ossietzky Medal from the International League for Human Rights. Currently, he serves as president of the board of directors of the Freedom of the Press Foundation.

PERMANENT RECORD

EDWARD SNOWDEN

PAN BOOKS

First published 2019 by Metropolitan Books, Henry Holt and Company, LLC

First published in the UK 2019 by Macmillan

This paperback edition first published 2020 by Pan Books
an imprint of Pan Macmillan
The Smithson, 6 Briset Street, London EC1M 5NR
Associated companies throughout the world
www.panmacmillan.com

ISBN 978-1-5290-3569-8

1 3 5 7 9 8 6 4 2

A CIP catalogue record for this book is available from the British Library.

Printed and bound by CPI Group (UK) Ltd, Croydon CR0 4YY

Visit www.panmacmillan.com to read more about all our books
and to buy them. You will also find features, author interviews and
news of any author events, and you can sign up for e-newsletters
so that you're always first to hear about our new releases.

To L

CONTENTS

Preface   1

PART ONE

1. Looking Through the Window   11
2. The Invisible Wall   19
3. Beltway Boy   33
4. American Online   39
5. Hacking   51
6. Incomplete   61
7. 9/11   69
8. 9/12   77
9. X-Rays   83
10. Cleared and in Love   93

PART TWO

11. The System   105
12. *Homo contractus*   111

13. Indoc 121

14. The Count of the Hill 137

15. Geneva 149

16. Tokyo 163

17. Home on the Cloud 187

18. On the Couch 203

PART THREE

19. The Tunnel 213

20. Heartbeat 219

21. Whistleblowing 227

22. Fourth Estate 241

23. Read, Write, Execute 255

24. Encrypt 265

25. The Boy 275

26. Hong Kong 287

27. Moscow 299

28. From the Diaries of Lindsay Mills 311

29. Love and Exile 325

Acknowledgments 337

PERMANENT RECORD

Preface

My name is Edward Joseph Snowden. I used to work for the government, but now I work for the public. It took me nearly three decades to recognize that there was a distinction, and when I did, it got me into a bit of trouble at the office. As a result, I now spend my time trying to protect the public from the person I used to be—a spy for the Central Intelligence Agency (CIA) and National Security Agency (NSA), just another young technologist out to build what I was sure would be a better world.

My career in the American Intelligence Community (IC) only lasted a short seven years, which I'm surprised to realize is just one year longer than the time I've spent since in exile in a country that wasn't my choice. During that seven-year stint, however, I participated in the most significant change in the history of American espionage—the change from the targeted surveillance of individuals to the mass surveillance of entire populations. I helped make it technologically feasible for a single government to collect all the world's digital communications, store them for ages, and search through them at will.

After 9/11, the IC was racked with guilt for failing to protect

America, for letting the most devastating and destructive attack on the country since Pearl Harbor occur on its watch. In response, its leaders sought to build a system that would prevent them from being caught off guard ever again. At its foundation was to be technology, a foreign thing to their army of political science majors and masters of business administration. The doors to the most secretive intelligence agencies were flung wide open to young technologists like myself. And so the geek inherited the earth.

If I knew anything back then, I knew computers, so I rose quickly. At twenty-two, I got my first top secret clearance from the NSA, for a position at the very bottom of the org chart. Less than a year later, I was at the CIA, as a systems engineer with sprawling access to some of the most sensitive networks on the planet. The only adult supervision was a guy who spent his shifts reading paperbacks by Robert Ludlum and Tom Clancy. The agencies were breaking all of their own rules in their quest to hire technical talent. They'd normally never hire anybody without a bachelor's degree, or later at least an associate's, neither of which I had. By all rights, I should never have even been let into the building.

From 2007 to 2009, I was stationed at the US Embassy in Geneva as one of the rare technologists deployed under diplomatic cover, tasked with bringing the CIA into the future by bringing its European stations online, digitizing and automating the network by which the US government spied. My generation did more than reengineer the work of intelligence; we entirely redefined what intelligence was. For us, it was not about clandestine meetings or dead drops, but about data.

By age twenty-six, I was a nominal employee of Dell, but once again working for the NSA. Contracting had become my cover, as it was for nearly all the tech-inclined spies of my cohort. I was sent to Japan, where I helped to design what amounted to the agency's global backup—a massive covert network that ensured that even if the NSA's headquarters was reduced to ash in a nuclear blast, no data would ever be lost. At the time, I didn't realize that engineering a system that would keep a permanent record of everyone's life was a tragic mistake.

I came back to the States at age twenty-eight, and received a stratospheric promotion to the technical liaison team handling Dell's relationship with the CIA. My job was to sit down with the heads of the technical divisions of the CIA in order to design and sell the solution to any problem that they could imagine. My team helped the agency build a new type of computing architecture—a "cloud," the first technology that enabled every agent, no matter where they were physically located, to access and search any data they needed, no matter the distance.

In sum, a job managing and connecting the flow of intelligence gave way to a job figuring out how to store it forever, which in turn gave way to a job making sure it was universally available and searchable. These projects came into focus for me in Hawaii, where I moved to take a new contract with the NSA at the age of twenty-nine. Up until then, I'd been laboring under the doctrine of Need to Know, unable to understand the cumulative purpose behind my specialized, compartmentalized tasks. It was only in paradise that I was finally in a position to see how all my work fit together, meshing like the gears of a giant machine to form a system of global mass surveillance.

Deep in a tunnel under a pineapple field—a subterranean Pearl Harbor–era former airplane factory—I sat at a terminal from which I had practically unlimited access to the communications of nearly every man, woman, and child on earth who'd ever dialed a phone or touched a computer. Among those people were about 320 million of my fellow American citizens, who in the regular conduct of their everyday lives were being surveilled in gross contravention of not just the Constitution of the United States, but the basic values of any free society.

The reason you're reading this book is that I did a dangerous thing for a man in my position: I decided to tell the truth. I collected internal IC documents that gave evidence of the US government's lawbreaking and turned them over to journalists, who vetted and published them to a scandalized world.

This book is about what led up to that decision, the moral and ethical principles that informed it, and how they came to be—which means that it's also about my life.

What makes a life? More than what we say; more, even, than what we do. A life is also what we love, and what we believe in. For me, what I love and believe in the most is connection, human connection, and the technologies by which that is achieved. Those technologies include books, of course. But for my generation, connection has largely meant the Internet.

Before you recoil, knowing well the toxic madness that infests that hive in our time, understand that for me, when I came to know it, the Internet was a very different thing. It was a friend, and a parent. It was a community without border or limit, one voice and millions, a common frontier that had been settled but not exploited by diverse tribes living amicably enough side by side, each member of which was free to choose their own name and history and customs. Everyone wore masks, and yet this culture of anonymity-through-polyonymy produced more truth than falsehood, because it was creative and cooperative rather than commercial and competitive. Certainly, there was conflict, but it was outweighed by goodwill and good feelings—the true pioneering spirit.

You will understand, then, when I say that the Internet of today is unrecognizable. It's worth noting that this change has been a conscious choice, the result of a systematic effort on the part of a privileged few. The early rush to turn commerce into e-commerce quickly led to a bubble, and then, just after the turn of the millennium, to a collapse. After that, companies realized that people who went online were far less interested in spending than in sharing, and that the human connection the Internet made possible could be monetized. If most of what people wanted to do online was to be able to tell their family, friends, and strangers what they were up to, and to be told what their family, friends, and strangers were up to in return, then all companies had to do was figure out how to put themselves in the middle of those social exchanges and turn them into profit.

This was the beginning of surveillance capitalism, and the end of the Internet as I knew it.

Now, it was the creative Web that collapsed, as countless beautiful, difficult, individualistic websites were shuttered. The promise of convenience led people to exchange their personal sites—which demanded constant and laborious upkeep—for a Facebook page and a Gmail account. The appearance of ownership was easy to mistake for the reality of it. Few of us understood it at the time, but none of the things that we'd go on to share would belong to us anymore. The successors to the e-commerce companies that had failed because they couldn't find anything we were interested in buying now had a new product to sell.

That new product was Us.

Our attention, our activities, our locations, our desires—everything about us that we revealed, knowingly or not, was being surveilled and sold in secret, so as to delay the inevitable feeling of violation that is, for most of us, coming only now. And this surveillance would go on to be actively encouraged, and even funded by an army of governments greedy for the vast volume of intelligence they would gain. Aside from log-ins and financial transactions, hardly any online communications were encrypted in the early twenty-aughts, which meant that in many cases governments didn't even need to bother approaching the companies in order to know what their customers were doing. They could just spy on the world without telling a soul.

The American government, in total disregard of its founding charter, fell victim to precisely this temptation, and once it had tasted the fruit of this poisonous tree it became gripped by an unrelenting fever. In secret, it assumed the power of mass surveillance, an authority that by definition afflicts the innocent far more than the guilty.

It was only when I came to a fuller understanding of this surveillance and its harms that I became haunted by the awareness
that we the public—the public of not just one country but of all
the world—had never been granted a vote or even a chance to
voice our opinion in this process. The system of near-universal
surveillance had been set up not just without our consent, but in
a way that deliberately hid every aspect of its programs from our
knowledge. At every step, the changing procedures and their consequences were kept from everyone, including most lawmakers.
To whom could I turn? Who could I talk to? Even to whisper the
truth, even to a lawyer or a judge or to Congress, had been made
so severe a felony that just a basic outlining of the broadest facts
would invite a lifetime sentence in a federal cell.

I was lost, and fell into a dark mood while I struggled with my
conscience. I love my country, and I believe in public service—my
whole family, my whole family line for centuries, is filled with men
and women who have spent their lives serving this country and its
citizens. I myself had sworn an oath of service not to an agency,
nor even a government, but to the public, in support and defense
of the Constitution, whose guarantee of civil liberties had been so
flagrantly violated. Now I was more than part of that violation:
I was party to it. All of that work, all of those years—who was I
working for? How was I to balance my contract of secrecy with
the agencies that employed me and the oath I'd sworn to my country's founding principles? To whom, or what, did I owe the greater
allegiance? At what point was I morally obliged to break the law?

Reflecting on those principles brought me my answers. I realized that coming forward and disclosing to journalists the extent
of my country's abuses wouldn't be advocating for anything radical, like the destruction of the government, or even of the IC. It
would be a return to the pursuit of the government's, and the IC's,
own stated ideals.

The freedom of a country can only be measured by its respect
for the rights of its citizens, and it's my conviction that these rights
are in fact limitations of state power that define exactly where

and when a government may not infringe into that domain of personal or individual freedoms that during the American Revolution was called "liberty" and during the Internet Revolution is called "privacy."

It's been six years since I came forward because I witnessed a decline in the commitment of so-called advanced governments throughout the world to protecting this privacy, which I regard—and the United Nations regards—as a fundamental human right. In the span of those years, however, this decline has only continued as democracies regress into authoritarian populism. Nowhere has this regression been more apparent than in the relationship of governments to the press.

The attempts by elected officials to delegitimize journalism have been aided and abetted by a full-on assault on the principle of truth. What is real is being purposefully conflated with what is fake, through technologies that are capable of scaling that conflation into unprecedented global confusion.

I know this process intimately enough, because the creation of irreality has always been the Intelligence Community's darkest art. The same agencies that, over the span of my career alone, had manipulated intelligence to create a pretext for war—and used illegal policies and a shadow judiciary to permit kidnapping as "extraordinary rendition," torture as "enhanced interrogation," and mass surveillance as "bulk collection"—didn't hesitate for a moment to call me a Chinese double agent, a Russian triple agent, and worse: "a millennial."

They were able to say so much, and so freely, in large part because I refused to defend myself. From the moment I came forward to the present, I was resolute about never revealing any details of my personal life that might cause further distress to my family and friends, who were already suffering enough for my principles.

It was out of a concern for increasing that suffering that I hesitated to write this book. Ultimately, the decision to come forward with evidence of government wrongdoing was easier for me to make than the decision, here, to give an account of my life. The abuses I witnessed demanded action, but no one writes a memoir because they're unable to resist the dictates of their conscience. This is why I have tried to seek the permission of every family member, friend, and colleague who is named, or otherwise publicly identifiable, in these pages.

Just as I refuse to presume to be the sole arbiter of another's privacy, I never thought that I alone should be able to choose which of my country's secrets should be made known to the public and which should not. That is why I disclosed the government's documents only to journalists. In fact, the number of documents that I disclosed directly to the public is zero.

I believe, just as those journalists believe, that a government may keep some information concealed. Even the most transparent democracy in the world may be allowed to classify, for example, the identity of its undercover agents and the movements of its troops in the field. This book includes no such secrets.

To give an account of my life while protecting the privacy of my loved ones and not exposing legitimate government secrets is no simple task, but it is my task. Between those two responsibilities— that is where to find me.

PART ONE

1

Looking Through the Window

The first thing I ever hacked was bedtime.

It felt unfair, being forced by my parents to go to sleep—before they went to sleep, before my sister went to sleep, when I wasn't even tired. Life's first little injustice.

Many of the first 2,000 or so nights of my life ended in civil disobedience: crying, begging, bargaining, until—on night 2,193, the night I turned six years old—I discovered direct action. The authorities weren't interested in calls for reform, and I wasn't born yesterday. I had just had one of the best days of my young life, complete with friends, a party, and even gifts, and I wasn't about to let it end just because everyone else had to go home. So I went about covertly resetting all the clocks in the house by several hours. The microwave's clock was easier than the stove's to roll back, if only because it was easier to reach.

When the authorities—in their unlimited ignorance—failed to notice, I was mad with power, galloping laps around the living room. I, the master of time, would never again be sent to bed. I was free. And so it was that I fell asleep on the floor, having finally seen the sunset on June 21, the summer solstice, the longest day of the year. When I awoke, the clocks in the house once again matched my father's watch.

IF ANYBODY BOTHERED to set a watch today, how would they know what to set it to? If you're like most people these days, you'd set it to the time on your smartphone. But if you look at your phone, and I mean really look at it, burrowing deep through its menus into its settings, you'll eventually see that the phone's time is "automatically set." Every so often, your phone quietly—silently— asks your service provider's network, "Hey, do you have the time?" That network, in turn, asks a bigger network, which asks an even bigger network, and so on through a great succession of towers and wires until the request reaches one of the true masters of time, a Network Time Server run by or referenced against the atomic clocks kept at places like the National Institute of Standards and Technology in the United States, the Federal Institute of Meteorology and Climatology in Switzerland, and the National Institute of Information and Communications Technology in Japan. That long invisible journey, accomplished in a fraction of a second, is why you don't see a blinking 12:00 on your phone's screen every time you power it up again after its battery runs out.

I was born in 1983, at the end of the world in which people set the time for themselves. That was the year that the US Department of Defense split its internal system of interconnected computers in half, creating one network for the use of the defense establishment, called MILNET, and another network for the public, called the Internet. Before the year was out, new rules defined the boundaries of this virtual space, giving rise to the Domain Name System that we still use today—the .govs, .mils, .edus, and, of course, .coms—and the country codes assigned to the rest of the world: .uk, .de, .fr, .cn, .ru, and so on. Already, my country (and so I) had an advantage, an edge. And yet it would be another six years before the World Wide Web was invented, and about nine years before my family got a computer with a modem that could connect to it.

Of course, the Internet is not a single entity, although we tend to refer to it as if it were. The technical reality is that there are new networks born every day on the global cluster of interconnected communications networks that you—and about three billion other people, or roughly 42 percent of the world's population—use regularly. Still, I'm going to use the term in its broadest sense, to mean the universal network of networks connecting the majority of the world's computers to one another via a set of shared protocols.

Some of you may worry that you don't know a protocol from a hole in the wall, but all of us have made use of many. Think of protocols as languages for machines, the common rules they follow to be understood by one another. If you're around my age, you might remember having to type the "http" at the beginning of a website's address into the address bar of your Web browser. This refers to the Hypertext Transfer Protocol, the language you use to access the World Wide Web, that massive collection of mostly text-based but also audio- and video-capable sites like Google and YouTube and Facebook. Every time you check your email, you use a language like IMAP (Internet Message Access Protocol), SMTP (Simple Mail Transfer Protocol), or POP3 (Post Office Protocol). File transfers pass through the Internet using FTP (File Transfer Protocol). And as for the time-setting procedure on your phone that I mentioned, those updates get fetched through NTP (Network Time Protocol).

All these protocols are known as application protocols, and comprise just one family of protocols among the myriad online. For example, in order for the data in any of these application protocols to cross the Internet and be delivered to your desktop, or laptop, or phone, it first has to be packaged up inside a dedicated transport protocol—think of how the regular snail-mail postal service prefers you to send your letters and parcels in their standard-size envelopes and boxes. TCP (Transmission Control Protocol) is used to route, among other applications, Web pages and email. UDP (User Datagram Protocol) is used to route more time-sensitive, real-time applications, such as Internet telephony and live broadcasts.

Any recounting of the multilayered workings of what in my childhood was called cyberspace, the Net, the Infobahn, and the Information Superhighway is bound to be incomplete, but the takeaway is this: these protocols have given us the means to digitize and put online damn near everything in the world that we don't eat, drink, wear, or dwell in. The Internet has become almost as integral to our lives as the air through which so many of its communications travel. And, as we've all been reminded—every time our social media feeds alert us to a post that tags us in a compromising light—to digitize something is to record it, in a format that will last forever.

Here's what strikes me when I think back to my childhood, particularly those first nine Internet-less years: I can't account for everything that happened back then, because I have only my memory to rely on. The data just doesn't exist. When I was a child, "the unforgettable experience" was not yet a threateningly literal technological description, but a passionate metaphorical prescription of significance: my first words, my first steps, my first lost tooth, my first time riding a bicycle.

My generation was the last in American and perhaps even in world history for which this is true—the last undigitized generation, whose childhoods aren't up on the cloud but are mostly trapped in analog formats like handwritten diaries and Polaroids and VHS cassettes, tangible and imperfect artifacts that degrade with age and can be lost irretrievably. My schoolwork was done on paper with pencils and erasers, not on networked tablets that logged my keystrokes. My growth spurts weren't tracked by smart-home technologies, but notched with a knife into the wood of the door frame of the house in which I grew up.

WE LIVED IN a grand old redbrick house on a little patch of lawn shaded by dogwood trees and strewn in summer with white magnolia flowers that served as cover for the plastic army men I used to crawl around with. The house had an atypical layout: its main entrance was on the second floor, accessed by a massive brick staircase. This floor was the primary living space, with the kitchen, dining room, and bedrooms.

Above this main floor was a dusty, cobwebbed, and forbidden attic given over to storage, haunted by what my mother promised me were squirrels, but what my father insisted were vampire werewolves that would devour any child foolish enough to venture up there. Below the main floor was a more or less finished basement—a rarity in North Carolina, especially so close to the coast. Basements tend to flood, and ours, certainly, was perennially damp, despite the constant workings of the dehumidifier and sump pump.

At the time my family moved in, the back of the main floor was extended and divided up into a laundry room, a bathroom, my bedroom, and a den outfitted with a TV and a couch. From my bedroom, I had a view of the den through the window set into what had originally been the exterior wall of the house. This window, which once looked outside, now looked inside.

For nearly all the years that my family spent in that house in Elizabeth City, this bedroom was mine, and its window was, too. Though the window had a curtain, it didn't provide much, if any, privacy. From as far back as I can remember, my favorite activity was to tug the curtain aside and peek through the window into the den. Which is to say, from as far back as I can remember, my favorite activity was spying.

I spied on my older sister, Jessica, who was allowed to stay up later than I was and watch the cartoons that I was still too young for. I spied on my mother, Wendy, who'd sit on the couch to fold the laundry while watching the nightly news. But the person

I spied on the most was my father, Lon—or, as he was called in the Southern style, Lonnie—who'd commandeer the den into the wee hours.

My father was in the Coast Guard, though at the time I didn't have the slightest clue what that meant. I knew that sometimes he wore a uniform and sometimes he didn't. He left home early and came home late, often with new gadgets—a Texas Instruments TI-30 scientific calculator, a Casio stopwatch on a lanyard, a single speaker for a home stereo system—some of which he'd show me, and some of which he'd hide. You can imagine which I was more interested in.

The gadget I was most interested in arrived one night, just after bedtime. I was in bed and about to drift off, when I heard my father's footsteps coming down the hall. I stood up on my bed, tugged aside the curtain, and watched. He was holding a mysterious box, close in size to a shoe box, and he removed from it a beige object that looked like a cinder block, from which long black cables snaked like the tentacles of some deep-sea monster out of one of my nightmares.

Working slowly and methodically—which was partially his disciplined, engineer's way of doing everything, and partially an attempt to stay quiet—my father untangled the cables and stretched one across the shag carpet from the back of the box to the back of the TV. Then he plugged the other cable into a wall outlet behind the couch.

Suddenly the TV lit up, and with it my father's face lit up, too. Normally he would just spend his evenings sitting on the couch, cracking Sun Drop sodas and watching the people on TV run around a field, but this was different. It took me only a moment to come to the most amazing realization of my whole entire, though admittedly short, life: *my father was controlling what was happening on TV.*

I had come face-to-face with a Commodore 64—one of the first home computer systems on the market.

I had no idea what a computer was, of course, let alone whether what my father was doing on it was playing a game or working. Although he was smiling and seemed to be having fun, he was also applying himself to what was happening on-screen with the same intensity with which he applied himself to every mechanical task around the house. I knew only one thing: whatever he was doing, I wanted to do it, too.

After that, whenever my father came into the den to break out the beige brick, I'd stand up on my bed, tug away the curtain, and spy on his adventures. One night the screen showed a falling ball and a bar at the bottom; my father had to move the bar horizontally to hit the ball, bounce it up, and knock down a wall of multicolored bricks (*Arkanoid*). On another night, he sat before a screen of multicolored bricks in different shapes; they were always falling, and as they fell he moved and rotated them to assemble them into perfect rows, which immediately vanished (*Tetris*). I was truly confused, however, about what my father was doing—recreation or part of his job—when I peeked through the window one night and saw him flying.

My father—who'd always delighted me by pointing out the real helicopters from the Coast Guard Air Base when they flew by the house—was piloting his own helicopter right here, right in front of me, in our den. He took off from a little base, complete with a tiny waving American flag, into a black night sky full of twinkling stars, and then immediately crashed to the ground. He gave a little cry that masked my own, but just when I thought the fun was over, he was right back at the little base again with the tiny flag, taking off one more time.

The game was called *Choplifter!* and that exclamation point wasn't just part of its name, it was also part of the experience of playing it. *Choplifter!* was thrilling. Again and again I watched these sorties fly out of our den and over a flat desert moon, shooting at, and being shot at by, enemy jets and enemy tanks. The helicopter kept landing and lifting off, as my father tried to rescue a flashing crowd of people and ferry them to safety. That was my earliest sense of my father: he was a hero.

The cheer that came from the couch the first time that the diminutive helicopter touched down intact with a full load of miniature people was just a little too loud. My father's head snapped to the window to check whether he'd disturbed me, and he caught me dead in the eyes.

I leaped into bed, pulled up the blanket, and lay perfectly still as my father's heavy steps approached my room.

He tapped on the window. "It's past your bedtime, buddy. Are you still up?"

I held my breath. Suddenly, he opened the window, reached into my bedroom, picked me up—blanket and all—and pulled me through into the den. It all happened so quickly, my feet never even touched the carpet.

Before I knew it, I was sitting on my father's lap as his copilot. I was too young and too excited to realize that the joystick he'd given me wasn't plugged in. All that mattered was that I was flying alongside my father.

2

The Invisible Wall

Elizabeth City is a quaint, midsize port town with a relatively intact historic core. Like most other early American settlements, it grew around the water, in this case around the banks of the Pasquotank River, whose name is an English corruption of an Algonquin word meaning "where the current forks." The river flows down from Chesapeake Bay, through the swamps of the Virginia–North Carolina border, and empties into Albemarle Sound alongside the Chowan, the Perquimans, and other rivers. Whenever I consider what other directions my life might have taken, I think of that watershed: no matter the particular course the water travels from its source, it still ultimately arrives at the same destination.

My family has always been connected to the sea, my mother's side in particular. Her heritage is straight Pilgrim—her first ancestor on these shores was John Alden, the *Mayflower*'s cooper, or barrelmaker. He became the husband of a fellow passenger named Priscilla Mullins, who had the dubious distinction of being the only single woman of marriageable age onboard, and so the only single woman of marriageable age in the whole first generation of the Plymouth Colony.

John and Priscilla's Thanksgiving-time coupling almost never happened, however, due to the meddling of the commander of the Plymouth Colony, Myles Standish. His love for Priscilla, and Priscilla's rejection of him and eventual marriage to John, became the basis of a literary work that was referenced throughout my youth, *The Courtship of Miles Standish* by Henry Wadsworth Longfellow (himself an Alden-Mullins descendant):

> Nothing was heard in the room but the hurrying pen of the
>   stripling,
> Busily writing epistles important, to go by the Mayflower,
> Ready to sail on the morrow, or next day at latest, God willing!
> Homeward bound with the tidings of all that terrible winter,
> Letters written by Alden, and full of the name of Priscilla,
> Full of the name and the fame of the Puritan maiden Priscilla!

John and Priscilla's daughter, Elizabeth, was the first Pilgrim child born in New England. My mother, whose birth name is also Elizabeth, is her direct descendant. Because the lineage is almost exclusively through the women, though, the surnames changed with nearly every generation—with an Alden marrying a Pabodie marrying a Grinnell marrying a Stephens marrying a Jocelin. These seafaring ancestors of mine sailed down the coast from what's now Massachusetts to Connecticut and New Jersey—plying trade routes and dodging pirates between the Colonies and the Caribbean—until, with the Revolutionary War, the Jocelin line settled in North Carolina.

Amaziah Jocelin, also spelled Amasiah Josselyn, among other variants, was a privateer and war hero. As captain of the ten-gun barque *The Firebrand*, he was credited with the defense of Cape Fear. Following American independence, he became the US Navy Agent, or supply officer, of the Port of Wilmington, where he also established the city's first chamber of commerce, which he called, funnily enough, the Intelligence-Office. The Jocelins and their descendants—the Moores and Halls and Meylands and Howells and Stevens and Restons and Stokleys—who comprise the rest of my mother's side fought in every war in my country's history, from the Revolution and the Civil War (in which the Carolinian relatives fought for the Confederacy against their New England/Union cousins), to both world wars. Mine is a family that has always answered the call of duty.

My maternal grandfather, whom I call Pop, is better known as Rear Admiral Edward J. Barrett. At the time of my birth he was deputy chief, aeronautical engineering division, Coast Guard Headquarters, Washington, DC. He'd go on to hold various engineering and operational commands, from Governors Island, New York City, to Key West, Florida, where he was director of the Joint Interagency Task Force East (a multiagency, multinational US Coast Guard–led force dedicated to the interdiction of narcotics trafficking in the Caribbean). I wasn't aware of how high up the ranks Pop was rising, but I knew that the welcome-to-command ceremonies became more elaborate as time went on, with longer speeches and larger cakes. I remember the souvenir I was given by the artillery guard at one of them: the shell casing of a 40mm round, still warm and smelling like powdered hell, which had just been fired in a salute in Pop's honor.

Then there's my father, Lon, who at the time of my birth was a chief petty officer at the Coast Guard's Aviation Technical Training Center in Elizabeth City, working as a curriculum designer and electronics instructor. He was often away, leaving my mother at home to raise my sister and me. To give us a sense of responsibility, she gave us chores; to teach us how to read, she labeled all our dresser drawers with their contents—SOCKS, UNDERWEAR. She would load us into our Red Flyer wagon and tow us to the local library, where I immediately made for my favorite section, the one that I called "Big Masheens." Whenever my mother asked me if I was interested in any specific "Big Masheen," I was unstoppable: "Dump trucks and steamrollers and forklifts and cranes and—"

"Is that all, buddy?"

"Oh," I'd say, "and also cement mixers and bulldozers and—"

My mother loved giving me math challenges. At Kmart or Winn-Dixie, she'd have me pick out books and model cars and trucks and buy them for me if I was able to mentally add together their prices. Over the course of my childhood, she kept escalating the difficulty, first having me estimate and round to the nearest dollar, then having me figure out the precise dollar-and-cents amount, and then having me calculate 3 percent of that amount and add it on to the total. I was confused by that last challenge—not by the arithmetic so much as by the reasoning. "Why?"

"It's called tax," my mother explained. "Everything we buy, we have to pay three percent to the government."

"What do they do with it?"

"You like roads, buddy? You like bridges?" she said. "The government uses that money to fix them. They use that money to fill the library with books."

Some time later, I was afraid that my budding math skills had failed me, when my mental totals didn't match those on the cash register's display. But once again, my mother explained. "They raised the sales tax. Now you have to add four percent."

"So now the library will get even more books?" I asked.

"Let's hope," my mother said.

My grandmother lived a few streets over from us, across from the Carolina Feed and Seed Mill and a towering pecan tree. After stretching out my shirt to make a basket to fill with fallen pecans, I'd go up to her house and lie on the carpet beside the long low bookshelves. My usual company was an edition of *Aesop's Fables* and, perhaps my favorite, *Bulfinch's Mythology*. I would leaf through the pages, pausing only to crack a few nuts while I absorbed accounts of flying horses, intricate labyrinths, and serpent-haired Gorgons who turned mortals to stone. I was in awe of Odysseus, and liked Zeus, Apollo, Hermes, and Athena well enough, but the deity I admired most had to be Hephaestus: the ugly god of fire, volcanoes, blacksmiths, and carpenters, the god of tinkerers. I was proud of being able to spell his Greek name, and of knowing that his Roman name, Vulcan, was used for the home planet of Spock from *Star Trek*. The fundamental premise of the Greco-Roman pantheon always stuck with me. Up at the summit of some mountain there was this gang of gods and goddesses who spent most of their infinite existence fighting with each other and spying on the business of humanity. Occasionally, when they noticed something that intrigued or disturbed them, they disguised themselves, as lambs and swans and lions, and descended the slopes of Olympus to investigate and meddle. It was often a disaster—someone always drowned, or was struck by lightning, or was turned into a tree—whenever the immortals sought to impose their will and interfere in mortal affairs.

Once, I picked up an illustrated version of the legends of King Arthur and his knights, and found myself reading about another legendary mountain, this one in Wales. It served as the fortress of a tyrannical giant named Rhitta Gawr, who refused to accept that the age of his reign had passed and that in the future the world would be ruled by human kings, whom he considered tiny and weak. Determined to keep himself in power, he descended from his peak, attacking kingdom after kingdom and vanquishing their armies. Eventually he managed to defeat and kill every single king of Wales and Scotland. Upon killing them he shaved off their beards and wove them together into a cloak, which he wore as a gory trophy. Then he decided to challenge the strongest king of Britain, King Arthur, giving him a choice: Arthur could either shave off his own beard and surrender, or Rhitta Gawr would decapitate the king and remove the beard himself. Enraged at this hubris, Arthur set off for Rhitta Gawr's mountain fortress. The king and the giant met on the highest peak and battled each other for days, until Arthur was gravely wounded. Just as Rhitta Gawr grabbed the king by the hair and prepared to cut off his head, Arthur summoned a last measure of strength and sank his fabled sword through the eye of the giant, who toppled over dead. Arthur and his knights then went about piling up a funeral cairn atop

Rhitta Gawr's corpse, but before they could complete the work, snow began to fall. As they departed, the giant's bloodstained beard-cloak was returned to perfect whiteness.

The mountain was called Snaw Dun, which, a note explained, was Old English for "snow mound." Today, Snaw Dun is called Mount Snowdon. A long-extinct volcano, it is, at approximately 3,560 feet, the highest peak in Wales. I remember the feeling of encountering my name in this context—it was thrilling—and the archaic spelling gave me my first palpable sense that the world was older than I was, even older than my parents were. The name's association with the heroic exploits of Arthur and Lancelot and Gawain and Percival and Tristan and the other Knights of the Round Table gave me pride—until I learned that these exploits weren't historical, but legendary.

Years later, with my mother's help, I would scour the library in the hopes of separating the mythical from the factual. I found out that Stirling Castle in Scotland had been renamed Snowdon Castle, in honor of this Arthurian victory, as part of an attempt by the Scots to shore up their claim to the throne of England. Reality, I learned, is nearly always messier and less flattering than we might want it to be, but also in some strange way often richer than the myths.

By the time I uncovered the truth about Arthur, I had long been obsessed with a new and different type of story, or a new and different type of storytelling. On Christmas 1989, a Nintendo appeared in the house. I took to that two-tone-gray console so completely that my alarmed mother imposed a rule: I could only rent a new game when I finished reading a book. Games were expensive, and, having already mastered the ones that had come with the console—a single cartridge combining *Super Mario Bros.* and *Duck Hunt*—I was eager for other challenges. The only snag was that, at six years old, I couldn't read as fast as I could complete a game. It was time for another of my neophyte hacks. I started coming home from the library with shorter books, and books with lots of pictures. There were visual encyclopedias of inventions, with crazy drawings of velocipedes and blimps, and comic books that I realized only later were abridged, for-kids versions of Jules Verne and H. G. Wells.

It was the NES—the janky but genius 8-bit Nintendo Entertainment System—that was my real education. From *The Legend of Zelda*, I learned that the world exists to be explored; from *Mega Man*, I learned that my enemies have much to teach; and from *Duck Hunt*, well, *Duck Hunt* taught me that even if someone laughs at your failures, it doesn't mean you get to shoot them in the face. Ultimately, though, it was *Super Mario Bros.* that taught me what remains perhaps the most important lesson of my life. I am being perfectly sincere. I am asking you to consider this seriously. *Super Mario Bros.*, the 1.0 edition, is perhaps the all-time masterpiece of side-scrolling games. When the game begins, Mario is standing all the way to the left of the legendary opening screen, and he can only go in one direction: He can only move to the right, as new scenery and enemies scroll in from that side. He progresses through eight worlds of four levels each, all of them governed by time constraints, until he reaches the evil Bowser and frees the captive Princess Toadstool. Throughout all thirty-two levels, Mario exists in front of what in gaming parlance is called "an invisible wall," which doesn't allow him to go backward. There is no turning back, only going forward—for Mario and Luigi, for me, and for you. Life only scrolls in one direction, which is the direction of time, and no matter how far we might manage to go, that invisible wall will always be just behind us, cutting us off from the past, compelling us on into the unknown. A small kid growing up in small-town North Carolina in the 1980s has to get a sense of mortality from somewhere, so why not from two Italian-immigrant plumber brothers with an appetite for sewer mushrooms?

One day my much-used *Super Mario Bros.* cartridge wasn't loading, no matter how much I blew into it. That's what you had to do back then, or what we thought you had to do: you had to blow into the open mouth of the cartridge to clear it of the dust, debris, and pet hair that tended to accumulate there. But no matter how much I blew, both into the cartridge and into the cartridge slot of the console itself, the TV screen was full of blotches and waves, which were not reassuring in the least.

In retrospect, the Nintendo was probably just suffering from a faulty pin connection, but given that my seven-year-old self didn't even know what a pin connection was, I was frustrated and desperate. Worst of all, my father had only just left on a Coast Guard trip and wouldn't be back to help me fix it for two weeks. I knew of no Mario-style time-warping tricks or pipes to dive into that would make those weeks pass quicker, so I resolved to fix the thing myself. If I succeeded, I knew my father would be impressed. I went out to the garage to find his gray metal toolbox.

I decided that to figure out what was wrong with the thing, first I had to take it apart. Basically, I was just copying, or trying to copy, the same motions that my father went through whenever he sat at the kitchen table repairing the house's VCR or cassette deck—the two household machines that, to my eye, the Nintendo console most closely resembled. It took me about an hour to dismantle the console, with my uncoordinated and very small hands trying to twist a flat screwdriver into Philips-head screws, but eventually I succeeded.

The console's exterior was a dull, monochrome gray, but the interior was a welter of colors. It seemed like there was an entire rainbow of wires and glints of silver and gold jutting out of the green-as-grass circuitboard. I tightened a few things here, loosened a few things there—more or less at random—and blew on every part. After that, I wiped them all down with a paper towel. Then I had to blow on the circuitboard again to remove the bits of paper towel that had gotten stuck to what I now know were the pins.

Once I'd finished my cleaning and repairs, it was time for reassembly. Our golden Lab, Treasure, might have swallowed one of the tiny screws, or maybe it just got lost in the carpet or under the couch. And I must not have put all the components back in the same way I'd found them, because they barely fit into the console's shell. The shell's lid kept popping off, so I found myself squeezing the components down, the way you try to shut an overstuffed suitcase. Finally the lid snapped into place, but only on one side. The other side bulged up, and snapping that side into place only caused the first side to bulge. I went back and forth like that for a while, until I finally gave up and plugged the unit in again.

I pressed the Power button—and nothing. I pressed the Reset button—and nothing. Those were the only two buttons on the console. Before my repairs, the light next to the buttons had always glowed molten red, but now even that was dead. The console just sat there lopsided and useless, and I felt a surge of guilt and dread.

My father, when he came home from his Coast Guard trip, wasn't going to be proud of me: he was going to jump on my head like a Goomba. But it wasn't his anger I feared so much as his disappointment. To his peers, my father was a master electronics systems engineer who specialized in avionics. To me, he was a household mad scientist who'd try to fix everything himself— electrical outlets, dishwashers, hot-water heaters, and AC units. I'd work as his helper whenever he'd let me, and in the process I'd come to know both the physical pleasures of manual work and the intellectual pleasures of basic mechanics, along with the fundamental principles of electronics—the differences between voltage and current, between power and resistance. Every job we undertook together would end either in a successful act of repair or a curse, as my father would fling the unsalvageable piece of equipment across the room and into the cardboard box of things-that-can't-be-unbroken. I never judged him for these failures—I was always too impressed by the fact that he had dared to hazard an attempt.

When he returned home and found out what I'd done to the NES, he wasn't angry, much to my surprise. He wasn't exactly pleased, either, but he was patient. He explained that understanding why and how things had gone wrong was every bit as important as understanding what component had failed: figuring out the why and how would let you prevent the same malfunction from happening again in the future. He pointed to each of the console's parts in turn, explaining not just what it was, but what it did, and how it interacted with all the other parts to contribute to the correct working of the mechanism. Only by analyzing a mechanism in its individual parts were you able to determine whether its design was the most efficient to achieve its task. If it was the most efficient, just malfunctioning, then you fixed it. But if not, then you made modifications to improve the mechanism. This was the only proper protocol for repair jobs, according to my father, and nothing about it was optional—in fact, this was the fundamental responsibility you had to technology.

Like all my father's lessons, this one had broad applications beyond our immediate task. Ultimately, it was a lesson in the principle of self-reliance, which my father insisted that America had forgotten sometime between his own childhood and mine. Ours was now a country in which the cost of replacing a broken machine with a newer model was typically lower than the cost of having it fixed by an expert, which itself was typically lower than the cost of sourcing the parts and figuring out how to fix it yourself. This fact alone virtually guaranteed technological tyranny, which was perpetuated not by the technology itself but by the ignorance of everyone who used it daily and yet failed to understand it. To refuse to inform yourself about the basic operation and maintenance of the equipment you depended on was to passively accept that tyranny and agree to its terms: when your equipment works, you'll work, but when your equipment breaks down you'll break down, too. Your possessions would possess you.

It turned out that I had probably just broken a solder joint, but to find out exactly which one, my father wanted to use special test equipment that he had access to at his laboratory at the Coast Guard base. I suppose he could have brought the test equipment home with him, but for some reason he brought me to work instead. I think he just wanted to show me his lab. He'd decided I was ready.

I wasn't. I'd never been anywhere so impressive. Not even the library. Not even the Radio Shack at the Lynnhaven Mall. What I remember most are the screens. The lab itself was dim and empty, the standard-issue beige and white of government construction, but even before my father hit the lights I couldn't help but be transfixed by the pulsating glow of electric green. *Why does this place have so many TVs?* was my first thought, quickly followed up by, *And why are they all tuned to the same channel?* My father explained that these weren't TVs but computers, and though I'd heard the word before, I didn't know what it meant. I think I initially assumed that the screens—the monitors—were the computers themselves.

He went on to show them to me, one by one, and tried to explain what they did: this one processed radar signals, and that one relayed radio transmissions, and yet another one simulated the electronic systems on aircraft. I won't pretend that I understood even half of it. These computers were more advanced than nearly everything in use at that time in the private sector, far ahead of almost anything I had ever imagined. Sure, their processing units took a full five minutes to boot, their displays only showed one color, and they had no speakers for sound effects or music. But those limitations only marked them as serious.

My father plopped me down in a chair, raising it until I could just about reach the desk, and the rectangular hunk of plastic that was on it. For the first time in my life, I found myself in front of a keyboard. My father had never let me type on his Commodore 64, and my screen time had been restricted to video game consoles with their purpose-built controllers. But these computers were professional, general-purpose machines, not gaming devices, and I didn't understand how to make them work. There was no controller, no joystick, no gun—the only interface was that flat hunk of plastic set with rows of keys printed with letters and numbers. The letters were even arranged in a different order than the one that I'd been taught at school. The first letter was not A but Q, followed by W, E, R, T, and Y. At least the numbers were in the same order in which I'd learned them.

My father told me that every key on the keyboard had a purpose—every letter, every number—and that their combinations had purposes, too. And just like with the buttons on a controller or joystick, if you could figure out the right combinations, you could work miracles. To demonstrate, he reached over me, typed a command, and pressed the Enter key. Something popped up on-screen that I now know is called a text editor. Then he grabbed a Post-it note and a pen and scribbled out some letters and numbers, and told me to type them up exactly while he went off to repair the broken Nintendo.

The moment he was gone, I began reproducing his scribbles on-screen by pecking away at the keys. A left-handed kid raised to be a rightie, I immediately found this to be the most natural method of writing I'd ever encountered.

10 INPUT "WHAT IS YOUR NAME?"; NAME$
20 PRINT "HELLO, " + NAME$ + "!"

It may sound easy to you, but you're not a young child. I was. I was a young child with chubby, stubby fingers who didn't even know what quotation marks were, let alone that I had to hold down the Shift key in order to type them. After a whole lot of trial, and a whole lot of error, I finally succeeded in finishing the file. I pressed Enter and, in a flash, the computer was asking me a question: WHAT IS YOUR NAME?

I was fascinated. The note didn't say what I was supposed do next, so I decided to answer, and pressed my new friend Enter once more. Suddenly, out of nowhere, HELLO, EDDIE! wrote itself on-screen in a radioactive green that floated atop the blackness.

This was my introduction to programming and to computing in general: a lesson in the fact that these machines do what they do because somebody tells them to, in a very special, very careful way. And that somebody can even be seven years old.

Almost immediately, I grasped the limitations of gaming systems. They were stifling in comparison to computer systems. Nintendo, Atari, Sega—they all confined you to levels and worlds that you could advance through, even defeat, but never change. The repaired Nintendo console went back to the den, where my father and I competed in two-player *Mario Kart*, *Double Dragon*, and *Street Fighter*. By that point, I was significantly better than him at all those games—the first pursuit at which I proved more adept than my father—but every so often I'd let him beat me. I didn't want him to think that I wasn't grateful.

I'm not a natural programmer, and I've never considered myself any good at it. But I did, over the next decade or so, become good enough to be dangerous. To this day, I still find the process magical: typing in the commands in all these strange languages that the processor then translates into an experience that's available not just to me but to everyone. I was fascinated by the thought that one individual programmer could code something universal, something bound by no laws or rules or regulations except those essentially reducible to cause and effect. There was an utterly logical relationship between my input and the output. If my input was flawed, the output was flawed; if my input was flawless, the computer's output was, too. I'd never before experienced anything so consistent and fair, so unequivocally unbiased. A computer would wait forever to receive my command but would process it the very moment I hit Enter, no questions asked. No teacher had ever been so patient, yet so responsive. Nowhere else—certainly not at school, and not even at home—had I ever felt so in control. That a perfectly written set of commands would perfectly execute the same operations time and again would come to seem to me—as it did to so many smart, tech-inclined children of the millennium—the one stable saving truth of our generation.

3

Beltway Boy

I was just shy of my ninth birthday when my family moved from North Carolina to Maryland. To my surprise, I found that my name had preceded me. "Snowden" was everywhere throughout Anne Arundel, the county we settled in, though it was a while before I learned why.

Richard Snowden was a British major who arrived in the province of Maryland in 1658 with the understanding that Lord Baltimore's guarantee of religious freedom for both Catholics and Protestants would also be extended to Quakers. In 1674, Richard was joined by his brother John, who'd agreed to leave Yorkshire in order to shorten his prison sentence for preaching the Quaker faith. When William Penn's ship, the *Welcome*, sailed up the Delaware in 1682, John was one of the few Europeans to greet it.

Three of John's grandsons went on to serve in the Continental Army during the Revolution. As the Quakers are pacifists, they came in for community censure for deciding to join the fight for independence, but their conscience demanded a reconsideration of their pacifism. William Snowden, my direct paternal ancestor, served as a captain, was taken prisoner by the British in the Battle of Fort Washington in New York, and died in custody at one of the notorious sugar house prisons in Manhattan. (Legend has it that the British killed their POWs by forcing them to eat gruel laced with ground glass.) His wife, Elizabeth née Moor, was a valued adviser to General Washington, and the mother to another John Snowden—a politician, historian, and newspaper publisher in Pennsylvania whose descendants dispersed southward to settle amid the Maryland holdings of their Snowden cousins.

Anne Arundel County encompasses nearly all of the 1,976 acres of woodland that King Charles II granted to the family of Richard Snowden in 1686. The enterprises the Snowdens established there include the Patuxent Iron Works, one of colonial America's most important forges and a major manufacturer of cannonballs and bullets, and Snowden Plantation, a farm and dairy run by Richard Snowden's grandsons. After serving in the heroic Maryland Line of the Continental Army, they returned to the plantation and—most fully living the principles of independence—abolished their family's practice of slavery, freeing their two hundred African slaves nearly a full century before the Civil War.

Today, the former Snowden fields are bisected by Snowden River Parkway, a busy four-lane commercial stretch of upmarket chain restaurants and car dealerships. Nearby, Route 32/Patuxent Freeway leads directly to Fort George G. Meade, the second-largest army base in the country and the home of the NSA. Fort Meade, in fact, is built atop land that was once owned by my Snowden cousins, and that was either bought from them (in one account) or expropriated from them (according to others) by the US government.

I knew nothing of this history at the time: my parents joked that the state of Maryland changed the name on the signs every time somebody new moved in. They thought that was funny but I just found it spooky. Anne Arundel County is only a bit more than 250 miles away from Elizabeth City via I-95, yet it felt like a different planet. We'd exchanged the leafy riverside for a concrete sidewalk, and a school where I'd been popular and academically successful for one where I was constantly mocked for my glasses, my disinterest in sports, and, especially, for my accent—a strong Southern drawl that led my new classmates to call me "retarded."

I was so sensitive about my accent that I stopped speaking in class and started practicing alone at home until I managed to sound "normal"—or, at least, until I managed not to pronounce the site of my humiliation as "Anglish clay-iss" or say that I'd gotten a paper cut on my "fanger." Meanwhile, all that time I'd been afraid to speak freely had caused my grades to plummet, and some of my teachers decided to have me IQ-tested as a way of diagnosing what they thought was a learning disability. When my score came back, I don't remember getting any apologies, just a bunch of extra "enrichment assignments." Indeed, the same teachers who'd doubted my ability to learn now began to take issue with my newfound interest in speaking up.

My new home was on the Beltway, which traditionally referred to Interstate 495, the highway that encircles Washington, DC, but now describes the vast and ever-expanding blast radius of bedroom communities around the nation's capital, stretching north to Baltimore, Maryland, and south to Quantico, Virginia. The inhabitants of these suburbs almost invariably either serve in the US government or work for one of the companies that do business with the US government. There is, to put it plainly, no other reason to be there.

We lived in Crofton, Maryland, halfway between Annapolis and Washington, DC, at the western edge of Anne Arundel County, where the residential developments are all in the vinyl-sided Federalist style and have quaint ye-olde names like Crofton Towne, Crofton Mews, The Preserve, The Ridings. Crofton itself is a planned community fitted around the curves of the Crofton Country Club. On a map, it resembles nothing so much as the human brain, with the streets coiling and kinking and folding around one another like the ridges and furrows of the cerebral cortex. Our street was Knights Bridge Turn, a broad, lazy loop of split-level housing, wide driveways, and two-car garages. The house we lived in was seven down from one end of the loop, seven down from the other—the house in the middle. I got a Huffy ten-speed bike and with it, a paper route, delivering the *Capital*, a venerable newspaper published in Annapolis, whose daily distribution became distressingly erratic, especially in the winter, especially between Crofton Parkway and Route 450, which, as it passed by our neighborhood, acquired a different name: Defense Highway.

For my parents this was an exciting time. Crofton was a step up for them, both economically and socially. The streets were tree-lined and pretty much crime-free, and the multicultural, multiracial, multilingual population, which reflected the diversity of the Beltway's diplomatic corps and intelligence community, was well-to-do and well educated. Our backyard was basically a golf course, with tennis courts just around the corner, and beyond those an Olympic-size pool. Commuting-wise, too, Crofton was ideal. It took my father just forty minutes to get to his new posting as a chief warrant officer in the Aeronautical Engineering Division at Coast Guard Headquarters, which at the time was located at Buzzard Point in southern Washington, DC, adjacent to Fort Lesley J. McNair. And it took my mother just twenty or so minutes to get to her new job at the NSA, whose boxy futuristic headquarters, topped with radomes and sheathed in copper to seal in the communications signals, forms the heart of Fort Meade.

I can't stress this enough, for outsiders: this type of employment was normal. Neighbors to our left worked for the Defense Department; neighbors to the right worked in the Department of Energy and the Department of Commerce. For a while, nearly every girl at school on whom I had a crush had a father in the FBI. Fort Meade was just the place where my mother worked, along with about 125,000 other employees, approximately 40,000 of whom resided on-site, many with their families. The base was home to over 115 government agencies, in addition to forces from all five branches of the military. To put it in perspective, in Anne Arundel County, population just over half a million, every eight hundredth person works for the post office, every thirtieth person works for the public school system, and every fourth person works for, or serves in, a business, agency, or branch connected to Fort Meade. The base has its own post offices, schools, police, and fire departments. Area children, military brats and civilians alike, would flock to the base daily to take golf, tennis, and swimming lessons. Though we lived off base, my mother still used its commissary as our grocery store, to stock up on items in bulk. She also took advantage of the base's PX, or Post Exchange, as a one-stop shop for the sensible and, most important, tax-free clothing that my sister and I were constantly outgrowing. Perhaps it's best, then, for readers not raised in this milieu to imagine Fort Meade and its environs, if not the entire Beltway, as one enormous boom-or-bust company town. It is a place whose monoculture has much in common with, say, Silicon Valley's, except that the Beltway's product isn't technology but government itself.

I should add that both my parents had top secret clearances, but my mother also had a full-scope polygraph—a higher-level security check that members of the military aren't subject to. The funny thing is, my mother was the farthest thing from a spy. She was a clerk at an independent insurance and benefits association that serviced employees of the NSA—essentially, providing spies with retirement plans. But still, to process pension forms she had to be vetted as if she were about to parachute into a jungle to stage a coup.

My father's career remains fairly opaque to me to this day, and the fact is that my ignorance here isn't anomalous. In the world I grew up in, nobody really talked about their jobs—not just to children, but to each other. It is true that many of the adults around me were legally prohibited from discussing their work, even with their families, but to my mind a more accurate explanation lies in the technical nature of their labor and the government's insistence on compartmentalization. Tech people rarely, if ever, have a sense of the broader applications and policy implications of the projects to which they're assigned. And the work that consumes them tends to require such specialized knowledge that to bring it up at a barbecue would get them disinvited from the next one, because nobody cared.

In retrospect, maybe that's what got us here.

4

American Online

It was soon after we moved to Crofton that my father brought home our first desktop computer, a Compaq Presario 425, list price $1,399 but purchased at his military discount, and initially set up—much to my mother's chagrin—smack in the middle of the dining-room table. From the moment it appeared, the computer and I were inseparable. If previously I'd been loath to go outside and kick around a ball, now the very idea seemed ludicrous. There was no outside greater than what I could find inside this drab clunky PC clone, with what felt at the time like an impossibly fast 25-megahertz Intel 486 CPU and an inexhaustible 200-megabyte hard disk. Also, get this, it had a color monitor—an 8-bit color monitor, to be precise, which means that it could display up to 256 different colors. (Your current device can probably display in the millions.)

This Compaq became my constant companion—my second sibling, and first love. It came into my life just at the age when I was first discovering an independent self and the multiple worlds that can simultaneously exist within this world. That process of exploration was so exciting that it made me take for granted and even neglect, for a while at least, the family and life that I already had. Another way of saying this is, I was just experiencing the early throes of puberty. But this was a technologized puberty, and the tremendous changes that it wrought in me were, in a way, being wrought everywhere, in everyone.

My parents would call my name to tell me to get ready for school, but I wouldn't hear them. They'd call my name to tell me to wash up for dinner, but I'd pretend not to hear them. And whenever I was reminded that the computer was a shared computer and not my personal machine, I'd relinquish my seat with such reluctance that as my father, or mother, or sister took their turn, they'd have to order me out of the room entirely lest I hover moodily over their shoulders and offer advice—showing my sister word-processing macros and shortcuts when she was writing a research paper, or giving my parents spreadsheet tips when they tried to do their taxes.

I'd try to rush them through their tasks, so I could get back to mine, which were so much more important—like playing *Loom*. As technology had advanced, games involving Pong paddles and helicopters—the kind my father had played on that by now superannuated Commodore—had lost ground to ones that realized that at the heart of every computer user was a book reader, a being with the desire not just for sensation but for story. The crude Nintendo, Atari, and Sega games of my childhood, with plots along the lines of (and this is a real example) rescuing the president of the United States from ninjas, now gave way to detailed reimaginings of the ancient tales that I'd paged through while lying on the carpet of my grandmother's house.

Loom was about a society of Weavers whose elders (named after the Greek Fates Clotho, Lachesis, and Atropos) create a secret loom that controls the world, or, according to the script of the game, that weaves "subtle patterns of influence into the very fabric of reality." When a young boy discovers the loom's power, he's forced into exile, and everything spirals into chaos until the world decides that a secret fate machine might not be such a great idea, after all.

Unbelievable, sure. But then again, it's just a game.

Still, it wasn't lost on me, even at that young age, that the titular machine of the game was a symbol of sorts for the computer on which I was playing it. The loom's rainbow-colored threads were like the computer's rainbow-colored internal wires, and the lone gray thread that foretold an uncertain future was like the long gray phone cord that came out of the back of the computer and connected it to the great wide world beyond. There, for me, was the true magic: with just this cord, the Compaq's expansion card and modem, and a working phone, I could dial up and connect to something new called the Internet.

Readers who were born postmillennium might not understand the fuss, but trust me, this was a goddamned miracle. Nowadays, connectivity is just presumed. Smartphones, laptops, desktops, everything's connected, always. Connected to what exactly? How? It doesn't matter. You just tap the icon your older relatives call "the Internet button" and boom, you've got it: the news, pizza delivery, streaming music, and streaming video that we used to call TV and movies. Back then, however, we walked uphill both ways, to and from school, and plugged our modems directly into the wall, with manly twelve-year-old hands.

I'm not saying that I knew much about what the Internet was, or how exactly I was connecting to it, but I did understand the miraculousness of it all. Because in those days, when you told the computer to connect, you were setting off an entire process wherein the computer would beep and hiss like a traffic jam of snakes, after which—and it could take lifetimes, or at least whole minutes—you could pick up any other phone in the house on an extension line and actually *hear the computers talking*. You couldn't actually understand what they were saying to each other, of course, since they were speaking in a machine language that transmitted up to fourteen thousand symbols per second. Still, even that incomprehension was an astonishingly clear indication that phone calls were no longer just for older teenage sisters.

Internet access, and the emergence of the Web, was my generation's big bang or Precambrian explosion. It irrevocably altered the course of my life, as it did the lives of everyone. From the age of twelve or so, I tried to spend my every waking moment online. Whenever I couldn't, I was busy planning my next session. The Internet was my sanctuary; the Web became my jungle gym, my treehouse, my fortress, my classroom without walls. If it were possible, I became more sedentary. If it were possible, I became more pale. Gradually, I stopped sleeping at night and instead slept by day in school. My grades went back into free fall.

I wasn't worried by this academic setback, however, and I'm not sure that my parents were, either. After all, the education that I was getting online seemed better and even more practical for my future career prospects than anything provided by school. That, at least, was what I kept telling my mother and father.

My curiosity felt as vast as the Internet itself: a limitless space that was growing exponentially, adding webpages by the day, by the hour, by the minute, on subjects I knew nothing about, on subjects I'd never heard of before—yet the moment that I did hear about them, I'd develop an insatiable desire to understand them in their every detail, with few rests or snacks or even toilet breaks allowed. My appetite wasn't limited to serious tech subjects like how to fix a CD-ROM drive, of course. I also spent plenty of time on gaming sites searching for god-mode cheat codes for *Doom* and *Quake*. But I was generally just so overwhelmed by the sheer amount of information immediately available that I'm not sure I was able to say where one subject ended and another began. A crash course on how to build my own computer led to a crash course in processor architecture, with side excursions into information about martial arts, guns, sports cars, and—full disclosure—softcore-ish goth-y porn.

I sometimes had the feeling that I had to know everything and wasn't going to sign off until I did. It was like I was in a race with the technology, in the same way that some of the teenage boys around me were in a race with one another to see who'd grow the tallest, or who'd get facial hair first. At school I was surrounded by kids, some from foreign countries, who were just trying to fit in and would expend enormous effort to seem cool, to keep up with the trends. But owning the latest No Fear hat and knowing how to bend its brim was child's play—literally, child's play—compared to what I was doing. I found it so thoroughly demanding to keep pace with all of the sites and how-to tutorials I followed that I started to resent my parents whenever they—in response to a particularly substandard report card or a detention I received—would force me off the computer on a school night. I couldn't bear to have those privileges revoked, disturbed by the thought that every moment that I wasn't online more and more material was appearing that I'd be missing. After repeated parental warnings and threats of grounding, I'd finally relent and print out whatever file I was reading and bring the dot-matrix pages up to bed. I'd continue studying in hard copy until my parents had gone to bed themselves, and then I'd tiptoe out into the dark, wary of the squeaky door and the creaky floorboards by the stairs. I'd keep the lights off and, guiding myself by the glow of the screen saver, I'd wake the computer up and go online, holding my pillows against the machine to stifle the dial tone of the modem and the ever-intensifying hiss of its connection.

How can I explain it, to someone who wasn't there? My younger readers, with their younger standards, might think of the nascent Internet as way too slow, the nascent Web as too ugly and un-entertaining. But that would be wrong. Back then, being online was another life, considered by most to be separate and distinct from Real Life. The virtual and the actual had not yet merged. And it was up to each individual user to determine for themselves where one ended and the other began.

It was precisely this that was so inspiring: the freedom to imagine something entirely new, the freedom to start over. Whatever Web 1.0 might've lacked in user-friendliness and design sensibility, it more than made up for by its fostering of experimentation and originality of expression, and by its emphasis on the creative primacy of the individual. A typical GeoCities site, for example, might have a flashing background that alternated between green and blue, with white text scrolling like an exclamatory chyron across the middle—Read *This* First!!!—below the .gif of a dancing hamster. But to me, all these kludgy quirks and tics of amateur production merely indicated that the guiding intelligence behind the site was human, and unique. Computer science professors and systems engineers, moonlighting English majors and mouth-breathing, basement-dwelling armchair political economists were all only too happy to share their research and convictions—not for any financial reward, but merely to win converts to their cause. And whether that cause was PC or Mac, macrobiotic diets or the abolition of the death penalty, I was interested. I was interested because they were enthused. Many of these strange and brilliant people could even be contacted and were quite pleased to answer my questions via the forms ("click this hyperlink or copy and paste it into your browser") and email addresses (@usenix.org, @frontier.net) provided on their sites.

As the millennium approached, the online world would become increasingly centralized and consolidated, with both governments and businesses accelerating their attempts to intervene in what had always been a fundamentally peer-to-peer relationship. But for one brief and beautiful stretch of time—a stretch that, fortunately for me, coincided almost exactly with my adolescence—the Internet was mostly made of, by, and for the people. Its purpose was to enlighten, not to monetize, and it was administered more by a provisional cluster of perpetually shifting collective norms than by exploitative, globally enforceable terms of service agreements. To this day, I consider the 1990s online to have been the most pleasant and successful anarchy I've ever experienced.

I was especially involved with the Web-based bulletin-board systems or BBSes. On these, you could pick a username and type out whatever message you wanted to post, either adding to a preexisting group discussion or starting a new one. Any and all messages that replied to your post would be organized by thread. Imagine the longest email chain you've ever been on, but in public. These were also chat applications, like Internet Relay Chat, which provided an immediate-gratification instant-message version of the same experience. There you could discuss any topic in real time, or at least as close to real time as a telephone conversation, live radio, or TV news.

Most of the messaging and chatting I did was in search of answers to questions I had about how to build my own computer, and the responses I received were so considered and thorough, so generous and kind, they'd be unthinkable today. My panicked query about why a certain chipset for which I'd saved up my allowance didn't seem to be compatible with the motherboard I'd already gotten for Christmas would elicit a two-thousand-word explanation and note of advice from a professional tenured computer scientist on the other side of the country. Not cribbed from any manual, this response was composed expressly for me, to troubleshoot my problems step-by-step until I'd solved them. I was twelve years old, and my correspondent was an adult stranger far away, yet he treated me like an equal because I'd shown respect for the technology. I attribute this civility, so far removed from our current social-media sniping, to the high bar for entry at the time. After all, the only people on these boards were the people who could be there—who wanted to be there badly enough—who had the proficiency and passion, because the Internet of the 1990s wasn't just one click away. It took significant effort just to log on.

Once, a certain BBS that I was on tried to coordinate casual in-the-flesh meetings of its regular members throughout the country: in DC, in New York, at the Consumer Electronics Show in Las Vegas. After being pressured rather hard to attend—and promised extravagant evenings of eating and drinking—I finally just told everyone how old I was. I was afraid that some of my correspondents might stop interacting with me, but instead they became, if anything, even more encouraging. I was sent updates from the electronics show and images of its catalog; one guy offered to ship me secondhand computer parts through the mail, free of charge.

I MIGHT HAVE told the BBSers my age, but I never told them my name, because one of the greatest joys of these platforms was that on them I didn't have to be who I was. I could be anybody. The anonymizing or pseudonymizing features brought equilibrium to all relationships, correcting their imbalances. I could take cover under virtually any handle, or "nym," as they were called, and suddenly become an older, taller, manlier version of myself. I could even be multiple selves. I took advantage of this feature by asking what I sensed were my more amateur questions on what seemed to me the more amateur boards, under different personas each time. My computer skills were improving so swiftly that instead of being proud of all the progress I'd made, I was embarrassed by my previous ignorance and wanted to distance myself from it. I wanted to disassociate my selves. I'd tell myself that squ33ker had been so dumb when "he" had asked that question about chipset compatibility way back, long ago, last Wednesday.

For all of this cooperative, collectivist free-culture ethos, I'm not going to pretend that the competition wasn't merciless, or that the population—almost uniformly male, heterosexual, and hormonally charged—didn't occasionally erupt into cruel and petty squabbles. But in the absence of real names, the people who claimed to hate you weren't real people. They didn't know anything about you beyond what you argued, and how you argued it. If, or rather when, one of your arguments incurred some online wrath, you could simply drop that screen name and assume another mask, under the cover of which you could even join in the mimetic pile-on, beating up on your disowned avatar as if it were a stranger. I can't tell you what sweet relief that sometimes was.

In the 1990s, the Internet had yet to fall victim to the greatest iniquity in digital history: the move by both government and businesses to link, as intimately as possible, users' online personas to their offline legal identity. Kids used to be able to go online and say the dumbest things one day without having to be held accountable for them the next. This might not strike you as the healthiest environment in which to grow up, and yet it is precisely the only environment in which you *can* grow up—by which I mean that the early Internet's dissociative opportunities actually encouraged me and those of my generation to change our most deeply held opinions, instead of just digging in and defending them when challenged. This ability to reinvent ourselves meant that we never had to close our minds by picking sides, or close ranks out of fear of doing irreparable harm to our reputations. Mistakes that were swiftly punished but swiftly rectified allowed both the community and the "offender" to move on. To me, and to many, this felt like freedom.

Imagine, if you will, that you could wake up every morning and pick a new name and a new face by which to be known to the world. Imagine that you could choose a new voice and new words to speak in it, as if the "Internet button" were actually a reset button for your life. In the new millennium, Internet technology would be turned to very different ends: enforcing fidelity to memory, identarian consistency, and so ideological conformity. But back then, for a while at least, it protected us by forgetting our transgressions and forgiving our sins.

My most significant early encounters with online self-presentation happened not on BBSes, however, but in a more fantastical realm: the pseudo-feudal lands and dungeons of role-playing games, MMORPGs (massively multiplayer online role-playing games) in particular. In order to play *Ultima Online*, which was my favorite MMORPG, I had to create and assume an alternative identity, or "alt." I could choose, for example, to be a wizard or warrior, a tinkerer or thief, and I could toggle between these alts with a freedom that was unavailable to me in off-line life, whose institutions tend to regard all mutability as suspicious.

I'd roam the *Ultima* gamescape as one of my alts, interacting with the alts of others. As I got to know these other alts, by collaborating with them on certain quests, I'd sometimes come to realize that I'd met their users before, just under different identities, while they, in turn, might realize the same about me. They'd read my messages and figure out, through a characteristic phrase I'd used, or a particular quest that I'd suggest, that I—who was currently, say, a knight who called herself Shrike—was also, or had also been, a bard who called himself Corwin, and a smith who called himself Belgarion. Sometimes I just enjoyed these interactions as opportunities for banter, but more often than not I treated them competitively, measuring my success by whether I was able to identify more of another user's alts than they were able to identify of mine. These contests to determine whether I could unmask others without being unmasked myself required me to be careful not to fall into any messaging patterns that might expose me, while simultaneously engaging others and remaining alert to the ways in which they might inadvertently reveal their true identities.

While the alts of *Ultima* were multifarious in name, they were essentially stabilized by the nature of their roles, which were well defined, even archetypal, and so enmeshed within the game's established social order as to make playing them sometimes feel like discharging a civic duty. After a day at school or at a job that might seem purposeless and unrewarding, it could feel as if you were performing a useful service by spending the evening as a healer or shepherd, a helpful alchemist or mage. The relative stability of the *Ultima* universe—its continued development according to defined laws and codes of conduct—ensured that each alt had their role-specific tasks, and would be judged according to their ability, or willingness, to complete them and fulfill the societal expectations of their function.

I loved these games and the alternative lives they let me live, though love wasn't quite as liberating for the other members of my family. Games, especially of the massively multiplayer variety, are notoriously time-consuming, and I was spending so many hours playing *Ultima* that our phone bills were becoming exorbitant and no calls were getting through. The line was always busy.

My sister, now deep into her teen years, became furious when she found out that my online life had caused her to miss some crucial high-school gossip. However, it didn't take her long to figure out that all she had to do to get her revenge was pick up the phone, which would break the Internet connection. The modem's hiss would stop, and before she'd even received a normal dial tone, I'd be screaming my head off downstairs.

If you're interrupted in the middle of, say, reading the news online, you can always go back and pick up wherever you left off. But if you're interrupted while playing a game that you can't pause or save—because a hundred thousand others are playing it at the same time—you're ruined. You could be on top of the world, some legendary dragon-slayer with your own castle and an army, but after just thirty seconds of CONNECTION LOST you'd find yourself reconnecting to a bone-gray screen that bore a cruel epitaph: YOU ARE DEAD.

I'm a bit embarrassed nowadays at how seriously I took all of this, but I can't avoid the fact that I felt, at the time, as if my sister was intent on destroying my life—particularly on those occasions when she'd make sure to catch my eye from across the room and smile before picking up the downstairs receiver, not because she wanted to make a phone call but purely because she wanted to remind me who was boss. Our parents got so fed up with our shouting matches that they did something uncharacteristically in-dulgent. They switched our Internet billing plan from pay-by-the-minute to flat-fee unlimited access, and installed a second phone line.

Peace smiled upon our abode.

5

Hacking

All teenagers are hackers. They have to be, if only because their life circumstances are untenable. They think they're adults, but the adults think they're kids.

Remember, if you can, your own teen years. You were a hacker, too, willing to do anything to evade parental supervision. Basically, you were fed up with being treated like a child.

Recall how it felt when anyone older and bigger than you sought to control you, as if age and size were identical with authority. At one time or another, your parents, teachers, coaches, scoutmasters, and clergy would all take advantage of their position to invade your private life, impose their expectations on your future, and enforce your conformity to past standards. Whenever these adults substituted their hopes, dreams, and desires for your own, they were doing so, by their account, "for your own good" or "with your best interests at heart." And while sometimes this was true, we all remember those other times when it wasn't— when "because I said so" wasn't enough and "you'll thank me one day" rang hollow. If you've ever been an adolescent, you've surely been on the receiving end of one of these clichés, and so on the losing end of an imbalance of power.

To grow up is to realize the extent to which your existence has been governed by systems of rules, vague guidelines, and increasingly unsupportable norms that have been imposed on you without your consent and are subject to change at a moment's notice. There were even some rules that you'd only find out about after you'd violated them.

If you were anything like me, you were scandalized.

If you were anything like me, you were nearsighted, scrawny, and, age-wise, barely entering the double digits when you first started to wonder about politics.

In school, you were told that in the system of American politics, citizens give consent through the franchise to be governed by their equals. This is democracy. But democracy certainly wasn't in place in my US history class, where, if my classmates and I had the vote, Mr. Martin would have been out of a job. Instead, Mr. Martin made the rules for US history, Ms. Evans made the rules for English, Mr. Sweeney made the rules for science, Mr. Stockton made the rules for math, and all of those teachers constantly changed those rules to benefit themselves and maximize their power. If a teacher didn't want you to go to the bathroom, you'd better hold it in. If a teacher promised a field trip to the Smithsonian Institution but then canceled it for an imaginary infraction, they'd offer no explanation beyond citing their broad authority and the maintenance of proper order. Even back then, I realized that any opposition to this system would be difficult, not least because getting its rules changed to serve the interests of the majority would involve persuading the rule makers to put themselves at a purposeful disadvantage. That, ultimately, is the critical flaw or design defect intentionally integrated into every system, in both politics and computing: the people who create the rules have no incentive to act against themselves.

What convinced me that school, at least, was an illegitimate system was that it wouldn't recognize any legitimate dissent. I could plead my case until I lost my voice, or I could just accept the fact that I'd never had a voice to begin with.

However, the benevolent tyranny of school, like all tyrannies, has a limited shelf life. At a certain point, the denial of agency becomes a license to resist, though it's characteristic of adolescence to confuse resistance with escapism or even violence. The most common outlets for a rebellious teen were useless to me, because I was too cool for vandalism and not cool enough for drugs. (To this day, I've never even gotten drunk on liquor or smoked a cigarette.) Instead, I started hacking—which remains the sanest, healthiest, and most educational way I know for kids to assert autonomy and address adults on equal terms.

Like most of my classmates, I didn't like the rules but was afraid of breaking them. I knew how the system worked: you corrected a teacher's mistake, you got a warning; you confronted the teacher when they didn't admit the mistake, you got detention; someone cheated off your exam, and though you didn't expressly let them cheat, you got detention and the cheater got suspended. This is the origin of all hacking: the awareness of a systemic linkage between input and output, between cause and effect. Because hacking isn't just native to computing—it exists wherever rules do. To hack a system requires getting to know its rules better than the people who created it or are running it, and exploiting all the vulnerable distance between how those people had intended the system to work and how it actually works, or could be made to work. In capitalizing on these unintentional uses, hackers aren't breaking the rules as much as debunking them.

Humans are hardwired to recognize patterns. All the choices we make are informed by a cache of assumptions, both empirical and logical, unconsciously derived and consciously developed. We use these assumptions to assess the potential consequences of each choice, and we describe the ability to do all of this, quickly and accurately, as intelligence. But even the smartest among us rely on assumptions that we've never put to the test—and because we do, the choices we make are often flawed. Anyone who knows better, or thinks more quickly and more accurately than we do, can take advantage of those flaws to create consequences that we never expected. It's this egalitarian nature of hacking—which doesn't care who you are, just how you reason—that makes it such a reliable method of dealing with the type of authority figures so convinced of their system's righteousness that it never occurred to them to test it.

I didn't learn any of this at school, of course. I learned it online. The Internet gave me the chance to pursue all the topics I was interested in, and all the links between them, unconstrained by the pace of my classmates and my teachers. The more time I spent online, however, the more my schoolwork felt extracurricular.

The summer I turned thirteen, I resolved never to return, or at least to seriously reduce my classroom commitments. I wasn't quite sure how I'd swing that, though. All the plans I came up with were likely to backfire. If I was caught skipping class, my parents would revoke my computer privileges; if I decided to drop out, they'd bury my body deep in the woods and tell the neighbors I'd run away. I had to come up with a hack—and then, on the first day of the new school year, I found one. Indeed, it was basically handed to me.

At the start of each class, the teachers passed out their syllabi, detailing the material to be covered, the required reading, and the schedule of tests and quizzes and assignments. Along with these, they gave us their grading policies, which were essentially explanations of how As, Bs, Cs, and Ds were calculated. I'd never encountered information like this. Their numbers and letters were like a strange equation that suggested a solution to my problem.

After school that day, I sat down with the syllabi and did the math to figure out which aspects of each class I could simply ignore and still expect to receive a passing grade. Take my US history class, for example. According to the syllabus, quizzes were worth 25 percent, tests were worth 35 percent, term papers were worth 15 percent, homework was worth 15 percent, and class participation—that most subjective of categories, in every subject—was worth 10 percent. Because I usually did well on my quizzes and tests without having to do too much studying, I could count on them for a reliable pool of time-efficient points. Term papers and homework, however, were the major time-sucks: low-value, high-cost impositions on Me Time.

What all of those numbers told me was that if I didn't do any homework but aced everything else, I'd wind up with a cumulative grade of 85, a B. If I didn't do any homework or write any term papers but aced everything else, I'd wind up with a cumulative grade of 70, a C-minus. The 10 percent that was class participation would be my buffer. Even if the teacher gave me a zero in that—if they interpreted my participation as disruption—I could still manage a 65, a D-minus. I'd still pass.

My teachers' systems were terminally flawed. Their instructions for how to achieve the highest grade could be used as instructions for how to achieve the highest freedom—a key to how to avoid doing what I didn't like to do and still slide by.

The moment I figured that out, I stopped doing homework completely. Every day was bliss, the kind of bliss forbidden to anybody old enough to work and pay taxes, until Mr. Stockton asked me in front of the entire class why I hadn't handed in the past half-dozen or so homework assignments. Untouched as I was by the guile of age—and forgetting for a moment that by giving away my hack, I was depriving myself of an advantage—I cheerfully offered my equation to the math teacher. My classmates' laughter lasted just a moment before they set about scribbling, calculating whether they, too, could afford to adopt a post-homework life.

"Pretty clever, Eddie," Mr. Stockton said, moving on to the next lesson with a smile.

I was the smartest kid in school—until about twenty-four hours later, when Mr. Stockton passed out the new syllabus. This stated that any student who failed to turn in more than six homeworks by the end of the semester would get an automatic F.

Pretty clever, Mr. Stockton.

Then, he took me aside after class and said, "You should be

using that brain of yours not to figure out how to avoid work, but how to do the best work you can. You have so much potential, Ed. But I don't think you realize that the grades you get here will follow you for the rest of your life. You have to start thinking about your permanent record."

UNSHACKLED FROM HOMEWORK, at least for a while, and so with more time to spare, I also did some more conventional—computer-based—hacking. As I did, my abilities improved. At the bookstore, I'd page through tiny, blurrily photocopied, stapled-together hacker zines with names like *2600* and *Phrack*, absorbing their techniques, and in the process absorbing their antiauthoritarian politics.

I was at the bottom of the technical totem pole, a script kiddie n00b working with tools I didn't understand that functioned according to principles that were beyond me. People still ask me why, when I finally did gain some proficiency, I didn't race out to empty bank accounts or steal credit card numbers. The honest answer is that I was too young and dumb to even know that this was an option, let alone to know what I'd do with the stolen loot. All I wanted, all I needed, I already had for free. Instead, I figured out simple ways to hack some games, giving myself extra lives and letting me do things like see through walls. Also, there wasn't a lot of money on the Internet back then, at least not by today's standards. The closest that anyone I knew or anything I read ever came to theft was "phreaking," or making free phone calls.

If you asked some of the big-shot hackers of the day why, for example, they'd hacked into a major news site only to do nothing more meaningful than replace the headlines with a trippy GIF proclaiming the skills of Baron von Hackerface that would be taken down in less than half an hour, the reply would've been a version of the answer given by the mountaineer who was asked his reason for climbing Mount Everest: "Because it's there." Most hackers, particularly young ones, set out to search not for lucre or power, but for the limits of their talent and any opportunity to prove the impossible possible.

I was young, and while my curiosity was pure, it was also, in retrospect, pretty psychologically revealing, in that some of my earliest hacking attempts were directed toward allaying my neuroses. The more I came to know about the fragility of computer security, the more I worried over the consequences of trusting the wrong machine. As a teenager, my first hack that ever courted trouble dealt with a fear that suddenly became all I could think about: the threat of a full-on, scorched-earth nuclear holocaust.

I'd been reading some article about the history of the American nuclear program, and before I knew it, with just a couple of clicks, I was at the website of the Los Alamos National Laboratory, the country's nuclear research facility. That's just the way the Internet works: you get curious, and your fingers do the thinking for you. But suddenly I was legitimately freaked out: the website of America's largest and most significant scientific research and weapons development institution, I noticed, had a glaring security hole. Its vulnerability was basically the virtual version of an unlocked door: an open directory structure.

I'll explain. Imagine I sent you a link to download a .pdf file that's kept on its own page of a multipage website. The URL for this file would typically be something like website.com/files/pdfs/filename.pdf. Now, as the structure of a URL derives directly from directory structure, each part of this URL represents a distinct "branch" of the directory "tree." In this instance, within the directory of website.com is a folder of files, within which is a subfolder of pdfs, within which is the specific filename.pdf that you're seeking to download. Today, most websites will confine your visit to that specific file, keeping their directory structures closed and private. But back in those dinosaur days, even major websites were created and run by folks who were new to the technology, and they often left their directory structures wide open, which meant that if you truncated your file's URL—if you simply changed it to something like website.com/files—you'd be able to access every

file on the site, pdf or otherwise, including those that weren't necessarily meant for visitors. This was the case with the Los Alamos
site.

In the hacking community, this is basically Baby's First Hack—a
totally rudimentary traversal procedure known as "dirwalking,"
or "directory walking." And that's just what I did: I walked as fast
as I could from file to subfolder to upper-level folder and back
again, a teen let loose through the parent directories. Within a
half hour of reading an article about the threat of nuclear weapons, I'd stumbled upon a trove of files meant only for the lab's
security-cleared workers.

To be sure, the documents I accessed weren't exactly the classified plans for building a nuclear device in my garage. (And, anyway, it's not as if those plans weren't already available on about
a dozen DIY websites.) Instead, what I got was more along the
lines of confidential interoffice memoranda and other personal
employee information. Still, as someone suddenly acutely worried
about mushroom clouds on the horizon, and also—especially—as
the child of military parents, I did what I figured I was supposed
to: I told an adult. I sent an explanatory email to the laboratory's
webmaster about the vulnerability, and waited for a response that
never came.

Every day after school I visited the site to check if the directory structure had changed, and it hadn't—nothing had changed,
except my capacity for shock and indignation. I finally got on the
phone, my house's second line, and called the general information
phone number listed at the bottom of the laboratory's site.

An operator picked up, and the moment she did I started stam-
mering. I don't even think I got to the end of the phrase "directory
structure" before my voice broke. The operator interrupted with a
curt "please hold for IT," and before I could thank her she'd transferred me to a voice mail.

By the time the beep came, I'd regained some modicum of confidence and, with a steadier larynx, I left a message. All I recall
now of that message was how I ended it—with relief, and by re-

peating my name and phone number. I think I even spelled out my name, like my father sometimes did, using the military phonetic alphabet: "Sierra November Oscar Whiskey Delta Echo November." Then I hung up and went on with my life, which for a week consisted pretty much exclusively of checking the Los Alamos website.

Nowadays, given the government's cyberintelligence capabilities, anyone who was pinging the Los Alamos servers a few dozen times a day would almost certainly become a person of interest. Back then, however, I was merely an interested person. I couldn't understand—didn't anybody care?

Weeks passed—and weeks can feel like months to a teenager—until one evening, just before dinner, the phone rang. My mother, who was in the kitchen making dinner, picked up.

I was at the computer in the dining room when I heard it was for me: "Yes, uh-huh, he's here." Then, "May I ask who's calling?"

I turned around in my seat and she was standing over me, holding the phone against her chest. All the color had left her face. She was trembling.

Her whisper had a mournful urgency I'd never heard before, and it terrified me: "What did you do?"

Had I known, I would have told her. Instead, I asked, "Who is it?"

"Los Alamos, the nuclear laboratory."

"Oh, thank God."

I gently pried the phone away from her and sat her down. "Hello?"

On the line was a friendly representative from Los Alamos IT, who kept calling me Mr. Snowden. He thanked me for reporting the problem and informed me that they'd just fixed it. I restrained myself from asking what had taken so long—I restrained myself from reaching over to the computer and immediately checking the site.

My mother hadn't taken her eyes off me. She was trying to piece together the conversation, but could only hear one side. I gave her a thumbs-up, and then, to further reassure her, I affected an older, serious, and unconvincingly deep voice and stiffly explained to the IT rep what he already knew: how I'd found the directory traversal problem, how I'd reported it, how I hadn't received any response until now. I finished up with, "I really appreciate you telling me. I hope I didn't cause any problems."

"Not at all," the IT rep said, and then asked what I did for a living.

"Nothing really," I said.

He asked whether I was looking for a job and I said, "During the school year, I'm pretty busy, but I've got a lot of vacation and the summers are free."

That's when the lightbulb went off, and he realized that he was dealing with a teenager. "Well, kid," he said, "you've got my contact. Be sure and get in touch when you turn eighteen. Now pass me along to that nice lady I spoke to."

I handed the phone to my anxious mother and she took it back with her into the kitchen, which was filling up with smoke. Dinner was burnt, but I'm guessing the IT rep said enough complimentary things about me that any punishment I was imagining went out the window.

6

Incomplete

I don't remember high school very well, because I spent so much of it asleep, compensating for all my insomniac nights on the computer. At Arundel High most of my teachers didn't mind my little napping habit, and left me alone so long as I wasn't snoring, though there were still a cruel, joyless few who considered it their duty to always wake me—with the screech of chalk or the clap of erasers—and ambush me with a question: "And what do *you* think, Mr. Snowden?"

I'd lift my head off my desk, sit up in my chair, yawn, and—as my classmates tried to stifle their laughter—I'd have to answer.

The truth is, I loved these moments, which were among the greatest challenges high school had to offer. I loved being put on the spot, groggy and dazed, with thirty pairs of eyes and ears trained on me and expecting my failure, while I searched for a clue on the half-empty blackboard. If I could think quickly enough to come up with a good answer, I'd be a legend. But if I was too slow, I could always crack a joke—it's never too late for a joke. In the absolute worst case, I'd sputter, and my classmates would think I was stupid. Let them. You should always let people underestimate you. Because when people misappraise your intelligence and abilities, they're merely pointing out their own vulnerabilities—the gaping holes in their judgment that need to stay open if you want to cartwheel through later on a flaming horse, correcting the record with your sword of justice.

When I was a teen, I think I was a touch too enamored of the idea that life's most important questions are binary, meaning that one answer is always Right, and all the rest of the answers are Wrong. I think I was enchanted by the model of computer programming, whose questions can only be answered in one of two ways: 1 or 0, the machine-code version of Yes or No, True or False. Even the multiple-choice questions of my quizzes and tests could be approached through the oppositional logic of the binary. If I didn't immediately recognize one of the possible answers as correct, I could always try to reduce my choices by a process of elimination, looking for terms such as "always" or "never" and seeking out invalidating exceptions.

Toward the end of my freshman year, however, I was faced with a very different kind of assignment—a question that couldn't be answered by filling in bubbles with a #2 pencil, but only by rhetoric: full sentences in full paragraphs. In plain terms, it was an English class assignment, a writing prompt: "Please produce an autobiographical statement of no fewer than 1,000 words." I was being ordered by strangers to divulge my thoughts on perhaps the only subject on which I didn't have any thoughts: the subject of me, whoever he was. I just couldn't do it. I was blocked. I didn't turn anything in and received an Incomplete.

My problem, like the prompt itself, was personal. I couldn't "produce an autobiographical statement" because my life at the time was too confusing. This was because my family was falling apart. My parents were getting a divorce. It all happened so fast. My father moved out and my mother put the house in Crofton on the market, and then moved with my sister and me into an apartment, and then into a condominium in a development in nearby Ellicott City. I've had friends tell me that you aren't really an adult until you bury a parent or become one yourself. But what no one ever mentions is that for kids of a certain age, divorce is like both of those happening simultaneously. Suddenly, the invulnerable icons of your childhood are gone. In their stead, if there's anyone at all, is a person even more lost than you are, full of tears and rage, who craves your reassurance that everything will turn out okay. It won't, though, at least not for a while.

As the custody and visitation rights were being sorted by the courts, my sister threw herself into college applications, was accepted, and started counting down the days until she'd leave for the University of North Carolina at Wilmington. Losing her meant losing my closest tie to what our family had been.

I reacted by turning inward. I buckled down and willed myself into becoming another person, a shape-shifter putting on the mask of whoever the people I cared about needed at the time. Among family, I was dependable and sincere. Among friends, mirthful and unconcerned. But when I was alone, I was subdued, even morose, and constantly worried about being a burden. I was haunted by all the road trips to North Carolina I'd complained through, all the Christmases I'd ruined by bringing home bad report cards, all the times I'd refused to get off-line and do my chores. Every childhood fuss I'd ever made flickered in my mind like crime-scene footage, evidence that I was responsible for what had happened.

I tried to throw off the guilt by ignoring my emotions and feigning self-sufficiency, until I projected a sort of premature adulthood. I stopped saying that I was "playing" with the computer, and started saying that I was "working" on it. Just changing those words, without remotely changing what I was doing, made a difference in how I was perceived, by others and even by myself.

I stopped calling myself "Eddie." From now on, I was "Ed." I got my first cell phone, which I wore clipped to my belt like a grown-ass man.

The unexpected blessing of trauma—the opportunity for reinvention—taught me to appreciate the world beyond the four walls of home. I was surprised to find that as I put more and more distance between myself and the two adults who loved me the most, I came closer to others, who treated me like a peer. Mentors who taught me to sail, trained me to fight, coached me in public speaking, and gave me the confidence to stand onstage—all of them helped to raise me.

At the beginning of my sophomore year, though, I started getting tired a lot and falling asleep more than usual—not just at school anymore, but now even at the computer. I'd wake up in the middle of the night in a more or less upright position, the screen in front of me full of gibberish because I'd passed out atop the keys. Soon enough my joints were aching, my nodes were swollen, the whites of my eyes turned yellow, and I was too exhausted to get out of bed, even after sleeping for twelve hours or more at a stretch.

After having had more blood taken from me than I'd ever imagined was in my body, I was eventually diagnosed with infectious mononucleosis. It was both a seriously debilitating and seriously humiliating illness for me to have, not least because it's usually contracted through what my classmates called "hooking up," and at age fifteen the only "hooking up" I'd ever done involved a modem. School was totally forgotten, my absences piled up, and not even that made me happy. Not even an all-ice-cream diet made me happy. I barely had the energy to do anything but play the games my parents gave me—each of them trying to bring the cooler game, the newer game, as if they were in a competition to perk me up or mitigate their guilt about the divorce. When I no longer had it in me to even work a joystick, I wondered why I was alive. Sometimes I'd wake up unable to recognize my surroundings. It would take me a while to figure out whether the dimness meant that I was at my mother's condo or my father's one-bedroom, and I'd have no recollection of having been driven between them. Every day became the same.

It was a haze. I remember reading *The Conscience of a Hacker* (aka *The Hacker's Manifesto*), Neal Stephenson's *Snow Crash*, and reams of J. R. R. Tolkien, falling asleep midchapter and getting the characters and action confused, until I was dreaming that Gollum was by my bedside and whining, "Master, Master, information wants to be free."

While I was resigned to all the fever dreams sleep brought me, the thought of having to catch up on my schoolwork was the true nightmare. After I'd missed approximately four months of class, I got a letter in the mail from Arundel High informing me that I'd have to repeat my sophomore year. I'd say I was shocked, but the moment I read the letter, I realized that I'd known this was inevitable and had been dreading it for weeks. The prospect of returning to school, let alone of repeating two semesters, was unimaginable to me, and I was ready to do whatever it took to avoid it.

Just at the point when my glandular disease had developed into a full-on depression, receiving the school news shook me out of my slump. Suddenly I was upright and getting dressed in something other than pajamas. Suddenly I was online and on the phone, searching for the system's edges, searching for a hack. After a bit of research, and a lot of form-filling, my solution landed in the mailbox: I'd gotten myself accepted to college. Apparently, you don't need a high school diploma to apply.

Anne Arundel Community College was a local institution, certainly not as venerable as my sister's school, but it would do the trick. All that mattered was that it was accredited. I took the offer of admission to my high school administrators, who, with a curious and barely concealed mixture of resignation and glee, agreed to let me enroll. I'd attend college classes two days a week, which was just about the most that I could manage to stay upright and functional. By taking classes above my grade level, I wouldn't have to suffer through the year I'd missed. I'd just skip it.

AACC was about twenty-five minutes away, and the first few times I drove myself were perilous—I was a newly licensed driver who could barely stay awake at the wheel. I'd go to class and then come directly home to sleep. I was the youngest person in all my classes, and might even have been the youngest person at the school, alternately a mascot-like object of novelty and a discomfiting presence. This, along with the fact that I was still recovering, meant that I didn't hang out much. Also, because AACC was a commuter school, it had no active campus life. The anonymity of the school suited me fine, though, as did my classes, most of which were distinctly more interesting than anything I'd napped through at Arundel High.

BEFORE I GO any further and leave high school forever, I should note that I still owe that English class assignment, the one marked Incomplete. My autobiographical statement. The older I get, the heavier it weighs on me, and yet writing it hasn't gotten any easier.

The fact is, no one with a biography like mine ever comes comfortably to autobiography. It's hard to have spent so much of my life trying to avoid identification, only to turn around completely and share "personal disclosures" in a book. The Intelligence Community tries to inculcate in its workers a baseline anonymity, a sort of blank-page personality upon which to inscribe secrecy and the art of imposture. You train yourself to be inconspicuous, to look and sound like others. You live in the most ordinary house, you drive the most ordinary car, you wear the same ordinary clothes as everyone else. The difference is, you do it on purpose: normalcy, the ordinary, is your cover. This is the perverse reward of a self-denying career that brings no public glory: the private glory comes not during work, but after, when you can go back out among other people again and successfully convince them that you're one of them.

Though there are a score of more popular and surely more accurate psychological terms for this type of identity split, I tend to think of it as human encryption. As in any process of encryption, the original material—your core identity—still exists, but only in a locked and scrambled form. The equation that enables this ciphering is a simple proportion: the more you know about others, the less you know about yourself. After a time, you might forget your likes and even your dislikes. You can lose your politics, along with any and all respect for the political process that you might have had. Everything gets subsumed by the job, which begins with a denial of character and ends with a denial of conscience. "Mission First."

Some version of the above served me for years as an explanation of my dedication to privacy, and my inability or unwillingness to get personal. It's only now, when I've been out of the IC almost as long as I was in it, that I realize: it isn't nearly enough. After all, I was hardly a spy—I wasn't even shaving—when I failed to turn in my English class assignment. Instead, I was a kid who'd been practicing spycraft for a while already—partly through my online experiments with game-playing identities, but more than anything through dealing with the silence and lies that followed my parents' divorce.

With that rupture, we became a family of secret-keepers, experts at subterfuge and hiding. My parents kept secrets from each other, and from me and my sister. My sister and I would eventually keep our own secrets, too, when one of us was staying with our father for the weekend and the other was staying with our mother. One of the most difficult trials that a child of divorce has to face is being interrogated by one parent about the new life of the other.

My mother would be gone for stretches, back on the dating scene. My father tried his best to fill the void, but, at times, he would become enraged by the protracted and expensive divorce process. Whenever that happened, it would seem to me as if our roles had reversed. I had to be assertive and stand up to him, to reason with him.

It's painful to write this, though not so much because the events of this period are painful to recall as because they're in no way indicative of my parents' fundamental decency—or of how, out of love for their children, they were eventually able to bury their differences, reconcile with respect, and flourish separately in peace.

This kind of change is constant, common, and human. But an autobiographical statement is static, the fixed document of a person in flux. This is why the best account that someone can ever give of themselves is not a statement but a pledge—a pledge to the principles they value, and to the vision of the person they hope to become.

I'd enrolled in community college to save myself time after a setback, not because I intended to continue with my higher education. But I made a pledge to myself that I'd at least complete my high school degree. It was a weekend when I finally kept that promise, driving out to a public school near Baltimore to take the last test I'd ever take for the state of Maryland: the exam for the General Education Development (GED) degree, which the US government recognizes as the standard equivalent to a high school diploma.

I remember leaving the exam feeling lighter than ever, having satisfied the two years of schooling that I still owed to the state just by taking a two-day exam. It felt like a hack, but it was more than that. It was me staying true to my word.

7

9/11

From the age of sixteen, I was pretty much living on my own. With my mother throwing herself into her work, I often had her condo to myself. I set my own schedule, cooked my own meals, and did my own laundry. I was responsible for everything but paying the bills.

I had a 1992 white Honda Civic and drove it all over the state, listening to the indie alternative 99.1 WHFS—"Now Hear This" was one of its catchphrases—because that's what everybody else did. I wasn't very good at being normal, but I was trying.

My life became a circuit, tracing a route between my home, my college, and my friends, particularly a new group that I met in Japanese class. I'm not quite sure how long it took us to realize that we'd become a clique, but by the second semester we attended class as much to see each other as to learn the language. This, by the way, is the best way to "seem normal": surround yourself with people just as weird, if not weirder, than you are. Most of these friends were aspiring artists and graphic designers obsessed with then controversial anime, or Japanese animation. As our friendships deepened, so, too, did my familiarity with anime genres, until I could rattle off relatively informed opinions about a new library of shared experiences with titles like *Grave of the Fireflies*, *Revolutionary Girl Utena*, *Neon Genesis Evangelion*, *Cowboy Bebop*, *The Vision of Escaflowne*, *Rurouni Kenshin*, *Nausicaa of the Valley of the Wind*, *Trigun*, *The Slayers*, and my personal favorite, *Ghost in the Shell*.

One of these new friends—I'll call her Mae—was an older woman, much older, at a comfortably adult twenty-five. She was something of an idol to the rest of us, as a published artist and avid cosplayer. She was my Japanese conversation partner and, I was impressed to find out, also ran a successful Web-design business that I'll call Squirrelling Industries, after the pet sugar gliders she occasionally carried around in a purple felt Crown Royal bag.

That's the story of how I became a freelancer: I started working as a Web designer for the girl I met in class. She, or I guess her business, hired me under the table at the then lavish rate of $30/hour in cash. The trick was how many hours I'd actually get paid for.

Of course, Mae could've paid me in smiles—because I was smitten, just totally in love with her. And though I didn't do a particularly good job of concealing that, I'm not sure that Mae minded, because I never missed a deadline or even the slightest opportunity to do a favor for her. Also, I was a quick learner. In a company of two, you've got to be able to do everything. Though I could, and did, conduct my Squirrelling Industries business anywhere—that, after all, is the point of working online—she preferred that I come into the office, by which I mean her house, a two-story town house that she shared with her husband, a neat and clever man whom I'll call Norm.

Yes, Mae was married. What's more, the town house that she and Norm lived in was located on base at the southwestern edge of Fort Meade, where Norm worked as an air force linguist assigned to the NSA. I can't tell you if it's legal to run a business out of your home if your home is federal property on a military installation, but as a teenager infatuated with a married woman who was also my boss, I wasn't exactly going to be a stickler for propriety.

It's nearly inconceivable now, but at the time Fort Meade was almost entirely accessible to anyone. It wasn't all bollards and barricades and checkpoints trapped in barbed wire. I could just drive onto the army base housing the world's most secretive intelligence agency in my '92 Civic, windows down, radio up, without having to stop at a gate and show ID. It seemed like every other weekend or so a quarter of my Japanese class would congregate in Mae's little house behind NSA headquarters to watch anime and create comics. That's just the way it was, in those bygone days when "It's a free country, isn't it?" was a phrase you heard in every schoolyard and sitcom.

On workdays I'd show up at Mae's in the morning, pulling into her cul-de-sac after Norm left for the NSA, and I'd stay through the day, until just before he returned. On the occasions that Norm and I happened to overlap during the two years or so I spent working for his wife, he was, all things considered, kind and generous to me. At first, I assumed that he was oblivious to my infatuation, or had such a low opinion of my chances as a seducer that he didn't mind leaving me alone with his wife. But one day, when we happened to pass each other—him going, me coming—he politely mentioned that he kept a gun on the nightstand.

Squirrelling Industries, which was really just Mae and me, was pretty typical of basement start-ups circa the dot-com boom, small enterprises competing for scraps before everything went bust. How it worked was that a large company—a carmaker, for instance— would hire a major ad agency or PR firm to build their website and just generally spiff up their Internet presence. The large company would know nothing about building websites, and the ad agency or PR firm would know only slightly more—just enough to post a job description seeking a Web designer at one of the then proliferating freelance work portals.

Mom-and-pop operations—or, in this case, older-married-woman/young-single-man operations—would then bid for the jobs, and the competition was so intense that the quotes would be driven ridiculously low. Factor in the cut that the winning contractor would have to pay to the work portal, and the money was barely enough for an adult to survive on, let alone a family. On top of the lack of financial reward, there was also a humiliating lack of credit: the freelancers could rarely mention what projects they'd done, because the ad agency or PR firm would claim to have developed it all in-house.

I got to know a lot about the world, particularly the business world, with Mae as my boss. She was strikingly canny, working twice as hard as her peers to make it in what was then a fairly macho industry, where every other client was out to screw you for free labor. This culture of casual exploitation incentivized freelancers to find ways to hack around the system, and Mae had a talent for managing her relationships in such a way as to bypass the work portals. She tried to cut out the middlemen and third parties and deal directly with the largest clients possible. She was wonderful at this, particularly after my help on the technical side allowed her to focus exclusively on the business and art. She parlayed her illustration skills into logo design and offered basic branding services. As for my work, the methods and coding were simple enough for me to pick up on the fly, and although they could be brutally repetitive, I wasn't complaining. I took to even the most menial Notepad++ job with pleasure. It's amazing what you do for love, especially when it's unrequited.

I can't help but wonder whether Mae was fully aware of my feelings for her all along, and simply leveraged them to her best advantage. But if I was a victim, I was a willing one, and my time under her left me better off.

Still, about a year into my tenure with Squirrelling Industries, I realized I had to plan for my future. Professional industry certifications for the IT sector were becoming hard to ignore. Most job listings and contracts for advanced work were beginning to require that applicants be officially accredited by major tech companies like IBM and Cisco in the use and service of their products. At least, that was the gist of a radio commercial that I kept hearing. One day, coming home from my commute after hearing the commercial for what must have been the hundredth time, I found myself dialing the 1-800 number and signing up for the Microsoft certification course that was being offered by the Computer Career Institute at Johns Hopkins University. The entire operation, from its embarrassingly high cost to its location at a "satellite campus" instead of at the main university, had the faint whiff of a scam, but I didn't care. It was a nakedly transactional affair— one that would allow Microsoft to impose a tax on the massively rising demand for IT folks, HR managers to pretend that an expensive piece of paper could distinguish bona fide pros from filthy charlatans, and nobodies like me to put the magic words "Johns Hopkins" on their résumé and jump to the front of the hiring line.

The certification credentials were being adopted as industry standard almost as quickly as the industry could invent them. An "A+ Certification" meant that you were able to service and repair computers. A "Net+ Certification" meant that you were able to handle some basic networking. But these were just ways to become the guy who worked the Help Desk. The best pieces of paper were grouped under the rubric of the Microsoft Certified Professional series. There was the entry-level MCP, the Microsoft Certified Professional; the more accomplished MCSA, the Microsoft Certified Systems Administrator; and the top piece of printed-out technical credibility, the MCSE, Microsoft Certified Systems Engineer. This was the brass ring, the guaranteed meal ticket. At the lowest of the low end, an MCSE's starting salary was $40,000 per year, a sum that—at the turn of the millennium and the age of seventeen—I found astonishing. But why not? Microsoft was trading above $100 per share, and Bill Gates had just been named the richest man in the world.

In terms of technical know-how, the MCSE wasn't the easiest to get, but it also didn't require what most self-respecting hackers would consider unicorn genius either. In terms of time and money, the commitment was considerable. I had to take seven separate tests, which cost $150 each, and pay something like $18,000 in tuition to Hopkins for the full battery of prep classes, which—true to form—I didn't finish, opting to go straight to the testing after I felt I'd had enough. Unfortunately, Hopkins didn't give refunds.

With payments looming on my tuition loan, I now had a more practical reason to spend time with Mae: money. I asked her to give me more hours. She agreed, and asked me to start coming in at 9:00 a.m. It was an egregiously early hour, especially for a free-lancer, which was why I was running late one Tuesday morning.

I was speeding down Route 32 under a beautiful Microsoft-blue sky, trying not to get caught by any speed traps. With a little luck, I'd roll into Mae's sometime before 9:30, and—with my window down and my hand riding the wind—it felt like a lucky day. I had the talk radio cranked and was waiting for the news to switch to the traffic.

Just as I was about to take the Canine Road shortcut into Fort Meade, an update broke through about a plane crash in New York City.

Mae came to the door and I followed her up the stairs from the dim entryway to the cramped office next to her bedroom. There wasn't much to it: just our two desks side by side, a drawing table for her art, and a cage for her squirrels. Though I was slightly distracted by the news, we had work to do. I forced myself to focus on the task at hand. I was just opening the project's files in a simple text editor—we wrote the code for websites by hand—when the phone rang.

Mae picked up. "What? Really?"

Because we were sitting so close together, I could hear her husband's voice. And he was yelling.

Mae's expression turned to alarm, and she loaded a news site on her computer. The only TV was downstairs. I was reading the site's report about a plane hitting one of the Twin Towers of the

World Trade Center, when Mae said, "Okay. Wow. Okay," and hung up.

She turned to me. "A second plane just hit the other tower."

Until that moment, I'd thought it had been an accident.

Mae said, "Norm thinks they're going to close the base."

"Like, the gates?" I said. "Seriously?" The scale of what had happened had yet to hit me. I was thinking about my commute.

"Norm said you should go home. He doesn't want you to get stuck."

I sighed, and saved the work I'd barely started. Just when I got up to leave, the phone rang again, and this time the conversation was even shorter. Mae was pale.

"You're not going to believe this."

Pandemonium, chaos: our most ancient forms of terror. They both refer to a collapse of order and the panic that rushes in to fill the void. For as long as I live, I'll remember retracing my way up Canine Road—the road past the NSA's headquarters—after the Pentagon was attacked. Madness poured out of the agency's black glass towers, a tide of yelling, ringing cell phones, and cars revving up in the parking lots and fighting their way onto the street. At the moment of the worst terrorist attack in American history, the staff of the NSA—the major signals intelligence agency of the American IC—was abandoning its work by the thousands, and I was swept up in the flood.

NSA director Michael Hayden issued the order to evacuate before most of the country even knew what had happened. Subsequently, the NSA and the CIA—which also evacuated all but a skeleton crew from its own headquarters on 9/11—would explain their behavior by citing a concern that one of the agencies might potentially, possibly, perhaps be the target of the fourth and last hijacked airplane, United Airlines Flight 93, rather than, say, the White House or Capitol.

I sure as hell wasn't thinking about the next likeliest targets as I crawled through the gridlock, with everyone trying to get their cars out of the same parking lot simultaneously. I wasn't thinking about anything at all. What I was doing was obediently following along, in what today I recall as one totalizing moment—a clamor of horns (I don't think I'd ever heard a car horn at an American military installation before) and out-of-phase radios shrieking the news of the South Tower's collapse while the drivers steered with their knees and feverishly pressed redial on their phones. I can still feel it—the present-tense emptiness every time my call was dropped by an overloaded cell network, and the gradual realization that, cut off from the world and stalled bumper to bumper, even though I was in the driver's seat, I was just a passenger.

The stoplights on Canine Road gave way to humans, as the NSA's special police went to work directing traffic. In the ensuing hours, days, and weeks they'd be joined by convoys of Humvees topped with machine guns, guarding new roadblocks and checkpoints. Many of these new security measures became permanent, supplemented by endless rolls of wire and massive installations of surveillance cameras. With all this security, it became difficult for me to get back on base and drive past the NSA—until the day I was employed there.

These trappings of what would be called the War on Terror weren't the only reason I gave up on Mae after 9/11, but they certainly played a part. The events of that day had left her shaken. In time, we stopped working together and grew distant. I'd chat her up occasionally, only to find that my feelings had changed and I'd changed, too. By the time Mae left Norm and moved to California, she felt like a stranger to me. She was too opposed to the war.

8

9/12

Try to remember the biggest family event you've ever been to—maybe a family reunion. How many people were there? Maybe 30, 50? Though all of them together comprise your family, you might not really have gotten the chance to know each and every individual member. Dunbar's number, the famous estimate of how many relationships you can meaningfully maintain in life, is just 150. Now think back to school. How many people were in your class in grade school, and in high school? How many of them were friends, and how many others did you just know as acquaintances, and how many still others did you simply recognize? If you went to school in the United States, let's say it's a thousand. It certainly stretches the boundaries of what you could say are all "your people," but you may still have felt a bond with them.

Nearly three thousand people died on 9/11. Imagine everyone you love, everyone you know, even everyone with a familiar name or just a familiar face—and imagine they're gone. Imagine the empty houses. Imagine the empty school, the empty classrooms. All those people you lived among, and who together formed the fabric of your days, just not there anymore. The events of 9/11 left holes. Holes in families, holes in communities. Holes in the ground.

Now, consider this: over one million people have been killed in the course of America's response.

The two decades since 9/11 have been a litany of American destruction by way of American self-destruction, with the promulgation of secret policies, secret laws, secret courts, and secret wars, whose traumatizing impact—whose very existence—the US government has repeatedly classified, denied, disclaimed, and distorted. After having spent roughly half that period as an employee of the American Intelligence Community and roughly the other half in exile, I know better than most how often the agencies get things wrong. I know, too, how the collection and analysis of intelligence can inform the production of disinformation and propaganda, for use as frequently against America's allies as its enemies—and sometimes against its own citizens. Yet even given that knowledge, I still struggle to accept the sheer magnitude and speed of the change, from an America that sought to define itself by a calculated and performative respect for dissent to a security state whose militarized police demand obedience, drawing their guns and issuing the order for total submission now heard in every city: "Stop resisting."

This is why whenever I try to understand how the last two decades happened, I return to that September—to that ground-zero day and its immediate aftermath. To return to that fall means coming up against a truth darker than the lies that tied the Taliban to al-Qaeda and conjured up Saddam Hussein's illusory stockpile of WMDs. It means, ultimately, confronting the fact that the carnage and abuses that marked my young adulthood were born not only in the executive branch and the intelligence agencies, but also in the hearts and minds of all Americans, myself included.

I remember escaping the panicked crush of the spies fleeing Fort Meade just as the North Tower came down. Once on the highway, I tried to steer with one hand while pressing buttons with the other, calling family indiscriminately and never getting through. Finally I managed to get in touch with my mother, who at this point in her career had left the NSA and was working as a clerk for the federal courts in Baltimore. They, at least, weren't evacuating.

Her voice scared me, and suddenly the only thing in the world that mattered to me was reassuring her.

"It's okay. I'm headed off base," I said. "Nobody's in New York, right?"

"I don't—I don't know. I can't get in touch with Gran."

"Is Pop in Washington?"

"He could be in the Pentagon for all I know."

The breath went out of me. By 2001, Pop had retired from the Coast Guard and was now a senior official in the FBI, serving as one of the heads of its aviation section. This meant that he spent plenty of time in plenty of federal buildings throughout DC and its environs.

Before I could summon any words of comfort, my mother spoke again. "There's someone on the other line. It might be Gran. I've got to go."

When she didn't call me back, I tried her number endlessly but couldn't get through, so I went home to wait, sitting in front of the blaring TV while I kept reloading news sites. The new cable modem we had was quickly proving more resilient than all of the telecom satellites and cell towers, which were failing across the country.

My mother's drive back from Baltimore was a slog through crisis traffic. She arrived in tears, but we were among the lucky ones. Pop was safe.

The next time we saw Gran and Pop, there was a lot of talk—about Christmas plans, about New Year's plans—but the Pentagon and the towers were never mentioned.

My father, by contrast, vividly recounted his 9/11 to me. He was at Coast Guard Headquarters when the towers were hit, and

he and three of his fellow officers left their offices in the Operations Directorate to find a conference room with a screen so they
could watch the news coverage. A young officer rushed past them
down the hall and said, "They just bombed the Pentagon." Met
with expressions of disbelief, the young officer repeated, "I'm serious—they just bombed the Pentagon." My father hustled over
to a wall-length window that gave him a view across the Potomac
of about two-fifths of the Pentagon and swirling clouds of thick
black smoke.

The more that my father related this memory, the more intrigued I became by the line: "They just bombed the Pentagon."
Every time he said it, I recall thinking, "They"? Who were "They"?

America immediately divided the world into "Us" and "Them,"
and everyone was either with "Us" or against "Us," as President
Bush so memorably remarked even while the rubble was still smoldering. People in my neighborhood put up new American flags, as
if to show which side they'd chosen. People hoarded red, white,
and blue Dixie cups and stuffed them through every chain-link
fence on every overpass of every highway between my mother's
home and my father's, to spell out phrases like UNITED WE STAND
and STAND TOGETHER NEVER FORGET.

I sometimes used to go to a shooting range and now alongside
the old targets, the bull's-eyes and flat silhouettes, were effigies of
men in Arab headdress. Guns that had languished for years behind the dusty glass of the display cases were now marked SOLD.
Americans also lined up to buy cell phones, hoping for advance
warning of the next attack, or at least the ability to say good-bye
from a hijacked flight.

Nearly a hundred thousand spies returned to work at the
agencies with the knowledge that they'd failed at their primary
job, which was protecting America. Think of the guilt they were
feeling. They had the same anger as everybody else, but they also
felt the guilt. An assessment of their mistakes could wait. What
mattered most at that moment was that they redeem themselves.
Meanwhile, their bosses got busy campaigning for extraordinary

budgets and extraordinary powers, leveraging the threat of terror to expand their capabilities and mandates beyond the imagination not just of the public but even of those who stamped the approvals.

September 12 was the first day of a new era, which America faced with a unified resolve, strengthened by a revived sense of patriotism and the goodwill and sympathy of the world. In retrospect, my country could have done so much with this opportunity. It could have treated terror not as the theological phenomenon it purported to be, but as the crime it was. It could have used this rare moment of solidarity to reinforce democratic values and cultivate resilience in the now-connected global public.

Instead, it went to war.

The greatest regret of my life is my reflexive, unquestioning support for that decision. I was outraged, yes, but that was only the beginning of a process in which my heart completely defeated my rational judgment. I accepted all the claims retailed by the media as facts, and I repeated them as if I were being paid for it. I wanted to be a liberator. I wanted to free the oppressed. I embraced the truth constructed for the good of the state, which in my passion I confused with the good of the country. It was as if whatever individual politics I'd developed had crashed—the anti-institutional hacker ethos instilled in me online, and the apolitical patriotism I'd inherited from my parents, both wiped from my system—and I'd been rebooted as a willing vehicle of vengeance. The sharpest part of the humiliation comes from acknowledging how easy this transformation was, and how readily I welcomed it.

I wanted, I think, to be part of something. Prior to 9/11, I'd been ambivalent about serving because it had seemed pointless, or just boring. Everyone I knew who'd served had done so in the post–Cold War world order, between the fall of the Berlin Wall and the attacks of 2001. In that span, which coincided with my youth, America lacked for enemies. The country I grew up in was the sole global superpower, and everything seemed—at least to me, or to people like me—prosperous and settled. There were no new frontiers to conquer or great civic problems to solve, except online. The attacks of 9/11 changed all that. Now, finally, there was a fight.

My options dismayed me, however. I thought I could best serve my country behind a terminal, but a normal IT job seemed too comfortable and safe for this new world of asymmetrical conflict. I hoped I could do something like in the movies or on TV—those hacker-versus-hacker scenes with walls of virus-warning blinken-lights, tracking enemies and thwarting their schemes. Unfortunately for me, the primary agencies that did that—the NSA, the CIA—had their hiring requirements written a half century ago and often rigidly required a traditional college degree, meaning that though the tech industry considered my AACC credits and MCSE certification acceptable, the government wouldn't. The more I read around online, however, the more I realized that the post-9/11 world was a world of exceptions. The agencies were growing so much and so quickly, especially on the technical side, that they'd sometimes waive the degree requirement for military veterans. It's then that I decided to join up.

You might be thinking that my decision made sense, or was inevitable, given my family's record of service. But it didn't and it wasn't. By enlisting, I was as much rebelling against that well-established legacy as I was conforming to it—because after talking to recruiters from every branch, I decided to join the army, whose leadership some in my Coast Guard family had always considered the crazy uncles of the US military.

When I told my mother, she cried for days. I knew better than to tell my father, who'd already made it very clear during hypothetical discussions that I'd be wasting my technical talents there. I was twenty years old; I knew what I was doing.

The day I left, I wrote my father a letter—handwritten, not typed—that explained my decision, and slipped it under the front door of his apartment. It closed with a statement that still makes me wince. "I'm sorry, Dad," I wrote, "but this is vital for my personal growth."

X-Rays

I joined the army, as its slogan went, to be all I could be, and also because it wasn't the Coast Guard. It didn't hurt that I'd scored high enough on its entrance exams to qualify for a chance to come out of training as a Special Forces sergeant, on a track the recruiters called 18 X-Ray, which was designed to augment the ranks of the small flexible units that were doing the hardest fighting in America's increasingly shadowy and disparate wars. The 18 X-Ray program was a considerable incentive, because traditionally, before 9/11, I would've had to already be in the army before being given a shot at attending the Special Forces' exceedingly demanding qualification courses. The new system worked by screening prospective soldiers up front, identifying those with the highest levels of fitness, intelligence, and language-learning ability—the ones who might make the cut—and using the inducements of special training and a rapid advance in rank to enlist promising candidates who might otherwise go elsewhere. I'd put in a couple of months of grueling runs to prepare—I was in great shape, but I always hated running—before my recruiter called to say that my paperwork was approved: I was in, I'd made it. I was the first candidate he'd ever signed up for the program, and I could hear the pride and cheer in his voice when he told me that after training, I'd probably be made a Special Forces Communications, Engineering, or Intelligence sergeant.

Probably.

But first, I had to get through basic training at Fort Benning, Georgia.

I sat next to the same guy the whole way down there, from bus to plane to bus, Maryland to Georgia. He was enormous, a puffy bodybuilder somewhere between two and three hundred pounds. He talked nonstop, his conversation alternating between describing how he'd slap the drill sergeant in the face if he gave him any lip and recommending the steroid cycles I should take to most effectively bulk up. I don't think he took a breath until we arrived at Fort Benning's Sand Hill training area—which in hindsight, I have to say, didn't actually seem to have that much sand.

The drill sergeants greeted us with withering fury and gave us nicknames based on our initial infractions and grave mistakes, like getting off the bus wearing a brightly colored floral-patterned shirt, or having a name that could be modified slightly into something funnier. Soon I was Snowflake and my seatmate was Daisy and all he could do was clench his jaw—nobody dared to clench a fist—and fume.

Once the drill sergeants noticed that Daisy and I were already acquainted, and that I was the lightest in the platoon, at five foot nine and 124 pounds, and he the heaviest, they decided to entertain themselves by pairing us together as often as possible. I still remember the buddy carry, an exercise where you had to carry your supposedly wounded partner the length of a football field using a number of different methods like the "neck drag," the "fireman," and the especially comedic "bridal carry." When I had to carry Daisy, you couldn't see me beneath his bulk. It would look like Daisy was floating, though I'd be under him sweating and cursing, straining to get his gigantic ass to the other side of the goal line before collapsing myself. Daisy would then get up with a laugh, drape me around his neck like a damp towel, and go skipping along like a child in the woods.

We were always dirty and always hurting, but within weeks I was in the best shape of my life. My slight build, which had seemed like a curse, soon became an advantage, because so much of what we did were body-weight exercises. Daisy couldn't climb a rope, which I scampered up like a chipmunk. He struggled to lift his incredible bulk above the bar for the bare minimum of pull-ups, while I could do twice the number with one arm. He could barely manage a handful of push-ups before breaking a sweat, whereas I could do them with claps, or with just a single thumb. When we did the two-minute push-up tests, they stopped me early for maxing the score.

Everywhere we went, we marched—or ran. We ran constantly. Miles before mess, miles after mess, down roads and fields and around the track, while the drill sergeant called cadence:

I went to the desert
where the terrorists run
pulled out my machete
pulled out my gun.

Left, right, left, right—kill kill kill!
Mess with us and you know we will!

I went to the caves
where the terrorists hide
pulled out a grenade
and threw it inside.

Left, right, left, right—kill kill kill!
Mess with us and you know we will!

———

RUNNING IN UNIT formation, calling cadence—it lulls you, it puts you outside yourself, filling your ears with the din of dozens of men echoing your own shouting voice and forcing your eyes to fix on the footfalls of the runner in front of you. After a while you don't think anymore, you merely count, and your mind dissolves into the rank and file as you pace out mile after mile. I would say it was serene if it wasn't so deadening. I would say I was at peace if I weren't so tired. This was precisely as the army intended. The drill sergeant goes unslapped not so much because of fear but because of exhaustion: he's never worth the effort. The army makes its fighters by first training the fight out of them until they're too weak to care, or to do anything besides obey.

It was only at night in the barracks that we could get some respite, which we had to earn by toeing the line in front of our bunks, reciting the Soldier's Creed, and then singing "The Star-Spangled Banner." Daisy would always forget the words. Also, he was tone-deaf.

Some guys would stay up late talking about what they were going to do to bin Laden once they found him, and they were all sure they were going to find him. Most of their fantasies had to do with decapitation, castration, or horny camels. Meanwhile, I'd have dreams about running, not through the lush and loamy Georgia landscape but through the desert.

Sometime during the third or fourth week we were out on a land navigation movement, which is when your platoon goes into the woods and treks over variegated terrain to predetermined coordinates, clambering over boulders and wading across streams, with just a map and a compass—no GPS, no digital technology. We'd done versions of this movement before, but never in full kit, with each of us lugging a rucksack stuffed with around fifty pounds of gear. Worse still, the raw boots the army had issued me were so wide that I floated in them. I felt my toes blister even as I set out, loping across the range.

Toward the middle of the movement, I was on point and scrambled atop a storm-felled tree that arched over the path at about chest height so that I could shoot an azimuth to check our bearings. After confirming that we were on track, I went to hop down, but with one foot extended I noticed the coil of a snake directly below me. I'm not exactly a naturalist, so I don't know what species of snake it was, but then again, I didn't really care. Kids in North Carolina grow up being told that all snakes are deadly and I wasn't about to start doubting it now.

Instead, I started trying to walk on air. I widened the stride of my outstretched foot, once, twice, twisting for the extra distance, when suddenly I realized I was falling. When my feet hit the ground, some distance beyond the snake, a fire shot up my legs that was more painful than any viper bite I could imagine. A few stumbling steps, which I had to take in order to regain my balance, told me that something was wrong. Grievously wrong. I was in excruciating pain, but I couldn't stop, because I was in the army and the army was in the middle of the woods. I gathered my resolve, pushed the pain away, and just focused on maintaining a steady pace—left, right, left, right—relying on the rhythm to distract me.

It got harder to walk as I went on, and although I managed to tough it out and finish, the only reason was that I didn't have a choice. By the time I got back to the barracks, my legs were numb. My rack, or bunk, was up top, and I could barely get myself into it. I had to grab its post, hoist up my torso like I was getting out of a pool, and drag my lower half in after.

The next morning I was torn from a fitful sleep by the clanking of a metal trash can being thrown down the squad bay, a wake-up call that meant someone hadn't done their job to the drill sergeant's satisfaction. I shot up automatically, swinging myself over the edge and springing to the floor. When I landed, my legs gave way. They crumpled and I fell. It was like I had no legs at all.

I tried to get up, grabbing for the lower bunk to try my hoist-by-the-arms maneuver again, but as soon as I moved my legs every muscle in my body seized and I sank down immediately.

Meanwhile a crowd had gathered around me, with laughter that turned to concern and then to silence as the drill sergeant approached. "What's the matter with you, broke-dick?" he said. "Get up off my floor before I make you a part of it, permanently." When he saw the agony flash across my face as I immediately and unwisely struggled to respond to his commands, he put his hand to my chest to stop me. "Daisy! Get Snowflake here down to the bench." Then he crouched down over me, as if he didn't want the others to hear him being gentle, and said in a quiet rasp, "As soon as it opens, Private, you're going to crutch your broken ass to Sick Call," which is where the army sends its injured to be abused by professionals.

There's a major stigma about getting injured in the army, mostly because the army is dedicated to making its soldiers feel invincible but also because it likes to protect itself from accusations of mis-training. This is why almost all training-injury victims are treated like whiners or, worse, malingerers.

After he carried me down to the bench, Daisy had to go. He wasn't hurt, and those of us who were had to be kept separated. We were the untouchables, the lepers, the soldiers who couldn't train because of anything from sprains, lacerations, and burns to broken ankles and deep necrotized spider bites. My new battle buddies would now come from this bench of shame. A battle buddy is the person who, by policy, goes everywhere you go, just as you go everywhere they go, if there's even the remotest chance that either of you might be alone. Being alone might lead to thinking, and thinking can cause the army problems.

The battle buddy assigned to me was a smart, handsome, former catalog model Captain America type who'd injured his hip about a week earlier but hadn't attended to it until the pain had become unbearable and left him just as gimpy as me. Neither of us felt up to talking, so we crutched along in grim silence—left, right, left, right, but slowly. At the hospital I was X-rayed and told that I had bilateral tibial fractures. These are stress fractures, fissures on the surface of the bones that can deepen with time and pressure until they crack the bones down to the marrow. The only thing I could do to help my legs heal was to get off my feet and stay off them. It was with those orders that I was dismissed from the examination room to get a ride back to the battalion.

Except I couldn't go yet, because I couldn't leave without my battle buddy. He'd gone in to be X-rayed after me and hadn't returned. I assumed he was still being examined, so I waited. And waited. Hours passed. I spent the time reading newspapers and magazines, an unthinkable luxury for someone in basic training.

A nurse came over and said my drill sergeant was on the phone at the desk. By the time I hobbled over to take the call, he was livid. "Snowflake, you enjoying your reading? Maybe you could get some pudding while you're at it, and some copies of *Cosmo* for the girls? Why in the hell haven't you two dirtbags left yet?"

"Drill Sarn"—that's how everybody said it in Georgia, where my Southern accent had resurfaced for the moment—"I'm still waiting on my battle buddy, Drill Sarn."

"And where the fuck is he, Snowflake?"

"Drill Sarn, I don't know. He went into the examination room and hasn't come out, Drill Sarn."

He wasn't happy with the answer, and barked even louder. "Get off your crippled ass and go fucking find him, goddamnit."

I got up and crutched over to the intake counter to make inquiries. My battle buddy, they told me, was in surgery.

It was only toward evening, after a barrage of calls from the drill sergeant, that I found out what had happened. My battle buddy had been walking around on a broken hip for the past week, apparently, and if he hadn't been taken into surgery immediately and had it screwed back together, he might have been incapacitated for life. Major nerves could have been severed, because the break was as sharp as a knife.

I was sent back to Fort Benning alone, back to the bench. Anybody on the bench for more than three or four days was at serious risk of being "recycled"—forced to start basic training over from scratch—or, worse, of being transferred to the Medical Unit and sent home. These were guys who'd dreamed of being in the army their entire lives, guys for whom the army had been their only way out of cruel families and dead-end careers, who now had to face the prospect of failure and a return to civilian life irreparably damaged.

We were the cast-offs, the walking wounded hellguard who had no other duty than to sit on a bench in front of a brick wall twelve hours a day. We had been judged by our injuries as unfit for the army and now had to pay for this fact by being separated and shunned, as if the drill sergeants feared we'd contaminate others with our weakness or with the ideas that had occurred to us while benched. We were punished beyond the pain of our injuries themselves, excluded from petty joys like watching the fireworks on the Fourth of July. Instead, we pulled "fire guard" that night for the empty barracks, a task that involved watching to make sure that the empty building didn't burn down.

We pulled fire guard two to a shift, and I stood in the dark on my crutches, pretending to be useful, alongside my partner. He was a sweet, simple, beefy eighteen-year-old with a dubious, perhaps self-inflicted injury. By his own account, he should never have enlisted to begin with. The fireworks were bursting in the distance while he told me how much of a mistake he'd made, and how agonizingly lonely he was—how much he missed his parents and his home, their family farm somewhere way out in Appalachia.

I sympathized, though there wasn't much I could do but send him to speak to the chaplain. I tried to offer advice, suck it up, it might be better once you're used to it. But then he put his bulk in front of me and, in an endearingly childlike way, told me point-blank that he was going AWOL—a crime in the military—and asked me whether I would tell anybody. It was only then that I noticed he'd brought his laundry bag. He meant that he was going AWOL that very moment.

I wasn't sure how to deal with the situation, beyond trying to talk some sense into him. I warned him that going AWOL was a bad idea, that he'd end up with a warrant out for his arrest and any cop in the country could pick him up for the rest of his life. But the guy only shook his head. Where he lived, he said, deep in the mountains, they didn't even have cops. This, he said, was his last chance to be free.

I understood, then, that his mind was made up. He was much more mobile than I was, and he was big. If he ran, I couldn't chase him; if I tried to stop him, he might snap me in half. All I could do was report him, but if I did, I'd be penalized for having let the conversation get this far without calling for reinforcements and beating him with a crutch.

I was angry. I realized I was yelling at him. Why didn't he wait until I was in the latrine to make a break for it? Why was he putting me in this position?

He spoke softly. "You're the only one who listens," he said, and began to cry.

The saddest part of that night is that I believed him. In the company of a quarter thousand, he was alone. We stood in silence as the fireworks popped and snapped in the distance. I sighed and said, "I've got to go to the latrine. I'm going to be a while." Then I limped away and didn't look back.

That was the last I ever saw of him. I think I realized, then and there, that I wasn't long for the army, either.

My next doctor's appointment was merely confirmation.

The doctor was a tall, lanky Southerner with a wry demeanor. After examining me and a new set of X-rays, he said that I was in no condition to continue with my company. The next phase of training was airborne, and he told me, "Son, if you jump on those legs, they're going to turn into powder."

I was despondent. If I didn't finish the basic training cycle on time, I'd lose my slot in 18X, which meant that I'd be reassigned according to the needs of the army. They could make me into whatever they wanted: regular infantry, a mechanic, a desk jockey, a potato peeler, or—in my greatest nightmare—doing IT at the army's help desk.

The doctor must have seen how dejected I was, because he cleared his throat and gave me a choice: I could get recycled and try my luck with reassignment, or he could write me a note putting me out on what was called "administrative separation." This, he explained, was a special type of severance, not characterized as either honorable or dishonorable, only available to enlistees who'd been in the services fewer than six months. It was a clean break, more like an annulment than a divorce, and could be taken care of rather quickly.

I'll admit, the idea appealed to me. In the back of my mind, I even thought it might be some kind of karmic reward for the mercy I'd shown to the Appalachian who'd gone AWOL. The doctor left me to think, and when he came back in an hour I accepted his offer.

Shortly thereafter I was transferred to the Medical Unit, where I was told that in order for the administrative separation to go through I had to sign a statement attesting that I was all better, that my bones were all healed. My signature was a requirement, but it was presented as a mere formality. Just a few scribbles and I could go.

As I held the statement in one hand and the pen in the other, a knowing smile crossed my face. I recognized the hack: what I'd thought was a kind and generous offer made by a caring army doctor to an ailing enlistee was the government's way of avoiding liability and a disability claim. Under the military's rules, if I'd received a medical discharge, the government would have had to pay the bills for any issues stemming from my injury, any treatments and therapies it required. An administrative discharge put the burden on me, and my freedom hinged on my willingness to accept that burden.

I signed, and left that same day, on crutches that the army let me keep.

Cleared and in Love

I can't remember exactly when, in the midst of my convalescence, I started thinking clearly again. First the pain had to ebb away, then gradually the depression ebbed, too, and after weeks of waking to no purpose beyond watching the clock change I slowly began paying attention to what everyone around me was telling me: I was still young and I still had a future. I only felt that way myself, however, once I was finally able to stand upright and walk on my own. It was one of the myriad things that, like the love of my family, I'd simply taken for granted before.

As I made my first forays into the yard outside my mother's condo, I came to realize that there was another thing I'd taken for granted: my talent for understanding technology.

Forgive me if I come off like a dick, but there's no other way to say this: I'd always been so comfortable with computers that I almost didn't take my abilities seriously, and didn't want to be praised for them or to succeed because of them. I'd wanted, instead, to be praised for and to succeed at something else—something that was harder for me. I wanted to show that I wasn't just a brain in a jar; I was also heart and muscle.

That explained my stint in the army. And over the course of my convalescence, I came to realize that although the experience had wounded my pride, it had improved my confidence. I was stronger now, not afraid of the pain as much as grateful to be improved by it. Life beyond the barbed wire was getting easier. In the final reckoning, all the army had cost me was my hair, which had grown back, and a limp, which was healing.

I was ready to face the facts: if I still had the urge to serve my country, and I most certainly did, then I'd have to serve it through my head and hands—through computing. That, and only that, would be giving my country my best. Though I wasn't much of a veteran, having passed through the military's vetting could only help my chances of working at an intelligence agency, which was where my talents would be most in demand and, perhaps, most challenged.

Thus I became reconciled to what in retrospect was inevitable: the need for a security clearance. There are, generally speaking, three levels of security clearance: from low to high, confidential, secret, and top secret. The last of these can be further extended with a Sensitive Compartmented Information qualifier, creating the coveted TS/SCI access required by positions with the top-tier agencies—CIA and NSA. The TS/SCI was by far the hardest access to get, but also opened the most doors, and so I went back to Anne Arundel Community College while I searched for jobs that would sponsor my application for the grueling Single Scope Background Investigation the clearance required. As the approval process for a TS/SCI can take a year or more, I heartily recommend it to anyone recovering from an injury. All it involves is filling out some paperwork, then sitting around with your feet up and trying not to commit too many crimes while the federal government renders its verdict. The rest, after all, is out of your hands.

On paper, I was a perfect candidate. I was a kid from a service family, nearly every adult member of which had some level of clearance; I'd tried to enlist and fight for my country until an unfortunate accident had laid me low. I had no criminal record, no drug habit. My only financial debt was the student loan for my Microsoft certification, and I hadn't yet missed a payment.

None of this stopped me, of course, from being nervous.

I drove to and from classes at AACC as the National Background Investigations Bureau rummaged through nearly every aspect of my life and interviewed almost everyone I knew: my parents, my extended family, my classmates and friends. They went through my spotty school transcripts and, I'm sure, spoke to a few of my teachers. I got the impression that they even spoke to Mae and Norm, and to a guy I'd worked with one summer at a snow cone stand at Six Flags America. The goal of all this background checking was not only to find out what I'd done wrong, but also to find out how I might be compromised or blackmailed. The most important thing to the IC is not that you're 100 percent perfectly clean, because if that were the case they wouldn't hire anybody. Instead, it's that you're robotically honest—that there's no dirty secret out there that you're hiding that could be used against you, and thus against the agency, by an enemy power.

This, of course, set me thinking—sitting stuck in traffic as all the moments of my life that I regretted went spinning around in a loop inside my head. Nothing I could come up with would have raised even an iota of eyebrow from investigators who are used to finding out that the middle-aged analyst at a think tank likes to wear diapers and get spanked by grandmothers in leather. Still, there was a paranoia that the process created, because you don't have to be a closet fetishist to have done things that embarrass you and to fear that strangers might misunderstand you if those things were exposed. I mean, I grew up on the Internet, for Christ's sake. If you haven't entered something shameful or gross into that search box, then you haven't been online very long—though I wasn't worried about the pornography. Everybody looks at porn, and for those of you who are shaking your heads, don't worry: your secret is safe with me. My worries were more personal, or felt more personal: the endless conveyor belt of stupid jingoistic things I'd said, and the even stupider misanthropic opinions I'd abandoned, in the process of growing up online. Specifically, I was worried about my chat logs and forum posts, all the supremely moronic commentary that I'd sprayed across a score of gaming and hacker sites. Writing pseudonymously had meant writing freely, but often thoughtlessly. And since a major aspect of early Internet culture was competing with others to say the most inflammatory thing, I'd never hesitate to advocate, say, bombing a country that taxed video games, or corralling people who didn't like anime into reeducation camps. Nobody on those sites took any of it seriously, least of all myself.

When I went back and reread the posts, I cringed. Half the things I'd said I hadn't even meant at the time—I'd just wanted attention—but I didn't fancy my odds of explaining that to a gray-haired man in horn-rimmed glasses peering over a giant folder labeled PERMANENT RECORD. The other half, the things I think I had meant at the time, were even worse, because I wasn't that kid anymore. I'd grown up. It wasn't simply that I didn't recognize the voice as my own—it was that I now actively opposed its overheated, hormonal opinions. I found that I wanted to argue with a ghost. I wanted to fight with that dumb, puerile, and casually cruel self of mine who no longer existed. I couldn't stand the idea of being haunted by him forever, but I didn't know the best way to express my remorse and put some distance between him and me, or whether I should even try to do that. It was heinous to be so inextricably, technologically bound to a past that I fully regretted but barely remembered.

This might be the most familiar problem of my generation, the first to grow up online. We were able to discover and explore our identities almost totally unsupervised, with hardly a thought spared for the fact that our rash remarks and profane banter were being preserved for perpetuity, and that one day we might be expected to account for them. I'm sure everyone who had an Internet connection before they had a job can sympathize with this—surely everyone has that one post that embarrasses them, or that text or email that could get them fired.

My situation was somewhat different, however, in that most of the message boards of my day would let you delete your old posts. I could put together one tiny little script—not even a real program—and all of my posts would be gone in under an hour. It would've been the easiest thing in the world to do. Trust me, I considered it.

But ultimately, I couldn't. Something kept preventing me. It just felt wrong. To blank my posts from the face of the earth wasn't illegal, and it wouldn't even have made me ineligible for a security clearance had anyone found out. But the prospect of doing so bothered me nonetheless. It would've only served to reinforce some of the most corrosive precepts of online life: that nobody is ever allowed to make a mistake, and anybody who does make a mistake must answer for it forever. What mattered to me wasn't so much the integrity of the written record but that of my soul. I didn't want to live in a world where everyone had to pretend that they were perfect, because that was a world that had no place for me or my friends. To erase those comments would have been to erase who I was, where I was from, and how far I'd come. To deny my younger self would have been to deny my present self's validity.

I decided to leave the comments up and figure out how to live with them. I even decided that true fidelity to this stance would require me to continue posting. In time, I'd outgrow these new opinions, too, but my initial impulse remains unshakable, if only because it was an important step in my own maturity. We can't erase the things that shame us, or the ways we've shamed ourselves, online. All we can do is control our reactions—whether we let the past oppress us, or accept its lessons, grow, and move on.

This was the first thing that you might call a principle that occurred to me during this idle but formative time, and though it would prove difficult, I've tried to live by it.

Believe it or not, the only online traces of my existence whose past iterations have never given me worse than a mild sense of embarrassment were my dating profiles. I suspect this is because I'd had to write them with the expectation that their words truly mattered—since the entire purpose of the enterprise was for somebody in Real Life to actually care about them, and, by extension, about me.

I'd joined a website called HotOrNot.com, which was the most popular of the rating sites of the early 2000s, like RateMyFace and AmIHot. (Their most effective features were combined by a young Mark Zuckerberg into a site called FaceMash, which later became Facebook.) HotOrNot was the most popular of these pre-Facebook rating sites for a simple reason: it was the best of the few that had a dating component.

Basically, how it worked was that users voted on each other's photos: Hot or Not. An extra function for registered users such as myself was the ability to contact other registered users, if each had rated the other's photos Hot and clicked "Meet Me." This banal and crass process is how I met Lindsay Mills, my partner and the love of my life.

Looking at the photos now, I'm amused to find that nineteen-year-old Lindsay was gawky, awkward, and endearingly shy. To me at the time, though, she was a smoldering blonde, absolutely volcanic. What's more, the photos themselves were beautiful: they had a serious artistic quality, self-portraits more than selfies. They caught the eye and held it. They played coyly with light and shade. They even had a hint of meta fun: there was one taken inside the photo lab where she worked, and another where she wasn't even facing the camera.

I rated her Hot, a perfect ten. To my surprise, we matched (she rated me an eight, the angel), and in no time we were chatting. Lindsay was studying fine art photography. She had her own website, where she kept a journal and posted more shots: forests, flowers, abandoned factories, and—my favorite—more of her.

I scoured the Web and used each new fact I found about her to create a fuller picture: the town she was born in (Laurel, Maryland), her school's name (MICA, the Maryland Institute College of

Art). Eventually, I admitted to cyberstalking her. I felt like a creep, but Lindsay cut me off. "I've been searching about you, too, mister," she said, and rattled off a list of facts about me.

These were among the sweetest words I'd ever heard, yet I was reluctant to see her in person. We scheduled a date, and as the days ticked down my nervousness grew. It's a scary proposition, to take an online relationship off-line. It would be scary even in a world without ax murderers and scammers. In my experience, the more you've communicated with someone online, the more disappointed you'll be by meeting them in person. Things that are the easiest to say on-screen become the most difficult to say face-to-face. Distance favors intimacy: no one talks more openly than when they're alone in a room, chatting with an unseen someone alone in a different room. Meet that person, however, and you lose your latitude. Your talk becomes safer and tamer, a common conversation on neutral ground.

Online, Lindsay and I had become total confidants, and I was afraid of losing our connection in person. In other words, I was afraid of being rejected.

I shouldn't have been.

Lindsay—who'd insisted on driving—told me that she'd pick me up at my mother's condo. The appointed hour found me standing outside in the twilight cold, guiding her by phone through the similarly named, identical-looking streets of my mother's development. I was keeping an eye out for a gold '98 Chevy Cavalier, when suddenly I was blinded, struck in the face by a beam of light from the curb. Lindsay was flashing her brights at me across the snow.

"Buckle up." Those were the first words that Lindsay said to me in person, as I got into her car. Then she said, "What's the plan?"

It's then that I realized that despite all the thinking I had been doing about her, I'd done no thinking whatsoever about our destination.

If I'd been in this situation with any other woman, I'd have improvised, covering for myself. But with Lindsay it was different.

With Lindsay, it didn't matter. She drove us down her favorite road—she had a favorite road—and we talked until we ran out of miles on Guilford and ended up in the parking lot of the Laurel Mall. We just sat in her car and talked.

It was perfection. Talking face-to-face turned out to be just an extension of all our phone calls, emails, and chats. Our first date was a continuation of our first contact online and the start of a conversation that will last as long as we will. We talked about our families, or what was left of them. Lindsay's parents were also divorced: her mother and father lived twenty minutes apart, and as a kid Lindsay had been shuttled back and forth between them. She'd lived out of a bag. Mondays, Wednesdays, and Fridays she slept in her room at her mother's house. Tuesdays, Thursdays, and Saturdays she slept in her room at her father's house. Sundays were the dramatic day, because she had to choose.

She told me how bad my taste was, and criticized my date apparel: a button-down shirt decorated with metallic flames over a wifebeater and jeans (I'm sorry). She told me about the two other guys she was dating, whom she'd already mentioned online, and Machiavelli would've blushed at the ways in which I set about undermining them (I'm not sorry). I told her everything, too, including the fact that I wouldn't be able to talk to her about my work—the work I hadn't even started. This was ludicrously pretentious, which she made obvious to me by nodding gravely.

I told her I was worried about the upcoming polygraph required for my clearance and she offered to practice with me—a goofy kind of foreplay. The philosophy she lived by was the perfect training: say what you want, say who you are, never be ashamed. If they reject you, it's their problem. I'd never been so comfortable around someone, and I'd never been so willing to be called out for my faults. I even let her take my photo.

I had her voice in my head on my drive to the NSA's oddly named Friendship Annex complex for the final interview for my security clearance. I found myself in a windowless room, bound like a hostage to a cheap office chair. Around my chest and stomach were pneumographic tubes that measured my breathing. Finger cuffs on my fingertips measured my electrodermal activity, a blood pressure cuff around my arm measured my heart rate, and a sensor pad on the chair detected my every fidget and shift. All of these devices—wrapped, clamped, cuffed, and belted tightly around me—were connected to the large black polygraph machine placed on the table in front of me.

Behind the table, in a nicer chair, sat the polygrapher. She reminded me of a teacher I once had—and I spent much of the test trying to remember the teacher's name, or trying not to. She, the polygrapher, began asking questions. The first ones were no-brainers: Was my name Edward Snowden? Was 6/21/83 my date of birth? Then: Had I ever committed a serious crime? Had I ever had a problem with gambling? Had I ever had a problem with alcohol or taken illegal drugs? Had I ever been an agent of a foreign power? Had I ever advocated the violent overthrow of the United States government? The only admissible answers were binary: "Yes" and "No." I answered "No" a lot, and kept waiting for the questions I'd been dreading. "Have you ever impugned the competence and character of the medical staff at Fort Benning online?" "What were you searching for on the network of the Los Alamos Nuclear Laboratory?" But those questions never came and, before I knew it, the test was over.

I'd passed with flying colors.

As required, I had to answer the series of questions three times in total, and all three times I passed, which meant that not only had I qualified for the TS/SCI, I'd also cleared the "full scope polygraph"—the highest clearance in the land.

I had a girlfriend I loved and I was on top of the world.

I was twenty-two years old.

PART TWO

11

The System

I'm going to press Pause here, for a moment, to explain something about my politics at age twenty-two: I didn't have any. Instead, like most young people, I had solid convictions that I refused to accept weren't truly mine but rather a contradictory cluster of inherited principles. My mind was a mash-up of the values I was raised with and the ideals I encountered online. It took me until my late twenties to finally understand that so much of what I believed, or of what I thought I believed, was just youthful imprinting. We learn to speak by imitating the speech of the adults around us, and in the process of that learning we wind up also imitating their opinions, until we've deluded ourselves into thinking that the words we're using are our own.

My parents were, if not dismissive of politics in general, then certainly dismissive of politicians. To be sure, this dismissal had little in common with the disaffection of nonvoters or partisan disdain. Rather, it was a certain bemused detachment particular to their class, which nobler ages have called the federal civil service or the public sector, but which our own time tends to refer to as the deep state or the shadow government. None of those epithets, however, really captures what it is: a class of career officials (incidentally, perhaps one of the last functional middle classes in American life) who—nonelected and non-appointed—serve or work in government, either at one of the independent agencies (from the CIA and NSA to the IRS, the FCC, and so on) or at one of the executive departments (State, Treasury, Defense, Justice, and the like).

These were my parents, these were my people: a nearly three-million-strong professional government workforce dedicated to assisting the amateurs chosen by the electorate, and appointed by the elected, in fulfilling their political duties—or, in the words of the oath, in faithfully executing their offices. These civil servants, who stay in their positions even as administrations come and go, work as diligently under Republicans as under Democrats because they ultimately work for the government itself, providing core continuity and stability of rule.

These were also the people who, when their country went to war, answered the call. That's what I had done after 9/11, and I found that the patriotism my parents had taught me was easily converted into nationalist fervor. For a time, especially in my run-up to joining the army, my sense of the world came to resemble the duality of the least sophisticated video games, where good and evil are clearly defined and unquestionable.

However, once I returned from the Army and rededicated myself to computing, I gradually came to regret my martial fantasies. The more I developed my abilities, the more I matured and realized that the technology of communications had a chance of succeeding where the technology of violence had failed. Democracy could never be imposed at the point of a gun, but perhaps it could be sown by the spread of silicon and fiber. In the early 2000s the Internet was still just barely out of its formative period, and, to my mind at least, it offered a more authentic and complete incarnation of American ideals than even America itself. A place where everyone was equal? Check. A place dedicated to life, liberty, and the pursuit of happiness? Check, check, check. It helped that nearly all the major founding documents of Internet culture framed it in terms reminiscent of American history: here was this wild, open new frontier that belonged to anyone bold enough to settle it, swiftly becoming colonized by governments and corporate interests that were seeking to regulate it for power and profit. The large companies that were charging large fees—for hardware, for software, for the long-distance phone calls that you needed back then to get online, and for knowledge itself, which was humanity's common inheritance and so, by all rights, should have been freely available—were irresistible contemporary avatars of the British, whose harsh taxation ignited the fervor for independence.

This revolution wasn't happening in history textbooks, but now, in my generation, and any of us could be part of it solely by dint of our abilities. This was thrilling—to participate in the founding of a new society, one based not on where we were born or how we grew up or our popularity at school but on our knowledge and technological ability. In school, I'd had to memorize the preamble to the U.S. Constitution: now its words were lodged in my memory alongside John Perry Barlow's "A Declaration of the Independence of Cyberspace," which employed the same self-evident, self-elect plural pronoun: "We are creating a world that all may enter without privilege or prejudice accorded by race, economic power, military force, or station of birth. We are creating a world where anyone, anywhere may express his or her beliefs, no matter how singular, without fear of being coerced into silence or conformity."

This technological meritocracy was certainly empowering, but it could also be humbling, as I came to understand when I first went to work in the Intelligence Community. The decentralization of the Internet merely emphasized the decentralization of computing expertise. I might have been the top computer person in my family, or in my neighborhood, but to work for the IC meant testing my skills against everyone in the country and the world. The

Internet showed me the sheer quantity and variety of talent that existed, and made clear that in order to flourish I had to specialize.

There were a few different careers available to me as a technologist. I could have become a software developer, or, as the job is more commonly called, a programmer, writing the code that makes computers work. Alternatively, I could have become a hardware or network specialist, setting up the servers in their racks and running the wires, weaving the massive fabric that connects every computer, every device, and every file. Computers and computer programs were interesting to me, and so were the networks that linked them together. But I was most intrigued by their total functioning at a deeper level of abstraction, not as individual components but as an overarching system.

I thought about this a lot while I was driving, to and from Lindsay's house and to and from AACC. Car time has always been thinking time for me, and commutes are long on the crowded Beltway. To be a software developer was to run the rest stops off the exits and to make sure that all the fast-food and gas station franchises accorded with each other and with user expectations; to be a hardware specialist was to lay the infrastructure, to grade and pave the roads themselves; while to be a network specialist was to be responsible for traffic control, manipulating signs and lights to safely route the time-crunched hordes to their proper destinations. To get into systems, however, was to be an urban planner, to take all of the components available and ensure their interaction to maximum effect. It was, pure and simple, like getting paid to play God, or at least a tinpot dictator.

There are two main ways to be a systems guy. One is that you take possession of the whole of an existing system and maintain it, gradually making it more efficient and fixing it when it breaks. That position is called a systems administrator, or sysadmin. The second is that you analyze a problem, such as how to store data or how to search across databases, and solve it by engineering a solution from a combination of existing components or by inventing entirely new ones. This position is called a systems engineer. I eventually would do both of these jobs, working my way into administration and from there into engineering, oblivious throughout about how this intense engagement with the deepest levels of integration of computing technology was exerting an influence on my political convictions.

I'll try not to be too abstract here, but I want you to imagine a system. It doesn't matter what system: it can be a computer system, an ecosystem, a legal system, or even a system of government. Remember, a system is just a bunch of parts that function together as a whole, which most people are only reminded of when something breaks. It's one of the great chastening facts of working with systems that the part of a system that malfunctions is almost never the part in which *you notice* the malfunction. In order to find what caused the system to collapse, you have to start from the point where you spotted the problem, and trace the problem's effects logically through all of the system's components. Because a sysadmin or engineer is responsible for such repairs, they have to be equally fluent in software, hardware, and networking. If the malfunction turns out to be a software issue, the repair might involve scrolling through line after line of code in a UN General Assembly's worth of programming languages. If it's a hardware issue, it might require going over a circuit board with a flashlight in the mouth and a soldering gun in hand, checking each connection. If networking is implicated, it might mean tracing every twist and turn of the cables that run above the ceiling and under the floor, connecting the distant data centers full of servers with an office full of laptops.

Because systems work according to instructions, or rules, such an analysis is ultimately a search for which rules failed, how, and why—an attempt to identify the specific points where the intention of a rule was not adequately expressed by its formulation or application. Did the system fail because something was not communicated, or because someone abused the system by accessing a resource they weren't allowed to, or by accessing a resource they were allowed to but using it exploitatively? Was the job of one component stopped, or impeded, by another? Did one program, or computer, or group of people take over more than their fair share of the system?

Over the course of my career, it became increasingly difficult for me to ask these questions about the technologies I was responsible for and not about my country. And it became increasingly frustrating to me that I was able to repair the former but not the latter. I ended my time in Intelligence convinced that my country's operating system—its government—had decided that it functioned best when broken.

12

Homo contractus

I had hoped to serve my country, but instead I went to work for it. This is not a trivial distinction. The sort of honorable stability offered to my father and Pop wasn't quite as available to me, or to anyone of my generation. Both my father and Pop entered the service of their country on the first day of their working lives and retired from that service on the last. That was the American government that was familiar to me, from earliest childhood—when it had helped to feed, clothe, and house me—to the moment when it had cleared me to go into the Intelligence Community. That government had treated a citizen's service like a compact: it would provide for you and your family, in return for your integrity and the prime years of your life.

But I came into the IC during a different age.

By the time I arrived, the sincerity of public service had given way to the greed of the private sector, and the sacred compact of the soldier, officer, and career civil servant was being replaced by the unholy bargain of *Homo contractus*, the primary species of US Government 2.0. This creature was not a sworn servant but a transient worker, whose patriotism was incentivized by a better

paycheck and for whom the federal government was less the ultimate authority than the ultimate client.

During the American Revolution, it had made sense for the
Continental Congress to hire privateers and mercenaries to protect the independence of what was then barely a functioning republic. But for third-millennium hyperpower America to rely on
privatized forces for the national defense struck me as strange and
vaguely sinister. Indeed, today contracting is most often associated with its major failures, such as the fighting-for-hire work of
Blackwater (which changed its name to Xe Services after its employees were convicted of killing fourteen Iraqi civilians, and then
changed its name again to Academi after it was acquired by a
group of private investors), or the torture-for-hire work of CACI
and Titan (both of which supplied personnel who terrorized prisoners at Abu Ghraib).

These sensationalist cases can lead the public to believe that the
government employs contractors in order to maintain cover and
deniability, off-loading the illegal or quasi-legal dirty work to keep
its hands clean and conscience clear. But that's not entirely true,
or at least not entirely true in the IC, which tends to focus less on
deniability and more on never getting caught in the first place. Instead, the primary purpose served by IC contracting is much more
mundane: it's a workaround, a loophole, a hack that lets agencies
circumvent federal caps on hiring. Every agency has a head count,
a legislative limit that dictates the number of people it can hire to
do a certain type of work. But contractors, because they're not directly employed by the federal government, aren't included in that
number. The agencies can hire as many of them as they can pay for,
and they can pay for as many of them as they want—all they have
to do is testify to a few select congressional subcommittees that
the terrorists are coming for our children, or the Russians are in
our emails, or the Chinese are in our power grid. Congress never
says no to this type of begging, which is actually a kind of threat,
and reliably capitulates to the IC's demands.

Among the documents that I provided to journalists was the

2013 Black Budget. This is a classified budget in which over 68 percent of its money, $52.6 billion, was dedicated to the IC, including funding for 107,035 IC employees—more than a fifth of whom, some 21,800 people, were full-time contractors. And that number doesn't even include the tens of thousands more employed by companies that have signed contracts (or subcontracts, or sub-subcontracts) with the agencies for a specific service or project. Those contractors are never counted by the government, not even in the Black Budget, because to add their ranks to the contracting total would make one disturbing fact extraordinarily clear: the work of American Intelligence is done as frequently by private employees as it is by government servants.

To be sure, there are many, even in government, who maintain that this trickle-down scheme is advantageous. With contractors, they say, the government can encourage competitive bidding to keep costs down, and isn't on the hook to pay pensions and benefits. But the real advantage for government officials is the conflict of interest inherent in the budgeting process itself. IC directors ask Congress for money to rent contract workers from private companies, congresspeople approve that money, and then those IC directors and congresspeople are rewarded, after they retire from office, by being given high-paying positions and consultancies with the very companies they've just enriched. From the vantage of the corporate boardroom, contracting functions as governmentally assisted corruption. It's America's most legal and convenient method of transferring public money to the private purse.

But however much the work of Intelligence is privatized, the federal government remains the only authority that can grant an individual clearance to access classified information. And because clearance candidates must be sponsored in order to apply for clearance—meaning they must already have a job offer for a position that requires clearance—most contractors begin their careers in a government position. After all, it's rarely worth the expense for a private company to sponsor your clearance application and then pay you to wait around for a year for the government's approval. It makes more financial sense for a company to just hire an already-cleared government employee. The situation created by this economy is one in which government bears all the burdens of background checks but reaps few of the benefits. It must do all of the work and assume all of the expense of clearing a candidate, who, the moment they have their clearance, more often than not bolts for the door, exchanging the blue badge of the government employee for the green badge of the contractor. The joke was that the green symbolized "money."

The government job that had sponsored me for my TS/SCI clearance wasn't the one I wanted, but the one I could find: I was officially an employee of the state of Maryland, working for the University of Maryland at College Park. The university was helping the NSA open a new institution called CASL, the Center for Advanced Study of Language.

CASL's ostensible mission was to study how people learned languages and to develop computer-assisted methods to help them do so more quickly and better. The hidden corollary of this mission was that the NSA also wanted to develop ways to improve computer comprehension of language. If the other agencies were having difficulties finding competent Arabic (and Farsi and Dari and Pashto and Kurdish) speakers who passed their often ridiculous security checks to translate and interpret on the ground—I know too many Americans rejected merely because they had an inconvenient distant cousin they'd never even met—the NSA was having its own tough time ensuring that its computers could comprehend and analyze the massive amount of foreign-language communications that they were intercepting.

I don't have a more granular idea of the kinds of things that CASL was supposed to do, for the simple reason that when I showed up for work with my bright, shiny clearance, the place wasn't even open yet. In fact, its building was still under construction. Until it was finished and the tech was installed, my job was essentially that of a night-shift security guard. My responsibilities were limited to showing up every day to patrol the empty halls after the construction workers—those other contractors—were finished, making sure that nobody burned down the building or broke in and bugged it. I spent hour after hour making rounds through the half-completed shell, inspecting the day's progress: trying out the chairs that had just been installed in the state-of-the-art auditorium, casting stones back and forth across the suddenly graveled roof, admiring the new drywall, and literally watching the paint dry.

This is the life of after-hours security at a top secret facility, and truthfully I didn't mind it. I was getting paid to do basically nothing but wander in the dark with my thoughts, and I had all the time in the world to use the one functioning computer that I had access to on the premises to search for a new position. During the daytime, I caught up on my sleep and went out on photography expeditions with Lindsay, who—thanks to my wooing and scheming—had finally dumped her other boyfriends.

At the time I was still naive enough to think that my position with CASL would be a bridge to a full-time federal career. But the more I looked around, the more I was amazed to find that there were very few opportunities to serve my country directly, at least in a meaningful technical role. I had a better chance of working as a contractor for a private company that served my country for profit; and I had the best chance, it turned out, of working as a subcontractor for a private company that contracted with another private company that served my country for profit. The realization was dizzying.

It was particularly bizarre to me that most of the systems engineering and systems administration jobs that were out there were private, because these positions came with almost universal access to the employer's digital existence. It's unimaginable that a major bank or even a social media outfit would hire outsiders for systems-level work. In the context of the US government, however, restructuring your intelligence agencies so that your most sensitive systems were being run by somebody who didn't really work for you was what passed for innovation.

———

THE AGENCIES WERE hiring tech companies to hire kids, and then they were giving them the keys to the kingdom, because—as Congress and the press were told—the agencies didn't have a choice. No one else knew how the keys, or the kingdom, worked. I tried to rationalize all this into a pretext for optimism. I swallowed my incredulity, put together a résumé, and went to the job fairs, which, at least in the early aughts, were the primary venues where contractors found new work and government employees were poached. These fairs went by the dubious name of "Clearance Jobs"—I think I was the only one who found that double meaning funny.

At the time, these events were held every month at the Ritz-Carlton in Tysons Corner, Virginia, just down the road from the CIA's headquarters, or at one of the grubbier Marriott-type hotels near the NSA's headquarters at Fort Meade. They were pretty much like any other job fair, I'm told, with one crucial exception: here, it always felt like there were more recruiters than there were recruits. That should give you an indication of the industry's appetite. The recruiters paid a lot of money to be at these fairs, because these were the only places in the country where everyone who walked through the door wearing their stickum name tag badge had supposedly already been prescreened online and cross-checked with the agencies—and so was presumed to already have a clearance, and probably also the requisite skills.

Once you left the well-appointed hotel lobby for the all-business ballroom, you entered Planet Contractor. Everybody would be there: this wasn't the University of Maryland anymore—this was Lockheed Martin, BAE Systems, Booz Allen Hamilton, DynCorp, Titan, CACI, SAIC, COMSO, as well as a hundred other different acronyms I'd never heard of. Some contractors had tables, but the larger ones had booths that were fully furnished and equipped with refreshments.

After you handed a prospective employer a copy of your résumé and small-talked a bit, in a sort of informal interview, they'd break out their binders, which contained lists of all the government billets they were trying to fill. But because this work touched on the clandestine, the billets were accompanied not by standardized job titles and traditional job descriptions but with intentionally obscure, coded verbiage that was often particular to each contractor. One company's Senior Developer 3 might or might not be equivalent to another company's Principal Analyst 2, for example. Frequently the only way to differentiate among these positions was to note that each specified its own requirements of years of experience, level of certifications, and type of security clearance.

After the 2013 revelations, the US government would try to disparage me by referring to me as "only a contractor" or "a former Dell employee," with the implication that I didn't enjoy the same kinds of clearance and access as a blue-badged agency staffer. Once that discrediting characterization was established, the government proceeded to accuse me of "job-hopping," hinting that I was some sort of disgruntled worker who didn't get along with superiors or an exceptionally ambitious employee dead-set on getting ahead at all costs. The truth is that these were both lies of convenience. The IC knows better than anyone that changing jobs is part of the career track of every contractor: it's a mobility situation that the agencies themselves created, and profit from.

In national security contracting, especially in tech contracting, you often find yourself physically working at an agency facility, but nominally—on paper—working for Dell, or Lockheed Martin, or one of the umpteen smaller firms that frequently get bought by a Dell or a Lockheed Martin. In such an acquisition, of course, the smaller firm's contracts get bought, too, and suddenly there's a different employer and job title on your business card. Your day-to-day work, though, remains the same: you're still sitting at the agency facility, doing your tasks. Nothing has changed at all. Meanwhile, the dozen coworkers sitting to your left and right—the same coworkers you work with on the same projects daily—might technically be employed by a dozen different companies, and those companies might still be a few degrees removed from the corporate entities that hold the primary contracts with the agency.

I wish I remembered the exact chronology of my contracting, but I don't have a copy of my résumé anymore—that file, Edward_Snowden_Resume.doc, is locked up in the Documents folder of one of my old home computers, since seized by the FBI. I do recall, however, that my first major contracting gig was actually a subcontracting gig: the CIA had hired BAE Systems, which had hired COMSO, which hired me.

BAE Systems is a midsize American subdivision of British Aerospace, set up expressly to win contracts from the American IC. COMSO was basically its recruiter, a few folks who spent all their time driving around the Beltway trying to find the actual contractors ("the asses") and sign them up ("put the asses in chairs"). Of all the companies I talked to at the job fairs, COMSO was the hungriest, perhaps because it was among the smallest. I never learned what the company's acronym stood for, or even if it stood for anything. Technically speaking, COMSO would be my employer, but I never worked a single day at a COMSO office, or at a BAE Systems office, and few contractors ever would. I'd only work at CIA headquarters.

In fact, I only ever visited the COMSO office, which was in Greenbelt, Maryland, maybe two or three times in my life. One of these was when I went down there to negotiate my salary and sign some paperwork. At CASL I'd been making around $30K/year, but that job didn't have anything to do with technology, so I felt comfortable asking COMSO for $50K. When I named that figure to the guy behind the desk, he said, "What about $60K?"

At the time I was so inexperienced, I didn't understand why he was trying to overpay me. I knew, I guess, that this wasn't ultimately COMSO's money, but I only later understood that some of the contracts that COMSO and BAE and others handled were of the type that's called "cost-plus." This meant that the middlemen contractors billed the agencies for whatever an employee got paid, plus a fee of 3 to 5 percent of that every year. Bumping up salaries was in everyone's interest—everyone's, that is, except the taxpayer's.

The COMSO guy eventually talked me, or himself, up to $62K, as a result of my once again agreeing to work the night shift. He held out his hand and, as I shook it, he introduced himself to me as my "manager." He went on to explain that the title was just a formality, and that I'd be taking my orders directly from the CIA. "If all goes well," he said, "we'll never meet again."

In the spy movies and TV shows, when someone tells you something like that, it usually means that you're about to go on a dangerous mission and might die. But in real spy life it just means, "Congratulations on the job." By the time I was out the door, I'm sure he'd already forgotten my face.

I left that meeting in a buoyant mood, but on the drive back, reality set in: this, I realized, was going to be my daily commute. If I was going to still live in Ellicott City, Maryland, in proximity to Lindsay, but work at the CIA in Virginia, my commute could be up to an hour and a half each way in Beltway gridlock, and that would be the end of me. I knew it wouldn't take long before I'd start to lose my mind. There weren't enough books on tape in the universe.

I couldn't ask Lindsay to move down to Virginia with me because she was still just in her sophomore year at MICA, and had class three days a week. We discussed this, and for cover referred to my job down there as COMSO—as in, "Why does COMSO have to be so far away?" Finally, we decided that I'd find a small place down there, *near* COMSO—just a small place to crash at during the days while I worked at night, *at* COMSO—and then I'd come up to Maryland again every weekend, or she'd come down to me.

I set off to find that place, something smack in the middle of that Venn diagram overlap of cheap enough that I could afford it and nice enough that Lindsay could survive it. It turned out to be a difficult search: Given the number of people who work at the CIA, and the CIA's location in Virginia—where the housing density is, let's say, semirural—the prices were through the roof. The 22100s are some of the most expensive zip codes in America.

Eventually, browsing on Craigslist, I found a room that was surprisingly within my budget, in a house surprisingly near—less than fifteen minutes from—CIA headquarters. I went to check it out, expecting a cruddy bachelor pad pigsty. Instead, I pulled up in front of a large glass-fronted McMansion, immaculately maintained with a topiary lawn that was seasonally decorated. I'm being completely serious when I say that as I approached the place, the smell of pumpkin spice got stronger.

A guy named Gary answered the door. He was older, which I expected from the "Dear Edward" tone of his email, but I hadn't expected him to be so well dressed. He was very tall, with buzz-cut gray hair, and was wearing a suit, and over the suit, an apron. He asked me very politely if I didn't mind waiting a moment. He was just then busy in the kitchen, where he was preparing a tray of apples, sticking cloves in them and dousing them with nutmeg, cinnamon, and sugar.

Once those apples were baking in the oven, Gary showed me the room, which was in the basement, and told me I could move in immediately. I accepted the offer and put down my security deposit and one month's rent.

Then he told me the house rules, which helpfully rhymed:

No mess.

No pets.

No overnight guests.

I confess that I almost immediately violated the first rule, and that I never had any interest in violating the second. As for the third, Gary made an exception for Lindsay.

13

Indoc

You know that one establishing shot that's in pretty much every spy movie and TV show that's subtitled "CIA Headquarters, Langley, Virginia"? And then the camera moves through the marble lobby with the wall of stars and the floor with the agency's seal? Well, Langley is the site's historical name, which the agency prefers Hollywood to use; CIA HQ is officially in McLean, Virginia; and nobody really comes through that lobby except VIPs or outsiders on a tour.

That building is the OHB, the Old Headquarters Building. The building where almost everybody who works at the CIA enters is far less ready for its close-up: the NHB, the New Headquarters Building. My first day was one of the very few I spent there in daylight. That said, I spent most of the day underground—in a grimy, cinder-block-walled room with all the charm of a nuclear fallout shelter and the acrid smell of government bleach.

"So this is the Deep State," one guy said, and almost everybody laughed. I think he'd been expecting a circle of Ivy League WASPs chanting in hoods, whereas I'd been expecting a group of normie civil service types who resembled younger versions of my parents.

Instead, we were all computer dudes—and yes, almost uniformly dudes—who were clearly wearing "business casual" for the first time in our lives. Some were tattooed and pierced, or bore evidence of having removed their piercings for the big day. One still had punky streaks of dye in his hair. Almost all wore contractor badges, as green and crisp as new hundred-dollar bills. We certainly didn't look like a hermetic power-mad cabal that controlled the actions of America's elected officials from shadowy subterranean cubicles.

This session was the first stage in our transformation. It was called the Indoc, or Indoctrination, and its entire point was to convince us that we were the elite, that we were special, that we had been chosen to be privy to the mysteries of state and to the truths that the rest of the country—and, at times, even its Congress and courts—couldn't handle.

I couldn't help but think while I sat through this Indoc that the presenters were preaching to the choir. You don't need to tell a bunch of computer whizzes that they possess superior knowledge and skills that uniquely qualify them to act independently and make decisions on behalf of their fellow citizens without any oversight or review. Nothing inspires arrogance like a lifetime spent controlling machines that are incapable of criticism.

This, to my thinking, actually represented the great nexus of the Intelligence Community and the tech industry: both are entrenched and unelected powers that pride themselves on maintaining absolute secrecy about their developments. Both believe that they have the solutions for everything, which they never hesitate to unilaterally impose. Above all, they both believe that these solutions are inherently apolitical, because they're based on data, whose prerogatives are regarded as preferable to the chaotic whims of the common citizen.

Being indoctrinated into the IC, like becoming expert at technology, has powerful psychological effects. All of a sudden you have access to the story behind the story, the hidden histories of well-known, or supposedly well-known, events. That can be intoxicating, at least for a teetotaler like me. Also, all of a sudden you have not just the license but the obligation to lie, conceal, dissemble, and dissimulate. This creates a sense of tribalism, which can lead many to believe that their primary allegiance is to the institution and not to the rule of law.

I wasn't thinking any of these thoughts at my Indoc session, of course. Instead, I was just trying to keep myself awake as the presenters proceeded to instruct us on basic operational security practices, part of the wider body of spy techniques the IC collectively describes as "tradecraft." These are often so obvious as to be mind-numbing: Don't tell anyone who you work for. Don't leave sensitive materials unattended. Don't bring your highly insecure cell phone into the highly secure office—or talk on it about work, ever. Don't wear your "Hi, I work for the CIA" badge to the mall.

Finally, the litany ended, the lights came down, the PowerPoint was fired up, and faces appeared on the screen that was bolted to the wall. Everyone in the room sat upright. These were the faces, we were told, of former agents and contractors who, whether through greed, malice, incompetence, or negligence failed to follow the rules. They thought they were above all this mundane stuff and their hubris resulted in their imprisonment and ruin. The people on the screen, it was implied, were now in basements even worse than this one, and some would be there until they died.

All in all, this was an effective presentation.

I'm told that in the years since my career ended, this parade of horribles—of incompetents, moles, defectors, and traitors—has been expanded to include an additional category: people of principle, whistleblowers in the public interest. I can only hope that the twenty-somethings sitting there today are struck by the government's conflation of selling secrets to the enemy and disclosing them to journalists when the new faces—when my face—pop up on the screen.

I came to work for the CIA when it was at the nadir of its morale. Following the intelligence failures of 9/11, Congress and the executive had set out on an aggressive reorganization campaign. It included stripping the position of director of Central Intelligence of its dual role as both head of the CIA and head of the entire American IC—a dual role that the position had held since the founding of the agency in the aftermath of World War II. When George Tenet was forced out in 2004, the CIA's half-century supremacy over all of the other agencies went with him.

The CIA's rank and file considered Tenet's departure and the directorship's demotion as merely the most public symbols of the agency's betrayal by the political class it had been created to serve. The general sense of having been manipulated by the Bush administration and then blamed for its worst excesses gave rise to a culture of victimization and retrenchment. This was only exacerbated by the appointment of Porter Goss, an undistinguished former CIA officer turned Republican congressman from Florida, as the agency's new director—the first to serve in the reduced position. The installation of a politician was taken as a chastisement and as an attempt to weaponize the CIA by putting it under partisan supervision. Director Goss immediately began a sweeping campaign of firings, layoffs, and forced retirements that left the agency understaffed and more reliant than ever on contractors. Meanwhile, the public at large had never had such a low opinion of the agency, or such insight into its inner workings, thanks to all the leaks and disclosures about its extraordinary renditions and black site prisons.

At the time, the CIA was broken into five directorates. There was the DO, the Directorate of Operations, which was responsible for the actual spying; the DI, the Directorate of Intelligence, which was responsible for synthesizing and analyzing the results of that spying; the DST, the Directorate of Science and Technology, which built and supplied computers, communications devices, and weapons to the spies and showed them how to use them; the DA, the Directorate of Administration, which basically meant lawyers, human resources, and all those who coordinated the daily business of the agency and served as a liaison to the government; and, finally, the DS, the Directorate of Support, which was a strange directorate and, back then, the largest. The DS included everyone who worked for the agency in a support capacity, from the majority of the agency's technologists and medical doctors to the personnel in the cafeteria and the gym and the guards at the gate. The primary function of the DS was to manage the CIA's global communications infrastructure, the platform ensuring that the spies' reports got to the analysts and that the analysts' reports got to the administrators. The DS housed the employees who provided technical support throughout the agency, maintained the servers, and kept them secure—the people who built, serviced, and protected the entire network of the CIA and connected it with the networks of the other agencies and controlled their access.

These were, in short, the people who used technology to link everything together. It should be no surprise, then, that the bulk of them were young. It should also be no surprise that most of them were contractors.

My team was attached to the Directorate of Support and our task was to manage the CIA's Washington-Metropolitan server architecture, which is to say the vast majority of the CIA servers in the continental United States—the enormous halls of expensive "big iron" computers that comprised the agency's internal networks and databases, all of its systems that transmitted, received, and stored intelligence. Though the CIA had dotted the country with relay servers, many of the agency's most important servers were situated on-site. Half of them were in the NHB, where my team was located; the other half were in the nearby OHB. They were set up on opposite sides of their respective buildings, so that if one side was blown up we wouldn't lose too many machines.

My TS/SCI security clearance reflected my having been "read into" a few different "compartments" of information. Some of these compartments were SIGINT (signals intelligence, or intercepted communications), and another was HUMINT (human intelligence, or the work done and reports filed by agents and analysts)—the CIA's work routinely involves both. On top of those, I was read into a COMSEC (communications security) compartment that allowed me to work with cryptographic key material, the codes that have traditionally been considered the most important agency secrets because they're used to protect all the other agency secrets. This cryptographic material was processed and stored on and around the servers I was responsible for managing. My team was one of the few at the agency permitted to actually lay hands on these servers, and likely the only team with access to log in to nearly all of them.

In the CIA, secure offices are called "vaults," and my team's vault was located a bit past the CIA's help desk section. During the daytime, the help desk was staffed by a busy contingent of older people, closer to my parents' age. They wore blazers and slacks and even blouses and skirts; this was one of the few places in the CIA tech world at the time where I recall seeing a sizable number of women. Some of them had the blue badges that identified them as government employees, or, as contractors called them, "govvies." They spent their shifts picking up banks of ringing phones and talking people in the building or out in the field through their tech issues. It was a sort of IC version of call-center work: resetting passwords, unlocking accounts, and going by rote through the troubleshooting checklists. "Can you log out and back in?" "Is the network cable plugged in?" If the govvies, with their minimal tech experience, couldn't deal with a particular issue themselves, they'd escalate it to more specialized teams, especially if the problem was happening in the "Foreign Field," meaning CIA stations overseas in places like Kabul or Baghdad or Bogotá or Paris.

I'm a bit ashamed to admit how proud I felt when I first walked through this gloomy array. I was decades younger than the help desk folks and heading past them into a vault to which they didn't have access and never would. At the time it hadn't yet occurred to me that the extent of my access meant that the process itself might be broken, that the government had simply given up on meaningfully managing and promoting its talent from within because the new contracting culture meant they no longer had to care. More than any other memory I have of my career, this route of mine past the CIA help desk has come to symbolize for me the generational and cultural change in the IC of which I was a part—the moment when the old-school prepster clique that traditionally staffed the agencies, desperate to keep pace with technologies they could not be bothered to understand, welcomed a new wave of young hackers into the institutional fold and let them develop, have complete access to, and wield complete power over unparalleled technological systems of state control.

In time I came to love the help desk govvies, who were kind and generous to me, and always appreciated my willingness to help even when it wasn't my job. I, in turn, learned much from them, in bits and pieces, about how the larger organization functioned beyond the Beltway. Some of them had actually worked out in the foreign field themselves once upon a time, like the agents they now assisted over the phone. After a while, they'd come back home to the States, not always with their families intact, and they'd been relegated to the help desk for the remaining years of their careers because they lacked the computer skills required to compete in an agency increasingly focused on expanding its technological capabilities.

I was proud to have won the govvies' respect, and I was never quite comfortable with how many of my team members condescendingly pitied and even made fun of these bright and committed folks—men and women who for low pay and little glory had given the agency years of their lives, often in inhospitable and even outright dangerous places abroad, at the end of which their ultimate reward was a job picking up phones in a lonely hallway.

AFTER A FEW weeks familiarizing myself with the systems on the day shift, I moved to nights—6:00 p.m. to 6:00 a.m.—when the help desk was staffed by a discreetly snoozing skeleton crew and the rest of the agency was pretty much dead.

At night, especially between, say, 10:00 p.m. and 4:00 a.m., the CIA was empty and lifeless, a vast and haunted complex with a postapocalyptic feel. All the escalators were stopped and you had to walk them like stairs. Only half of the elevators were working, and the pinging sounds they made, only barely audible during the bustle of daytime, now sounded alarmingly loud. Former CIA directors glared down from their portraits and the bald eagles seemed less like statues than like living predators waiting patiently to swoop in for the kill. American flags billowed like ghosts—spooks in red, white, and blue. The agency had recently committed to a new eco-friendly energy-saving policy and installed motion-sensitive overhead lights: the corridor ahead of you would be swathed in darkness and the lights would switch on when you approached, so that you felt followed, and your footsteps would echo endlessly.

For twelve hours each night, three days on and two days off, I sat in the secure office beyond the help desk, among the twenty desks each bearing two or three computer terminals reserved for the sysadmins who kept the CIA's global network online. Regardless of how fancy that might sound, the job itself was relatively banal, and can basically be described as waiting for catastrophe to happen. The problems generally weren't too difficult to solve. The moment something went wrong, I had to log in to try to fix it remotely. If I couldn't, I had to physically descend into the data center hidden a floor below my own in the New Headquarters Building—or walk the eerie half mile through the connecting tunnel over to the data center in the Old Headquarters Building—and tinker around with the machinery itself.

My partner in this task—the only other person responsible for the nocturnal functioning of the CIA's entire server architecture— was a guy I'm going to call Frank. He was our team's great outlier and an exceptional personality in every sense. Besides having a political consciousness (libertarian to the point of stockpiling Krugerrands) and an abiding interest in subjects outside of tech (he read vintage mysteries and thrillers in paperback), he was a fifty-something been-there-done-that ex-navy radio operator who'd managed to graduate from the call center's ranks thanks to being a contractor.

I have to say, when I first met Frank, I thought: *Imagine if my entire life were like the nights I spent at CASL.* Because, to put it frankly, Frank did hardly any work at all. At least, that was the impression he liked to project. He enjoyed telling me, and everyone else, that he didn't really know anything about computing and didn't understand why they'd put him on such an important team. He used to say that "contracting was the third biggest scam in Washington," after the income tax and Congress. He claimed he'd advised his boss that he'd be "next to useless" when they suggested moving him to the server team, but they moved him just the same. By his own account, all he'd done at work for the better part of the last decade was sit around and read books, though sometimes he'd also play games of solitaire—with a real deck of cards, not on the computer, of course—and reminisce about former wives ("she was a keeper") and girlfriends ("she took my car but it was worth it"). Sometimes he'd just pace all night and reload the Drudge Report.

When the phone rang to signal that something was broken, and bouncing a server didn't fix it, he'd just report it to the day shift. Essentially, his philosophy (if you could call it that) was that the night shift had to end sometime and the day shift had a deeper bench. Apparently, however, the day shift had gotten tired of coming in to work every morning to find Frank's feet up in front of the digital equivalent of a dumpster fire, and so I'd been hired.

For some reason, the agency had decided that it was preferable to bring me in than to let this old guy go. After a couple of weeks of working together, I was convinced that his continued employment had to be the result of some personal connection or favor. To test this hypothesis I tried to draw Frank out, and asked him which CIA directors or other agency brass he'd been with in the navy. But my question only provoked a tirade about how basically none of the navy vets high up at the agency had been enlisted men—they'd all been officers, which explained so much about the agency's dismal record. This lecture went on and on, until suddenly a panicked expression came over his face and he jumped up and said, "I gotta change the tape!"

I had no idea what he was talking about. But Frank was already heading to the gray door at the back of our vault, which opened onto a dingy stairwell that gave direct access to the data center itself—the humming, freezing night-black chamber that we sat directly on top of.

Going down into a server vault—especially the CIA's—can be a disorienting experience. You descend into darkness blinking with green and red LEDs like an evil Christmas, vibrating with the whir of the industrial fans cooling the precious rack-mounted machinery to prevent it from melting down. Being there was always a bit dizzying—even without a manic older guy cursing like the sailor he was as he dashed down the server hall.

Frank stopped by a shabby corner that housed a makeshift cubicle of reclaimed equipment, marked as belonging to the Directorate of Operations. Taking up almost the entirety of the sad, rickety desk was an old computer. On closer inspection, it was something from the early '90s, or even the late '80s, older than anything I remembered from my father's Coast Guard lab—a computer so ancient that it shouldn't even have been called a computer. It was more properly a *machine*, running a miniature tape format that I didn't recognize but was pretty sure would have been welcomed by the Smithsonian.

Next to this machine was a massive safe, which Frank unlocked.

He fussed with the tape that was in the machine, pried it free, and put it in the safe. Then he took another antique tape out of the safe and inserted it into the machine as a replacement, threading it through by touch alone. He carefully tapped a few times on the old keyboard—down, down, down, tab, tab, tab. He couldn't actually see the effect of those keystrokes, because the machine's monitor no longer worked, but he struck the Enter key with confidence.

I couldn't figure out what was going on. But the itty-bitty tape began to tick-tick-tick and then spin, and Frank grinned with satisfaction.

"This is the most important machine in the building," he said. "The agency doesn't trust this digital technology crap. They don't trust their own servers. You know they're always breaking. But when the servers break down they risk losing what they're storing, so in order not to lose anything that comes in during the day, they back everything up on tape at night."

"So you're doing a storage backup here?"

"A storage backup to tape. The old way. Reliable as a heart attack. Tape hardly ever crashes."

"But what's on the tape? Like personnel stuff, or like the actual incoming intelligence?"

Frank put a hand to his chin in a thinking pose and pretended to take the question seriously. Then he said, "Man, Ed, I didn't want to have to tell you. But it's field reports from your girlfriend, and we've got a lot of agents filing. It's raw intelligence. Very raw."

He laughed his way upstairs, leaving me speechless and blushing in the darkness of the vault.

It was only when Frank repeated this same tape-changing ritual the next night, and the night after that, and on every night we worked together thereafter, that I began to understand why the agency kept him around—and it wasn't just for his sense of humor. Frank was the only guy willing to stick around between 6:00 p.m. and 6:00 a.m. who was also old enough to know how to handle that proprietary tape system. All the other techs who'd come up in the dark ages when tape was the medium now had families and preferred to be home with them at night. But Frank was a bachelor and remembered the world before the Enlightenment.

After I found a way to automate most of my own work—writing scripts to automatically update servers and restore lost network connections, mostly—I started having what I came to call a Frank amount of time. Meaning, I had all night to do pretty much whatever I wanted. I passed a fair number of hours in long talks with Frank, especially about the more political stuff he was read-ing: books about how the country should return to the gold stan-dard, or about the intricacies of the flat tax. But there were always periods of every shift when Frank would disappear. He'd either put his head into a whodunit novel and not lift it until morning, or he'd go strolling the halls of the agency, hitting the cafeteria for a lukewarm slice of pizza or the gym to lift weights. I had my own way of keeping to myself, of course. I went online.

When you go online at the CIA, you have to check a box for a Consent to Monitoring Agreement, which basically says that ev-erything you do is being recorded and that you agree that you have no expectation of any privacy whatsoever. You end up check-ing this box so often that it becomes second nature. These agree-ments become invisible to you when you're working at the agency, because they pop up constantly and you're always trying to just click them down and get back to what you were doing. This, to my mind, is a major reason why most IC workers don't share civilian concerns about being tracked online: not because they have any insider information about how digital surveillance helps to protect America, but because to those in the IC, being tracked by the boss just comes with the job.

Anyway, it's not like there's a lot to be found out there on the public Internet that's more interesting than what the agency al-ready has internally. Few realize this, but the CIA has its own In-ternet and Web. It has its own kind of Facebook, which allows agents to interact socially; its own type of Wikipedia, which pro-vides agents with information about agency teams, projects, and missions; and its own internal version of Google—actually pro-vided by Google—which allows agents to search this sprawling classified network. Every CIA component has its own website on this network that discusses what it does and posts meeting min-utes and presentations. For hours and hours every night, this was my education.

According to Frank, the first things everyone looks up on the CIA's internal networks are aliens and 9/11, and that's why, also according to Frank, you'll never get any meaningful search results for them. I looked them up anyway. The CIA-flavored Google didn't return anything interesting for either, but hey—maybe the truth was out there on another network drive. For the record, as far as I could tell, aliens have never contacted Earth, or at least they haven't contacted US intelligence. But al-Qaeda did maintain unusually close ties with our allies the Saudis, a fact that the Bush White House worked suspiciously hard to suppress as we went to war with two other countries.

Here is one thing that the disorganized CIA didn't quite understand at the time, and that no major American employer outside of Silicon Valley understood, either: the computer guy knows everything, or rather can know everything. The higher up this employee is, and the more systems-level privileges he has, the more access he has to virtually every byte of his employer's digital existence. Of course, not everyone is curious enough to take advantage of this education, and not everyone is possessed of a sincere curiosity. My forays through the CIA's systems were natural extensions of my childhood desire to understand how everything works, how the various components of a mechanism fit together into the whole. And with the official title and privileges of a systems administrator, and technical prowess that enabled my clearance to be used to its maximum potential, I was able to satisfy my every informational deficiency and then some. In case you were wondering: Yes, man really did land on the moon. Climate change is real. Chemtrails are not a thing.

On the CIA's internal news sites I read top secret dispatches regarding trade talks and coups as they were still unfolding. These agency accounts of events were often very similar to the accounts that would eventually show up on network news, CNN, or Fox days later. The primary differences were merely in the sourcing and the level of detail. Whereas a newspaper or magazine account of an upheaval abroad might be attributed to "a senior official speaking on condition of anonymity," the CIA version would have explicit sourcing—say, "ZBSMACKTALK/1, an employee of the interior ministry who regularly responds to specific tasking, claims secondhand knowledge, and has proven reliable in the past." And the true name and complete personal history of ZBSMACK-TALK/1, called a case file, would be only a few clicks away.

Sometimes an internal news item would never show up in the media at all, and the excitement and significance of what I was reading both increased my appreciation of the importance of our work and made me feel like I was missing out by just sitting at a workstation. This may come off as naive, but I was surprised to learn how truly international the CIA was—and I don't mean its operations, I mean its workforce. The number of languages I heard in the cafeteria was astounding. I couldn't help feeling a sense of my own provincialism. Working at CIA Headquarters was a thrill, but it was still only a few hours away from where I'd grown up, which in many ways was a similar environment. I was in my early twenties and, apart from stints in North Carolina, childhood trips to visit my grandfather at Coast Guard bases where he'd held commands, and my few weeks in the army at Fort Benning, I'd never really left the Beltway.

As I read about events happening in Ouagadougou, Kinshasa, and other exotic cities I could never have found on a noncomputerized map, I realized that as long as I was still young I had to serve my country by doing something truly meaningful abroad. The alternative, I thought, was just becoming a more successful Frank: sitting at progressively bigger desks, making progressively more money, until eventually I, too, would be obsolesced and kept around only to handle the future's equivalent of a janky tape machine.

It was then that I did the unthinkable. I set about going govvy.

I think some of my supervisors were puzzled by this, but they were also flattered, because the typical route is the reverse: a public servant at the end of their tenure goes private and cashes in. No tech contractor just starting out goes public and takes a pay cut. To my mind, however, becoming a govvy was logical: I'd be getting paid to travel.

I got lucky, and a position opened up. After nine months as a systems administrator, I applied for a CIA tech job abroad, and in short order I was accepted.

My last day at CIA Headquarters was just a formality. I'd already done all my paperwork and traded in my green badge for a blue. All that was left to do was to sit through another indoctrination, which now that I was a govvy was held in an elegant conference room next to the cafeteria's Dunkin' Donuts. It was here that I performed the sacred rite in which contractors never participate. I raised my hand to swear an oath of loyalty—not to the government or agency that now employed me directly, but to the US Constitution. I solemnly swore to support and defend the Constitution of the United States against all enemies, foreign and domestic.

The next day, I drove my trusty old Honda Civic out into the Virginia countryside. In order to get to the foreign station of my dreams, I first had to go back to school—to the first sit-in-a-classroom schooling I'd ever really finish.

14

The Count of the Hill

My first orders as a freshly minted officer of the government were to head for the Comfort Inn in Warrenton, Virginia, a sad, dilapidated motel whose primary client was the "State Department," by which I mean the CIA. It was the worst motel in a town of bad motels, which was probably why the CIA chose it. The fewer other guests, the lower the chances that anybody would notice that this particular Comfort Inn served as a makeshift dormitory for the Warrenton Training Center—or, as folks who work there call it, the Hill.

When I checked in, the desk clerk warned me not to use the stairs, which were blocked off by police tape. I was given a room on the second floor of the main building, with a view of the inn's auxiliary buildings and parking lot. The room was barely lit, there was mold in the bathroom, the carpets were filthy with cigarette burns under the No Smoking sign, and the flimsy mattress was stained dark purple with what I hoped was booze. Nevertheless, I liked it—I was still at the age when I could find this seediness romantic—and I spent my first night lying awake in bed, watching the bugs swarm the single domed overhead light fixture and counting down the hours to the free continental breakfast I'd been promised.

The next morning, I discovered that on the continent of Warrenton, breakfast meant individual-size boxes of Froot Loops and sour milk. Welcome to the government.

The Comfort Inn was to be my home for the next six months. My fellow Innmates and I, as we called ourselves, were discouraged from telling our loved ones where we were staying and what we were doing. I leaned hard into those protocols, rarely heading back to Maryland or even talking to Lindsay on the phone. Anyway, we weren't allowed to take our phones to school, since class was classified, and we had classes all the time. Warrenton kept most of us too busy to be lonely.

If the Farm, down by Camp Peary, is the CIA's most famous training institution, chiefly because it's the only one that the agency's PR staff is allowed to talk to Hollywood about, the Hill is without a doubt the most mysterious. Connected via microwave and fiber optics to the satellite relay facility at Brandy Station—part of the Warrenton Training Center's constellation of sister sites—the Hill serves as the heart of the CIA's field communications network, carefully located just out of nuke range from DC. The salty old techs who worked there liked to say that the CIA could survive losing its headquarters to a catastrophic attack, but it would die if it ever lost Warrenton, and now that the top of the Hill holds two enormous top secret data centers—one of which I later helped to construct—I'm inclined to agree.

The Hill earned its name because of its location, which is atop, yes, a massive steepness. When I arrived, there was just one road that led in, past a purposely under-marked perimeter fence, and then up a grade so severe that whenever the temperature dropped and the road iced over, vehicles would lose traction and slide backward downhill.

Just beyond the guarded checkpoint lies the State Department's decaying diplomatic communications training facility, whose prominent location was meant to reinforce its role as cover: making the Hill appear as if it's merely a place where the American foreign service trains technologists. Beyond it, amid the back territory, were the various low, unlabeled buildings I studied in, and even farther on was the shooting range that the IC's trigger pullers used for special training. Shots would ring out, in a style of firing I wasn't familiar with: *pop-pop, pop; pop-pop, pop*. A doubletap meant to incapacitate, followed by an aimed shot meant to execute.

I was there as a member of class 6-06 of the BTTP, the Basic Telecommunications Training Program, whose intentionally beige name disguises one of the most classified and unusual curricula in existence. The purpose of the program is to train TISOs (Technical Information Security Officers)—the CIA's cadre of elite "communicators," or, less formally, "commo guys." A TISO is trained to be a jack-of-all-trades, a one-person replacement for previous generations' specialized roles of code clerk, radioman, electrician, mechanic, physical and digital security adviser, and computer technician. The main job of this undercover officer is to manage the technical infrastructure for CIA operations, most commonly overseas at stations hidden inside American missions, consulates, and embassies—hence the State Department connection. The idea is, if you're in an American embassy, which is to say if you're far from home and surrounded by untrustworthy foreigners—whether hostiles or allies, they're still untrustworthy foreigners to the CIA—you're going to have to handle all of your technical needs internally. If you ask a local repairman to fix your secret spy base, he'll definitely do it, even for cheap, but he's also going to install hard-to-find bugs on behalf of a foreign power.

As a result, TISOs are responsible for knowing how to fix basically every machine in the building, from individual computers and computer networks to CCTV and HVAC systems, solar panels, heaters and coolers, emergency generators, satellite hookups, military encryption devices, alarms, locks, and so on. The rule is that if it plugs in or gets plugged into, it's the TISO's problem.

TISOs also have to know how to build some of these systems

themselves, just as they have to know how to destroy them—when an embassy is under siege, say, after all the diplomats and most of their fellow CIA officers have been evacuated. The TISOs are always the last guys out. It's their job to send the final "off the air" message to headquarters after they've shredded, burned, wiped, degaussed, and disintegrated anything that has the CIA's fingerprints on it, from operational documents in safes to disks with cipher material, to ensure that nothing of value remains for an enemy to capture.

Why this was a job for the CIA and not for the State Department—the entity that actually owns the embassy building—is more than the sheer difference in competence and trust: the real reason is plausible deniability. The worst-kept secret in modern diplomacy is that the primary function of an embassy nowadays is to serve as a platform for espionage. The old explanations for why a country might try to maintain a notionally sovereign physical presence on another country's soil faded into obsolescence with the rise of electronic communications and jet-powered aircraft. Today, the most meaningful diplomacy happens directly between ministries and ministers. Sure, embassies do still send the occasional démarche and help support their citizens abroad, and then there are the consular sections that issue visas and renew passports. But those are often in a completely different building, and anyway, none of those activities can even remotely justify the expense of maintaining all that infrastructure. Instead, what justifies the expense is the ability for a country to use the cover of its foreign service to conduct and legitimize its spying.

TISOs work under diplomatic cover with credentials that hide them among these foreign service officers, usually under the identity of "attachés." The largest embassies would have maybe five of these people, the larger embassies would have maybe three, but most just have one. They're called "singletons," and I remember being told that of all the posts the CIA offers, these have the highest rates of divorce. To be a singleton is to be the lone technical officer, far from home, in a world where everything is always broken.

My class in Warrenton began with around eight members and lost only one before graduation—which I was told was fairly uncommon. And this motley crew was uncommon, too, though pretty well representative of the kind of malcontents who voluntarily sign up for a career track that all but guarantees they'll spend the majority of their service undercover in a foreign country. For the first time in my IC career, I wasn't the youngest in the room. At age twenty-four, I'd say I was around the mean, though my experience doing systems work at headquarters certainly gave me a boost in terms of familiarity with the agency's operations. Most of the others were just tech-inclined kids straight out of college, or straight off the street, who'd applied online.

In a nod to the paramilitary aspirations of the CIA's foreign field branches, we called each other by nicknames—quickly assigned based on eccentricities—more often than by our true names. Taco Bell was a suburb: wide, likable, and blank. At twenty years old, the only job he'd had prior to the CIA was as the night-shift manager at a branch of the eponymous restaurant in Pennsylvania. Rainman was in his late twenties and spent the term bouncing around the autism spectrum between catatonic detachment and shivering fury. He wore the name we gave him proudly and claimed it was a Native American honorific. Flute earned his name because his career in the Marines was far less interesting to us than his degree in panpipes from a music conservatory. Spo was one of the older guys, at thirty-five or so. He was called what he was called because he'd been an SPO—a Special Police Officer— at the CIA's headquarters, where he got so bored out of his mind guarding the gate at McLean that he was determined to escape overseas even if it meant cramming his entire family into a single motel room (a situation that lasted until the management found his kids' pet snake living in a dresser drawer). Our elder was the Colonel, a midforties former Special Forces commo sergeant who, after numerous tours in the sandbox, was trying out for his second act. We called him the Colonel, even though he was just an enlisted guy, not an officer, mostly out of his resemblance to that friendly

Kentuckian whose fried chicken we preferred to the regular fare of the Warrenton cafeteria.

My nickname—I guess I can't avoid it—was the Count. Not because of my aristocratic bearing or dandyish fashion sense, but because, like the felt vampire puppet of *Sesame Street*, I had a tendency to signal my intention to interrupt class by raising my forefinger, as if to say: *"One, two, three, ah, ha, ha, three things you forgot!"*

These were the folks with whom I'd cycle through some twenty different classes, each in its own specialty, but most having to do with how to make the technology available in any given environment serve the government of the United States, whether in an embassy or on the run.

One drill involved lugging the "off-site package," which was an eighty-pound suitcase of communications equipment that was older than I was, up onto a building's roof. With just a compass and a laminated sheet of coordinates, I'd have to find in all that vast sky of twinkling stars one of the CIA's stealth satellites, which would connect me to the agency's mothership, its Crisis Communications Center in McLean—call sign "Central"—and then I'd use the Cold War–era kit inside the package to establish an encrypted radio channel. This drill was a practical reminder of why the commo officer is always the first in and last out: the chief of station can steal the deepest secret in the world, but it doesn't mean squat until somebody gets it home.

That night I stayed on base after dark, and drove my car up to the very top of the Hill, parking outside the converted barn where we studied electrical concepts meant to prevent adversaries from monitoring our activities. The methods we learned about at times seemed close to voodoo—such as the ability to reproduce what's being displayed on any computer monitor by using only the tiny electromagnetic emissions caused by the oscillating currents in its internal components, which can be captured using a special antenna, a method called Van Eck phreaking. If this sounds hard to understand, I promise we all felt the same way. The instructor himself readily admitted he never fully comprehended the details and couldn't demonstrate it for us, but he knew the threat was real: the CIA was doing it to others, which meant others could do it to us.

I sat on the roof of my car, that same old white Civic, and, as I gazed out over what felt like all of Virginia, I called Lindsay for the first time in weeks, or even a month. We talked until my phone's battery died, my breath becoming visible as the night got colder. There was nothing I wanted more than to share the scene with her—the dark fields, the undulating hills, the high astral shimmer—but describing it to her was the best I could do. I was already breaking the rules by using my phone; I would've been breaking the law by taking a picture.

One of Warrenton's major subjects of study involved how to service the terminals and cables, the basic—in many ways, the primitive—components of any CIA station's communications infrastructure. A "terminal," in this context, is just a computer used to send and receive messages over a single secure network. In the CIA, the word "cables" tends to refer to the messages themselves, but technical officers know that "cables" are also far more tangible: they're the cords or wires that for the last half century or so have linked the agency's terminals—specifically its ancient Post Communications Terminals—all over the world, tunneling underground across national borders, buried at the bottom of the ocean.

Ours was the last year that TISOs had to be fluent in all of this: the terminal hardware, the multiple software packages, and the cables, too, of course. For some of my classmates, it felt a bit crazy to have to deal with issues of insulation and sheathing in what was supposed to be the age of wireless. But if any of them voiced doubts about the relevance of any of the seemingly antiquated tech that we were being taught, our instructors would remind us that ours was also the first year in the history of the Hill that TISOs weren't required to learn Morse code.

Closing in on graduation, we had to fill out what were called dream sheets. We were given a list of the CIA stations worldwide that needed personnel, and were told to rank them in the order of our preferences. These dream sheets then went to the Requirements Division, which promptly crumpled them up and tossed them in the trash—at least according to rumor.

My dream sheet started with what was called the SRD, the Special Requirements Division. This was technically a posting not at any embassy but here in Virginia, from which I would be sent out on periodic tours of all the uglier spots in the sandbox, places where the agency judged a permanent posting too harsh or too dangerous—tiny, isolated forward operating bases in Afghanistan, Iraq, and the border regions of Pakistan, for example. By choosing SRD, I was opting for challenge and variety over being stuck in just one city for the entire duration of what was supposed to be an up-to-three-years stint. My instructors were all pretty confident that SRD would jump at the chance to bring me on, and I was pretty confident in my newly honed abilities. But things didn't quite go as expected.

As was evident from the condition of the Comfort Inn, the school had been cutting some corners. Some of my classmates had begun to suspect that the administration was actually, believe it or not, violating federal labor laws. As a work-obsessed recluse, I initially wasn't bothered by this, nor was anyone around my age. For us, this was the sort of low-level exploitation we'd experienced so often that we already mistook it for normal. But unpaid overtime, denied leave, and refusals to honor family benefits made a difference to the older classmates. The Colonel had alimony payments, and Spo had a family: every dollar counted, every minute mattered.

These grievances came to a head when the decrepit stairs at the Comfort Inn finally collapsed. Luckily no one was injured, but everyone was spooked, and my classmates started grumbling that if the building had been bankrolled by any entity other than the CIA, it would've been condemned for fire-code violations years ago. The discontent spread, and soon enough what was basically a school for saboteurs was close to unionizing. Management, in response, dug in its heels and decided to wait us out, since everybody involved eventually had to either graduate or be fired.

A few of my classmates approached me. They knew that I was well liked by the instructors, since my skills put me near the top of my class. They were also aware, because I'd worked at headquarters, that I knew my way around the bureaucracy. Plus I could write pretty well—at least by tech standards. They wanted me to act as a sort of class representative, or class martyr, by formally bringing their complaints to the head of the school.

I'd like to say that I was motivated to take on this cause solely by my aggrieved sense of justice. But while that certainly did factor into the decision, I can't deny that for a young man who was suddenly excelling at nearly everything he attempted, challenging the school's crooked administration just sounded like fun. Within an hour I was compiling policies to cite from the internal network, and before the day was done my email was sent.

The next morning the head of the school had me come into his office. He admitted the school had gone off the rails, but said the problems weren't anything he could solve. "You're only here for twelve more weeks—do me a favor and just tell your classmates to suck it up. Assignments are coming up soon, and then you'll have better things to worry about. All you'll remember from your time here is who had the best performance review."

What he said had been worded in such a way that it might've been a threat, and it might've been a bribe. Either way, it bothered me. By the time I left his office the fun was over, and it was justice I was after.

I walked back into a class that had expected to lose. I remember Spo noticing my frown and saying, "Don't feel bad, man. At least you tried."

He'd been at the agency longer than any of my other classmates; he knew how it worked, and how ludicrous it was to trust management to fix something that management itself had broken. I was a bureaucratic innocent by comparison, disturbed by the loss and by the ease with which Spo and the others accepted it. I hated the feeling that the mere fiction of process was enough to dispel a genuine demand for results. It wasn't that my classmates didn't care enough to fight, it was that they couldn't afford to: the system was designed so that the perceived cost of escalation exceeded the expected benefit of resolution. At age twenty-four, though, I thought as little of the costs as I did of the benefits; I just cared about the system. I wasn't finished.

I rewrote and re-sent the email—not to the head of the school now, but to his boss, the director of Field Service Group. Though he was higher up the totem pole than the head of the school, the D/FSG was pretty much equivalent in rank and seniority to a few of the personnel I'd dealt with at headquarters. Then I copied the email to *his* boss, who definitely was not.

A few days later, we were in a class on something like false subtraction as a form of field-expedient encryption, when a front-office secretary came in and declared that the old regime had fallen. Unpaid overtime would no longer be required, and, effective in two weeks, we were all being moved to a much nicer hotel. I remember the giddy pride with which she announced, "A Hampton Inn!"

I had only a day or so to revel in my glory before class was interrupted again. This time, the head of the school was at the door, summoning me back to his office. Spo immediately leaped from his seat, enveloped me in a hug, mimed wiping away a tear, and declared that he'd never forget me. The head of the school rolled his eyes.

There, waiting in the school head's office was the director of the Field Service Group—the school head's boss, the boss of nearly everyone on the TISO career track, the boss whose boss I'd emailed. He was exceptionally cordial, and didn't project any of the school head's clenched-jaw irritation. This unnerved me.

I tried to keep a calm exterior, but inside I was sweating. The head of the school began our chat by reiterating how the issues the class had brought to light were in the process of being resolved. His superior cut him off. "But why we're here is not to talk about that. Why we're here is to talk about insubordination and the chain of command."

If he'd slapped me, I would've been less shocked.

I had no idea what the director meant by insubordination, but before I had the opportunity to ask, he continued. The CIA was quite different from the other civilian agencies, he said, even if, on paper, the regulations insisted it wasn't. And in an agency that did such important work, there was nothing more important than the chain of command.

Raising a forefinger, automatically but politely, I pointed out that before I emailed above my station, I'd *tried* the chain of command and been failed by it. Which was precisely the last thing I should have been explaining to the chain of command itself, personified just across a desk from me.

The head of the school just stared at his shoes and occasionally glanced out the window.

"Listen," his boss said. "Ed, I'm not here to file a 'hurt feelings report.' Relax. I recognize that you're a talented guy, and we've gone around and talked to all of your instructors and they say you're talented and sharp. Even volunteered for the war zone. That's something we appreciate. We want you here, but we need to know that we can count on you. You've got to understand that there's a system here. Sometimes we've all got to put up with things we don't like, because the mission comes first, and we can't complete that mission if every guy on the team is second-guessing." He took a pause, swallowed, and said, "Nowhere is this more true than in the desert. A lot of things happen out in the desert, and I'm not sure that we're at a stage yet where I'm comfortable you'll know how to handle them."

This was their gotcha, their retaliation. And though it was entirely self-defeating, the head of the school was now smiling at the parking lot. No one besides me—and I mean no one—had put down SRD, or any other active combat situation for that matter, as their first or second or even third choice on their dream sheets. Everyone else had prioritized all the stops on the European cham-

pagne circuit, all the neat sweet vacation-station burgs with wind-
mills and bicycles, where you rarely hear explosions.

Almost perversely, they now gave me one of these assignments.
They gave me Geneva. They punished me by giving me what I'd
never asked for, but what everybody else had wanted.

As if he were reading my mind, the director said, "This isn't a
punishment, Ed. It's an opportunity—really. Someone with your
level of expertise would be wasted in the war zone. You need a
bigger station, that pilots the newest projects, to really keep you
busy and stretch your skills."

Everybody in class who'd been congratulating me would later
turn jealous and think that I'd been bought off with a luxury position to avoid further complaints. My reaction, in the moment,
was the opposite: I thought that the head of the school must have
had an informant in the class, who'd told him exactly the type of
station I'd hoped to avoid.

The director got up with a smile, which signaled that the meeting was over. "All right, I think we've got a plan. Before I leave,
I just want to make sure we're clear here: I'm not going to have
another Ed Snowden moment, am I?"

15

Geneva

Mary Shelley's *Frankenstein*, written in 1818, is largely set in Geneva, the bustling, neat, clean, clockwork-organized Swiss city where I now made my home. Like many Americans, I'd grown up watching the various movie versions and TV cartoons, but I'd never actually read the book. In the days before I left the States, however, I'd been searching for what to read about Geneva, and in nearly all the lists I found online, *Frankenstein* stood out from among the tourist guides and histories. In fact, I think the only PDFs I downloaded for the flight over were *Frankenstein* and the Geneva Conventions, and I only finished the former. I did my reading at night over the long, lonely months I spent by myself before Lindsay moved over to join me, stretched out on a bare mattress in the living room of the comically fancy, comically vast, but still almost entirely unfurnished apartment that the embassy was paying for on the Quai du Seujet, in the Saint-Jean Falaises district, with the Rhône out one window and the Jura Mountains out the other.

Suffice it to say, the book wasn't what I expected. *Frankenstein* is an epistolary novel that reads like a thread of overwritten emails, alternating scenes of madness and gory murder with a cautionary account of the way technological innovation tends to outpace all moral, ethical, and legal restraints. The result is the creation of an uncontrollable monster.

In the Intelligence Community, the "Frankenstein effect" is widely cited, though the more popular military term for it is "blowback": situations in which policy decisions intended to advance American interests end up harming them irreparably. Prominent examples of the "Frankenstein effect" cited by after-the-fact civilian, governmental, military, and even IC assessments have included America's funding and training of the mujahideen to fight the Soviets, which resulted in the radicalization of Osama bin Laden and the founding of al-Qaeda, as well as the de-Baath-ification of the Saddam Hussein–era Iraqi military, which resulted in the rise of the Islamic state. Without a doubt, however, the major instance of the Frankenstein effect over the course of my brief career can be found in the US government's clandestine drive to restructure the world's communications. In Geneva, in the same landscape where Mary Shelley's creature ran amok, America was busy creating a network that would eventually take on a life and mission of its own and wreak havoc on the lives of its creators—mine very much included.

The CIA station in the American embassy in Geneva was one of the prime European laboratories of this decades-long experiment. This city, the refined Old World capital of family banking and an immemorial tradition of financial secrecy, also lay at the intersection of EU and international fiber-optic networks, and happened to fall just within the shadow of key communications satellites circling overhead.

The CIA is the primary American intelligence agency dedicated to HUMINT (human intelligence), or covert intelligence gathering by means of interpersonal contact—person to person, face-to-face, unmediated by a screen. The COs (case officers) who specialized in this were terminal cynics, charming liars who smoked, drank, and harbored deep resentment toward the rise of SIGINT (signals

intelligence), or covert intelligence gathering by means of intercepted communications, which with each passing year reduced
their privilege and prestige. But though the COs had a general
distrust of digital technology reminiscent of Frank's back at headquarters, they certainly understood how useful it could be, which
produced a productive camaraderie and a healthy rivalry. Even the
most cunning and charismatic CO will, over the course of their
career, come across at least a few zealous idealists whose loyalties
they can't purchase with envelopes stuffed with cash. That was
typically the moment when they'd turn to technical field officers
like myself—with questions, compliments, and party invitations.

To serve as a technical field officer among these people was to
be as much a cultural ambassador as an expert adviser, introduc-
ing the case officers to the folkways and customs of a new territory
no less foreign to most Americans than Switzerland's twenty-six
cantons and four official languages. On Monday, a CO might ask
my advice on how to set up a covert online communications channel with a potential turncoat they were afraid to spook. On Tuesday, another CO might introduce me to someone they'd say was a
"specialist" in from Washington—though this was in fact the same
CO from the day before, now testing out a disguise that I'm still
embarrassed to say I didn't suspect in the least, though I suppose
that was the point. On Wednesday, I might be asked how best
to destroy-after-transmitting (the technological version of burn-
after-reading) a disc of customer records that a CO had managed
to purchase from a crooked Swisscom employee. On Thursday, I
might have to write up and transmit security violation reports on
COs, documenting minor infractions like forgetting to lock the
door to a vault when they'd gone to the bathroom—a duty I'd
perform with considerable compassion, since I once had had to
write up myself for exactly the same mistake. Come Friday, the
chief of operations might call me into his office and ask me if, "hy-
pothetically speaking," headquarters could send over an infected
thumb drive that could be used by "someone" to hack the comput-

ers used by delegates to the United Nations, whose main building was just up the street—did I think there was much of a chance of this "someone" being caught?

I didn't and they weren't.

In sum, during my time in the field, the field was rapidly changing. The agency was increasingly adamant that COs enter the new millennium, and technical field officers like myself were tasked with helping them do that in addition to all of our other duties. We put them online, and they put up with us.

Geneva was regarded as ground zero for this transition because it contained the world's richest environment of sophisticated targets, from the global headquarters of the United Nations to the home offices of numerous specialized UN agencies and international nongovernmental organizations. There was the International Atomic Energy Agency, which promotes nuclear technology and safety standards worldwide, including those that relate to nuclear weaponry; the International Telecommunication Union, which—through its influence over technical standards for everything from the radio spectrum to satellite orbits—determines what can be communicated and how; and the World Trade Organization, which—through its regulation of the trade of goods, services, and intellectual property among participating nations—determines what can be sold and how. Finally, there was Geneva's role as the capital of private finance, which allowed great fortunes to be stashed and spent without much public scrutiny regardless of whether those fortunes were ill-gotten or well earned.

The notoriously slow and meticulous methods of traditional spycraft certainly had their successes in manipulating these systems for America's benefit, but ultimately too few to satisfy the ever-increasing appetite of the American policy makers who read the IC's reports, especially as the Swiss banking sector—along with the rest of the world—went digital. With the world's deepest secrets now stored on computers, which were more often than not connected to the open Internet, it was only logical that America's intelligence agencies would want to use those very same connections to steal them.

Before the advent of the Internet, if an agency wanted to gain access to a target's computer it had to recruit an asset who had physical access to it. This was obviously a dangerous proposition: the asset might be caught in the act of downloading the secrets, or of implanting the exploitative hardware and software that would radio the secrets to their handlers. The global spread of digital technology simplified this process enormously. This new world of "digital network intelligence" or "computer network operations" meant that physical access was almost never required, which reduced the level of human risk and permanently realigned the HUMINT/SIGINT balance. An agent now could just send the target a message, such as an email, with attachments or links that unleashed malware that would allow the agency to surveil not just the target's computer but its entire network. Given this innovation, the CIA's HUMINT would be dedicated to the identification of targets of interest, and SIGINT would take care of the rest. Instead of a CO cultivating a target into an asset—through cash-on-the-barrel bribery, or coercion and blackmail if the bribery failed—a few clever computer hacks would provide a similar benefit. What's more, with this method the target would remain unwitting, in what would inevitably be a cleaner process.

That, at least, was the hope. But as intelligence increasingly became "cyberintelligence" (a term used to distinguish it from the old phone-and-fax forms of off-line SIGINT), old concerns also had to be updated to the new medium of the Internet. For example: how to research a target while remaining anonymous online.

This issue would typically emerge when a CO would search the name of a person from a country like Iran or China in the agency's databases and come up empty-handed. For casual searches of prospective targets like these, No Results was actually a fairly common outcome: the CIA's databases were mostly filled with people already of interest to the agency, or citizens of friendly countries whose records were more easily available. When faced with No Results, a CO would have to do the same thing you do when you want to look someone up: they'd turn to the public Internet. This was risky.

Normally when you go online, your request for any website travels from your computer more or less directly to the server that hosts your final destination—the website you're trying to visit. At every stop along the way, however, your request cheerfully announces exactly where on the Internet it came from, and exactly where on the Internet it's going, thanks to identifiers called source and destination headers, which you can think of as the address information on a postcard. Because of these headers, your Internet browsing can easily be identified as yours by, among others, webmasters, network administrators, and foreign intelligence services.

It may be hard to believe, but the agency at the time had no good answer for what a case officer should do in this situation, beyond weakly recommending that they ask CIA headquarters to take over the search on their behalf. Formally, the way this ridiculous procedure was supposed to work was that someone back in McLean would go online from a specific computer terminal and use what was called a "nonattributable research system." This was set up to proxy—that is, fake the origin of—a query before sending it to Google. If anyone tried to look into who had run that particular search, all they would find would be an anodyne business located somewhere in America—one of the myriad fake executive-headhunter or personnel-services companies the CIA used as cover.

I can't say that anyone ever definitively explained to me why the agency liked to use "job search" businesses as a front; presumably they were the only companies that might plausibly look up a nuclear engineer in Pakistan one day and a retired Polish general the next. I can say with absolute certainty, however, that the process was ineffective, onerous, and expensive. To create just one of these covers, the agency had to invent the purpose and name of a company, secure a credible physical address somewhere in America, register a credible URL, put up a credible website, and then rent servers in the company's name. Furthermore, the agency had to create an encrypted connection from those servers that allowed it to communicate with the CIA network without anyone noticing the connection. Here's the kicker: After all of that effort and money was expended just to let us anonymously Google a name, whatever front business was being used as a proxy would immediately be burned—by which I mean its connection to the CIA would be revealed to our adversaries—the moment some analyst decided to take a break from their research to log in to their personal Facebook account on that same computer. Since few of the people at headquarters were undercover, that Facebook account would often openly declare, "I work at the CIA," or just as tellingly, "I work at the State Department, but in McLean."

Go ahead and laugh. Back then, it happened all the time.

During my stint in Geneva, whenever a CO would ask me if there was a safer, faster, and all-around more efficient way to do this, I introduced them to Tor.

The Tor Project was a creation of the state that ended up becoming one of the few effective shields against the state's surveillance. Tor is free and open-source software that, if used carefully, allows its users to browse online with the closest thing to perfect anonymity that can be practically achieved at scale. Its protocols were developed by the US Naval Research Laboratory throughout the mid-1990s, and in 2003 it was released to the public—to the worldwide civilian population on whom its functionality depends. This is because Tor operates on a cooperative community model, relying on tech-savvy volunteers all over the globe who run their own Tor servers out of their basements, attics, and garages. By routing its users' Internet traffic through these servers, Tor does the same job of protecting the origin of that traffic as the CIA's "non-attributable research" system, with the primary difference being that Tor does it better, or at least more efficiently. I was already convinced of this, but convincing the gruff COs was another matter altogether.

With the Tor protocol, your traffic is distributed and bounced around through randomly generated pathways from Tor server to Tor server, with the purpose being to replace your identity as the source of a communication with that of the last Tor server in the constantly shifting chain. Virtually none of the Tor servers, which are called "layers," know the identity of, or any identifying information about, the origin of the traffic. And in a true stroke of genius, the one Tor server that *does* know the origin—the very first server in the chain—*does not* know where that traffic is headed. Put more simply: the first Tor server that connects you to the Tor network, called a gateway, knows you're the one sending a request, but because it isn't allowed to read that request, it has no idea whether you're looking for pet memes or information about a protest, and the final Tor server that your request passes through, called an exit, knows exactly what's being asked for, but has no idea who's asking for it.

This layering method is called onion routing, which gives Tor its name: it's The Onion Router. The classified joke was that trying to surveil the Tor network makes spies want to cry. Therein lies the project's irony: here was a US military–developed technology that made cyberintelligence simultaneously harder and easier, applying hacker know-how to protect the anonymity of IC officers, but only at the price of granting that same anonymity to adversaries and to average users across the globe. In this sense, Tor was even more neutral than Switzerland. For me personally, Tor was a life changer, bringing me back to the Internet of my childhood by giving me just the slightest taste of freedom from being observed.

NONE OF THIS account of the CIA's pivot to cyberintelligence, or SIGINT on the Internet, is meant to imply that the agency wasn't still doing some significant HUMINT, in the same manner in which it had always done so, at least since the advent of the modern IC in the aftermath of World War II. Even I got involved, though my most memorable operation was a failure. Geneva was the first and only time in my intelligence career in which I made the personal acquaintance of a target—the first and only time that I looked directly into the eyes of a human being rather than just recording their life from afar. I have to say, I found the whole experience unforgettably visceral and sad.

Sitting around discussing how to hack a faceless UN complex was psychologically easier by a wide margin. Direct engagement, which can be harsh and emotionally draining, simply doesn't happen that much on the technical side of intelligence, and almost never in computing. There is a depersonalization of experience fostered by the distance of a screen. Peering at life through a window can ultimately abstract us from our actions and limit any meaningful confrontation with their consequences.

I met the man at an embassy function, a party. The embassy had lots of those, and the COs always went, drawn as much by the opportunities to spot and assess potential candidates for recruitment as by the open bars and cigar salons.

Sometimes the COs would bring me along. I'd lectured them on my specialty long enough, I guess, that now they were all too happy to lecture me on theirs, cross-training me to help them play "spot the sap" in an environment where there were always more people to meet than they could possibly handle on their own. My native geekiness meant I could get the young researchers from CERN (Conseil Européen pour la Recherche Nucléaire: European Council for Nuclear Research) talking about their work with a voluble excitement that the MBAs and political science majors who comprised the ranks of our COs had trouble provoking on their own.

As a technologist, I found it incredibly easy to defend my cover. The moment some bespoke-suited cosmopolite asked me what I did, and I responded with the four words "I work in IT" (or, in my improving French, *je travaille dans l'informatique*), their interest in me was over. Not that this ever stopped the conversation. When you're a fresh-faced professional in a conversation outside your field, it's never that surprising when you ask a lot of questions, and in my experience most people will jump at the chance to explain exactly how much more they know than you do about something they care about deeply.

The party I'm recalling took place on a warm night on the outside terrace of an upscale café on one of the side streets alongside Lake Geneva. Some of the COs wouldn't hesitate to abandon me at such a gathering if they had to in order to sit as close as possible to whatever woman happened to match their critical intelligence-value indicators of being highly attractive and no older than a student, but I wasn't about to complain. For me, spotting targets was a hobby that came with a free dinner.

I took my plate and sat down at a table next to a well-dressed Middle Eastern man in a cuff-linked, demonstratively Swiss pink shirt. He seemed lonely, and totally exasperated that no one seemed interested in him, so I asked him about himself. That's the usual technique: just be curious and let them talk. In this case, the man did so much talking that it was like I wasn't even there. He was Saudi, and told me about how much he loved Geneva, the relative beauties of the French and Arabic languages, and the absolute beauty of this one Swiss girl with whom he—yes—had a regular date playing laser tag. With a touch of a conspiratorial tone, he said that he worked in private wealth management. Within moments I was getting a full-on polished presentation about what, exactly, makes a private bank private, and the challenge of investing without moving markets when your clients are the size of sovereign wealth funds.

"Your clients?" I asked.

That's when he said, "Most of my work is on Saudi accounts."

After a few minutes, I excused myself to go to the bathroom, and on the way there I leaned over to tell the CO who worked finance targets what I'd learned. After a necessarily too-long interval "fixing my hair," or texting Lindsay in front of the bathroom mirror, I returned to find the CO sitting in my chair. I waved to my new Saudi friend before sitting down beside the CO's discarded, smoky-eyed date. Rather than feeling bad, I felt like I'd really earned the Pavés de Genève that were passed around for dessert. My job was done.

The next day, the CO, whom I'll call Cal, heaped me with praise and thanked me effusively. COs are promoted or passed over based primarily on how effective they are at recruiting assets with access to information on matters substantial enough to be formally reported back to headquarters, and given Saudi Arabia's suspected involvement in financing terror, Cal felt under tremendous pressure to cultivate a qualifying source. I was sure that in no time at all our fellow party guest would be getting a second paycheck from the agency.

That was not quite how it worked out, however. Despite Cal's regular forays with the banker to strip clubs and bars, the banker wasn't warming up to him—at least not to the point where a pitch could be made—and Cal was getting impatient.

After a month of failures, Cal was so frustrated that he took the banker out drinking and got him absolutely plastered. Then he pressured the guy to drive home drunk instead of taking a cab. Before the guy had even left the last bar of the night, Cal was calling the make and plate number of his car to the Geneva police, who not fifteen minutes later arrested him for driving under the influence. The banker faced an enormous fine, since in Switzerland fines aren't flat sums but based on a percentage of income, and his driver's license was suspended for three months—a stretch of time that Cal would spend, as a truly wonderful friend with a fake-guilty conscience, driving the guy back and forth between his home and work, daily, so that the guy could "keep his office from finding out." When the fine was levied, causing his friend cashflow problems, Cal was ready with a loan. The banker had become dependent, the dream of every CO.

There was only one hitch: when Cal finally made the pitch, the banker turned him down. He was furious, having figured out the planned crime and the engineered arrest, and felt betrayed that

Cal's generosity hadn't been genuine. He cut off all contact. Cal made a halfhearted attempt to follow up and do damage control, but it was too late. The banker who'd loved Switzerland had lost his job and was returning—or being returned—to Saudi Arabia. Cal himself was rotated back to the States.

Too much had been hazarded, too little had been gained. It was a waste, which I myself had put in motion and then was powerless to stop. After that experience, the prioritizing of SIGINT over HUMINT made all the more sense to me.

In the summer of 2008, the city celebrated its annual Fêtes de Genève, a giant carnival that culminates in fireworks. I remember sitting on the left bank of Lake Geneva with the local personnel of the SCS, or Special Collection Service, a joint CIA-NSA program responsible for installing and operating the special surveillance equipment that allows US embassies to spy on foreign signals. These guys worked down the hall from my vault at the embassy, but they were older than I was, and their work was not just way above my pay grade but way beyond my abilities—they had access to NSA tools that I didn't even know existed. Still, we were friendly: I looked up to them, and they looked out for me.

As the fireworks exploded overhead, I was talking about the banker's case, lamenting the disaster it had been, when one of the guys turned to me and said, "Next time you meet someone, Ed, don't bother with the COs—just give us his email address and we'll take care of it." I remember nodding somberly to this, though at the time I barely had a clue of the full implications of what that comment meant.

I steered clear of parties for the rest of the year and mostly just hung around the cafés and parks of Saint-Jean Falaises with Lindsay, taking occasional vacations with her to Italy, France, and Spain. Still, something had soured my mood, and it wasn't just the banker debacle. Come to think of it, maybe it was banking in general. Geneva is an expensive city and unabashedly posh, but as 2008 drew to a close its elegance seemed to tip over into extravagance, with a massive influx of the superrich—most of them from the Gulf states, many of them Saudi—enjoying the profits of peak oil prices on the cusp of the global financial crisis. These royal types were booking whole floors of five-star grand hotels and buying out the entire inventories of the luxury stores just across the bridge. They were putting on lavish banquets at the Michelin-starred restaurants and speeding their chrome-plated Lamborghinis down the cobbled streets. It would be hard at any time to miss Geneva's display of conspicuous consumption, but the profligacy now on display was particularly galling—coming as it did during the worst economic disaster, as the American media kept telling us, since the Great Depression, and as the European media kept telling us, since the interwar period and Versailles.

It wasn't that Lindsay and I were hurting: after all, our rent was being paid by Uncle Sam. Rather, it's that every time she or I would talk to our folks back home, the situation seemed grimmer. Both of our families knew people who'd worked their entire lives, some of them for the US government, only to have their homes taken away by banks after an unexpected illness made a few mortgage payments impossible.

To live in Geneva was to live in an alternative, even opposite, reality. As the rest of the world became more and more impoverished, Geneva flourished, and while the Swiss banks didn't engage in many of the types of risky trades that caused the crash, they gladly hid the money of those who'd profited from the pain and were never held accountable. The 2008 crisis, which laid so much of the foundation for the crises of populism that a decade later would sweep across Europe and America, helped me realize that something that is devastating for the public can be, and often is, beneficial to the elites. This was a lesson that the US government would confirm for me in other contexts, time and again, in the years ahead.

16

Tokyo

The Internet is fundamentally American, but I had to leave America to fully understand what that meant. The World Wide Web might have been invented in Geneva, at the CERN research laboratory in 1989, but the ways by which the Web is accessed are as American as baseball, which gives the American Intelligence Community the home field advantage. The cables and satellites, the servers and towers—so much of the infrastructure of the Internet is under US control that over 90 percent of the world's Internet traffic passes through technologies developed, owned, and/or operated by the American government and American businesses, most of which are physically located on American territory. Countries that traditionally worry about such advantages, like China and Russia, have attempted to make alternative systems, such as the Great Firewall, or the state-sponsored censored search engines, or the nationalized satellite constellations that provide selective GPS—but America remains the hegemon, the keeper of the master switches that can turn almost anyone on and off at will.

It's not just the Internet's infrastructure that I'm defining as fundamentally American—it's the computer software (Microsoft,

Google, Oracle) and hardware (HP, Apple, Dell), too. It's every-thing from the chips (Intel, Qualcomm), to the routers and mo-dems (Cisco, Juniper), to the Web services and platforms that provide email and social networking and cloud storage (Google, Facebook, and the most structurally important but invisible Am-azon, which provides cloud services to the US government along with half the Internet). Though some of these companies might manufacture their devices in, say, China, the companies them-selves are American and are subject to American law. The problem is, they're also subject to classified American policies that pervert law and permit the US government to surveil virtually every man, woman, and child who has ever touched a computer or picked up a phone.

Given the American nature of the planet's communications in-frastructure, it should have been obvious that the US government would engage in this type of mass surveillance. It should have been especially obvious to me. Yet it wasn't—mostly because the gov-ernment kept insisting that it did nothing of the sort, and generally disclaimed the practice in courts and in the media in a manner so adamant that the few remaining skeptics who accused it of lying were treated like wild-haired conspiracy junkies. Their suspicions about secret NSA programs seemed hardly different from para-noid delusions involving alien messages being beamed to the ra-dios in our teeth. We—me, you, all of us—were too trusting. But what makes this all the more personally painful for me was that the last time I'd made this mistake, I'd supported the invasion of Iraq and joined the army. When I arrived in the IC, I felt sure that I'd never be fooled again, especially given my top secret clearance. Surely that had to count for some degree of transparency. After all, why would the government keep secrets from its secret keepers? This is all to say that the obvious didn't even become the thinkable for me until some time after I moved to Japan in 2009 to work for the NSA, America's premier signals intelligence agency.

It was a dream job, not only because it was with the most ad-vanced intelligence agency on the planet, but also because it was based in Japan, a place that had always fascinated Lindsay and me. It felt like a country from the future. Though mine was officially a contractor position, its responsibilities and, especially, its location were more than enough to lure me. It's ironic that only by going private again was I put in a position to understand what my government was doing.

On paper, I was an employee of Perot Systems, a company founded by that diminutive hyperactive Texan who founded the Reform Party and twice ran for the presidency. But almost immediately after my arrival in Japan, Perot Systems was acquired by Dell, so on paper I became an employee of Dell. As in the CIA, this contractor status was all just formality and cover, and I only ever worked in an NSA facility.

The NSA's Pacific Technical Center (PTC) occupied one-half of a building inside the enormous Yokota Air Base. As the headquarters of US Forces Japan, the base was surrounded by high walls, steel gates, and guarded checkpoints. Yokota and the PTC were just a short bike ride from where Lindsay and I got an apartment in Fussa, a city at the western edge of Tokyo's vast metropolitan spread.

The PTC handled the NSA's infrastructure for the entire Pacific, and provided support for the agency's spoke sites in nearby countries. Most of these were focused on managing the secret relationships that let the NSA cover the Pacific Rim with spy gear, as long as the agency promised to share some of the intelligence it gleaned with regional governments—and so long as their citizens didn't find out what the agency was doing. Communications interception was the major part of the mission. The PTC would amass "cuts" from captured signals and push them back across the ocean to Hawaii, and Hawaii, in turn, would push them back to the continental United States.

My official job title was systems analyst, with responsibility for maintaining the local NSA systems, though much of my initial work was that of a systems administrator, helping to connect the NSA's systems architecture with the CIA's. Because I was the only one in the region who knew the CIA's architecture, I'd also travel out to US embassies, like the one I'd left in Geneva, establishing and maintaining the links that enabled the agencies to share intelligence in ways that hadn't previously been possible. This was the first time in my life that I truly realized the power of being the only one in a room with a sense not just of how one system functioned internally, but of how it functioned together with multiple systems—or didn't. Later, as the chiefs of the PTC came to recognize that I had a knack for hacking together solutions to their problems, I was given enough of a leash to propose projects of my own.

Two things about the NSA stunned me right off the bat: how technologically sophisticated it was compared with the CIA, and how much less vigilant it was about security in its every iteration, from the compartmentalization of information to data encryption. In Geneva, we'd had to haul the hard drives out of the computer every night and lock them up in a safe—and what's more, those drives were encrypted. The NSA, by contrast, hardly bothered to encrypt anything.

In fact, it was rather disconcerting to find out that the NSA was so far ahead of the game in terms of cyberintelligence yet so far behind it in terms of cybersecurity, including the most basic: disaster recovery, or backup. Each of the NSA's spoke sites collected its own intel, stored the intel on its own local servers, and, because of bandwidth restrictions—limitations on the amount of data that could be transmitted at speed—often didn't send copies back to the main servers at NSA headquarters. This meant that if any data were destroyed at a particular site, the intelligence that the agency had worked hard to collect could be lost.

My chiefs at the PTC understood the risks the agency was taking by not keeping copies of many of its files, so they tasked me with engineering a solution and pitching it to the decision makers at headquarters. The result was a backup and storage system that would act as a shadow NSA: a complete, automated, and constantly updating copy of all of the agency's most important material, which would allow the agency to reboot and be up and running again, with all its archives intact, even if Fort Meade were reduced to smoldering rubble.

The major problem with creating a global disaster-recovery system—or really with creating any type of backup system that involves a truly staggering number of computers—is dealing with duplicated data. In plain terms, you have to handle situations in which, say, one thousand computers all have copies of the same single file: you have to make sure you're not backing up that same file one thousand times, because that would require one thousand times the amount of bandwidth and storage space. It was this wasteful duplication, in particular, that was preventing the agency's spoke sites from transmitting daily backups of their records to Fort Meade: the connection would be clogged with a thousand copies of the same file containing the same intercepted phone call, 999 of which the agency did not need.

The way to avoid this was "deduplication": a method to evaluate the uniqueness of data. The system that I designed would constantly scan the files at every facility at which the NSA stored records, testing each "block" of data down to the slightest fragment of a file to find out whether or not it was unique. Only if the agency lacked a copy of it back home would the data be automatically queued for transmission—reducing the volume that flowed over the agency's transpacific fiber-optic connection from a waterfall to a trickle.

The combination of deduplication and constant improvements in storage technology allowed the agency to store intelligence data for progressively longer periods of time. Just over the course of my career, the agency's goal went from being able to store intelligence for days, to weeks, to months, to five years or more after its collection. By the time of this book's publication, the agency might already be able to store it for decades. The NSA's conventional wisdom was that there was no point in collecting anything unless they could store it until it was useful, and there was no way to predict when exactly that would be. This rationalization was fuel for the agency's ultimate dream, which is permanency—to store all of the files it has ever collected or produced for perpetuity, and so create a perfect memory. The permanent record.

The NSA has a whole protocol you're supposed to follow when you give a program a code name. It's basically an I Ching–like stochastic procedure that randomly picks words from two columns. An internal website throws imaginary dice to pick one name from column A, and throws again to pick one name from column B. This is how you end up with names that don't mean anything, like FOXACID and EGOTISTICALGIRAFFE. The point of a code name is that it's not supposed to refer to what the program does. (As has been reported, FOXACID was the code name for NSA servers that host malware versions of familiar websites; EGO-TISTICALGIRAFFE was an NSA program intended to exploit a vulnerability in certain Web browsers running Tor, since they couldn't break Tor itself.) But agents at the NSA were so confident of their power and the agency's absolute invulnerability that they rarely complied with the regulations. In short, they'd cheat and redo their dice throws until they got the name combination they wanted, whatever they thought was cool, TRAFFICTHIEF.

I swear I never did that when I went about finding a name for my backup system. I swear that I just rolled the bones and came up with EPICSHELTER.

Later, once the agency adopted the system, they renamed it something like the Storage Modernization Plan or Storage Modernization Program. Within two years of the invention of EP-ICSHELTER, a variant had been implemented and was in standard use under yet another name.

THE MATERIAL THAT I disseminated to journalists in 2013 documented such an array of abuses by the NSA, accomplished through such a diversity of technological capabilities, that no one agent in the daily discharge of their responsibilities was ever in the position to know about all of them—not even a systems administrator. To find out about even a fraction of the malfeasance, you had to go searching. And to go searching, you had to know that it existed.

It was something as banal as a conference that first clued me in to that existence, sparking my initial suspicion about the full scope of what the NSA was perpetrating.

In the midst of my EPICSHELTER work, the PTC hosted a conference on China sponsored by the Joint Counterintelligence Training Academy (JCITA) for the Defense Intelligence Agency (DIA), an agency connected to the Department of Defense that specializes in spying on foreign militaries and foreign military–related matters. This conference featured briefings given by experts from all the intelligence components, the NSA, CIA, FBI, and military, about how the Chinese intelligence services were targeting the IC and what the IC could do to cause them trouble. Though China certainly interested me, this wasn't the kind of work I would ordinarily have been involved in, so I didn't pay the conference much mind until it was announced that the only technology briefer was unable to attend at the last minute. I'm not sure what the reason was for that absence—maybe flu, maybe kismet—but the course chair for the conference asked if there was anyone at the PTC who might be able to step in as a replacement, since it was too late to reschedule. One of the chiefs mentioned my name, and when I was asked if I wanted to give it a shot, I said yes. I liked my boss, and wanted to help him out. Also, I was curious, and relished the opportunity to do something that wasn't about data deduplication for a change.

My boss was thrilled. Then he told me the catch: the briefing was the next day.

I called Lindsay and told her I wouldn't be home. I was going to be up all night preparing the presentation, whose nominal topic was the intersection between a very old discipline, counterintelligence, and a very new discipline, cyberintelligence, coming together to try to exploit and thwart the adversary's attempts to use the Internet to gather surveillance. I started pulling everything off the NSA network (and off the CIA network, to which I still had access), trying to read every top secret report I could find about what the Chinese were doing online. Specifically, I read up on so-called intrusion sets, which are bundles of data about particular types of attacks, tools, and targets. IC analysts used these intrusion sets to identify specific Chinese military cyberintelligence or hacking groups, in the same way that detectives might try to identify a suspect responsible for a string of burglaries by a common set of characteristics or modus operandi.

The point of my researching this widely dispersed material was to do more than merely report on how China was hacking us, however. My primary task was to provide a summary of the IC's assessment of China's ability to electronically track American officers and assets operating in the region.

Everyone knows (or thinks they know) about the draconian Internet measures of the Chinese government, and some people know (or think they know) the gravamen of the disclosures I gave to journalists in 2013 about my own government's capabilities. But listen: It's one thing to casually say, in a science-fiction dystopic type of way, that a government can theoretically see and hear everything that all of its citizens are doing. It's a very different thing for a government to actually try to implement such a system. What a science-fiction writer can describe in a sentence might take the concerted work of thousands of technologists and millions of dollars of equipment. To read the technical details of China's surveillance of private communications—to read a complete and accurate accounting of the mechanisms and machinery required for the constant collection, storage, and analysis of the billions of daily telephone and Internet communications of over a billion people—was utterly mind-boggling. At first I was so impressed by the system's sheer achievement and audacity that I almost forgot to be appalled by its totalitarian controls.

After all, China's government was an explicitly antidemocratic single-party state. NSA agents, even more than most Americans, just took it for granted that the place was an authoritarian hell-hole. Chinese civil liberties weren't my department. There wasn't anything I could do about them. I worked, I was sure of it, for the good guys, and that made me a good guy, too.

But there were certain aspects of what I was reading that disturbed me. I was reminded of what is perhaps the fundamental rule of technological progress: if something can be done, it probably will be done, and possibly already has been. There was simply no way for America to have so much information about what the Chinese were doing without having done some of the very same things itself, and I had the sneaking sense while I was looking through all this China material that I was looking at a mirror and seeing a reflection of America. What China was doing publicly to its own citizens, America might be—could be—doing secretly to the world.

And although you should hate me for it, I have to say that at the time I tamped down my unease. Indeed, I did my best to ignore it. The distinctions were still fairly clear to me. China's Great Firewall was domestically censorious and repressive, intended to keep its citizens in and America out in the most chilling and demonstrative way, while the American systems were invisible and purely defensive. As I then understood US surveillance, anyone in the world could come in through America's Internet infrastructure and access whatever content they pleased, unblocked and unfiltered—or at least only blocked and filtered by their home countries and American businesses, which are, presumptively, not under US government control. It was only those who'd been expressly targeted for visiting, for example, jihadist bombing sites or malware marketplaces who would find themselves tracked and scrutinized.

Understood this way, the US surveillance model was perfectly okay with me. It was more than okay, actually—I fully supported defensive and targeted surveillance, a "firewall" that didn't keep anybody out, but just burned the guilty.

But in the sleepless days after that sleepless night, some dim suspicion still stirred in my mind. Long after I gave my China briefing, I couldn't help but keep digging around.

AT THE START of my employment with the NSA, in 2009, I was only slightly more knowledgeable about its practices than the rest of the world. From journalists' reports, I was aware of the agency's myriad surveillance initiatives authorized by President George W. Bush in the immediate aftermath of 9/11. In particular, I knew about its most publicly contested initiative, the warrantless wiretapping component of the President's Surveillance Program (PSP), which had been disclosed by the *New York Times* in 2005 thanks to the courage of a few NSA and Department of Justice whistleblowers.

Officially speaking, the PSP was an "executive order," essentially a set of instructions set down by the American president that the government has to consider the equal of public law—even if they're just scribbled secretly on a napkin. The PSP empowered the NSA to collect telephone and Internet communications between the United States and abroad. Notably, the PSP allowed the NSA to do this without having to obtain a special warrant from a Foreign Intelligence Surveillance Court, a secret federal court established in 1978 to oversee IC requests for surveillance warrants after the agencies were caught domestically spying on the anti–Vietnam War and civil rights movements.

Following the outcry that attended the *Times* revelations, and American Civil Liberties Union challenges to the constitutionality of the PSP in non-secret, regular courts, the Bush administration claimed to have let the program expire in 2007. But the expiration turned out to be a farce. Congress spent the last two years of the Bush administration passing legislation that retroactively legalized the PSP. It also retroactively immunized from prosecution the telecoms and Internet service providers that had participated in it. This legislation—the Protect America Act of 2007 and the FISA Amendments Act of 2008—employed intentionally misleading language to reassure US citizens that their communications were not being explicitly targeted, even as it effectively extended the PSP's remit. In addition to collecting inbound communications coming from foreign countries, the NSA now also had policy approval for the warrantless collection of outbound telephone and Internet communications originating within American borders.

That, at least, was the picture I got after reading the government's own summary of the situation, which was issued to the public in an unclassified version in July 2009, the very same summer that I spent delving into Chinese cyber-capabilities. This summary, which bore the nondescript title *Unclassified Report on the President's Surveillance Program*, was compiled by the Offices of the Inspector Generals of five agencies (Department of Defense, Department of Justice, CIA, NSA, and the Office of the Director of National Intelligence) and was offered to the public in lieu of a full congressional investigation of Bush-era NSA overreach. The fact that President Obama, once in office, refused to call for a full congressional investigation was the first sign, to me at least, that the new president—for whom Lindsay had enthusiastically campaigned—intended to move forward without a proper reckoning with the past. As his administration rebranded and recertified PSP-related programs, Lindsay's hope in him, as well as my own, would prove more and more misplaced.

While the unclassified report was mostly just old news, I found it informative in a few respects. I remember being immediately struck by its curious, they-do-protest-too-much tone, along with more than a few twists of logic and language that didn't compute. As the report laid out its legal arguments in support of various agency programs—rarely named, and almost never described—I couldn't help but notice the fact that hardly any of the executive branch officials who had actually authorized these programs had agreed to be interviewed by the inspector generals. From Vice President Dick Cheney and his counsel David Addington to Attorney General John Ashcroft and DOJ lawyer John Yoo, nearly every major player had refused to cooperate with the very offices responsible for holding the IC accountable, and the IGs couldn't compel them to cooperate, because this wasn't a formal investigation involving testimony. It was hard for me to interpret their absence from the record as anything other than an admission of malfeasance.

Another aspect of the report that threw me was its repeated, obscure references to "Other Intelligence Activities" (the capitalization is the report's) for which no "viable legal rationale" or no "legal basis" could be found beyond President Bush's claim of executive powers during wartime—a wartime that had no end in sight. Of course, these references gave no description whatsoever of what these Activities might actually be, but the process of deduction pointed to warrantless domestic surveillance, as it was pretty much the only intelligence activity not provided for under the various legal frameworks that appeared subsequent to the PSP.

As I read on, I wasn't sure that anything disclosed in the report completely justified the legal machinations involved, let alone the threats by then deputy attorney general James Comey and then FBI director Robert Mueller to resign if certain aspects of the PSP were reauthorized. Nor did I notice anything that fully explained the risks taken by so many fellow agency members—agents much senior to me, with decades of experience—and DOJ personnel to contact the press and express their misgivings about how aspects of the PSP were being abused. If they were putting their careers, their families, and their lives on the line, it had to be over something graver than the warrantless wiretapping that had already made headlines.

That suspicion sent me searching for the classified version of the report, and it was not in the least dispelled by the fact that such a version appeared not to exist. I didn't understand. If the classified version was merely a record of the sins of the past, it should have been easily accessible. But it was nowhere to be found. I wondered whether I was looking in the wrong places. After a while of ranging fairly widely and still finding nothing, though, I decided to drop the issue. Life took over and I had work to do. When you get asked to give recommendations on how to keep IC agents and

assets from being uncovered and executed by the Chinese Ministry
of State Security, it's hard to remember what you were Googling
the week before.

It was only later, long after I'd forgotten about the missing IG
report, that the classified version came skimming across my desktop, as if in proof of that old maxim that the best way to find
something is to stop looking for it. Once the classified version
turned up, I realized why I hadn't had any luck finding it previously: it couldn't be seen, not even by the heads of agencies. It
was filed in an Exceptionally Controlled Information (ECI) compartment, an extremely rare classification used only to make sure
that something would remain hidden even from those holding top
secret clearance. Because of my position, I was familiar with most
of the ECIs at the NSA, but not this one. The report's full classification designation was TOP SECRET//STLW//HCS/COMINT//
ORCON/NOFORN, which translates to: pretty much only a few
dozen people in the world are allowed to read this.

I was most definitely not one of them. The report came to my
attention by mistake: someone in the NSA IG's office had left a
draft copy on a system that I, as a sysadmin, had access to. Its
caveat of STLW, which I didn't recognize, turned out to be what's
called a "dirty word" on my system: a label signifying a document
that wasn't supposed to be stored on lower-security drives. These
drives were being constantly checked for any newly appearing
dirty words, and the moment one was found I was alerted so that
I could decide how best to scrub the document from the system.
But before I did, I'd have to examine the offending file myself, just
to confirm that the dirty word search hadn't flagged anything accidentally. Usually I'd take just the briefest glance at the thing. But
this time, as soon I opened the document and read the title, I knew
I'd be reading it all the way through.

Here was everything that was missing from the unclassified
version. Here was everything that the journalism I'd read had
lacked, and that the court proceedings I'd followed had been denied: a complete accounting of the NSA's most secret surveillance

programs, and the agency directives and Department of Justice policies that had been used to subvert American law and contravene the US Constitution. After reading the thing, I could understand why no IC employee had ever leaked it to journalists, and no judge would be able to force the government to produce it in open court. The document was so deeply classified that anybody who had access to it who wasn't a sysadmin would be immediately identifiable. And the activities it outlined were so deeply criminal that no government would ever allow it to be released unredacted.

One issue jumped out at me immediately: it was clear that the unclassified version I was already familiar with wasn't a redaction of the classified version, as would usually be the practice. Rather, it was a wholly different document, which the classified version immediately exposed as an outright and carefully concocted lie. The duplicity was stupefying, especially given that I'd just dedicated months of my time to deduplicating files. Most of the time, when you're dealing with two versions of the same document, the differences between them are trivial—a few commas here, a few words there. But the only thing these two particular reports had in common was their title.

Whereas the unclassified version merely made reference to the NSA being ordered to intensify its intelligence-gathering practices following 9/11, the classified version laid out the nature, and scale, of that intensification. The NSA's historic brief had been fundamentally altered from targeted collection of communications to "bulk collection," which is the agency's euphemism for mass surveillance. And whereas the unclassified version obfuscated this shift, advocating for expanded surveillance by scaring the public with the specter of terror, the classified version made this shift explicit, justifying it as the legitimate corollary of expanded technological capability.

The NSA IG's portion of the classified report outlined what it called "a collection gap," noting that existing surveillance legislation (particularly the Foreign Intelligence Surveillance Act) dated from 1978, a time when most communications signals traveled via radio or telephone lines, rather than fiber-optic cables and satellites. In essence, the agency was arguing that the speed and volume of contemporary communication had outpaced, and outgrown, American law—no court, not even a secret court, could issue enough individually targeted warrants fast enough to keep up—and that a truly global world required a truly global intelligence agency. All of this pointed, in the NSA's logic, to the necessity of the bulk collection of Internet communications. The code name for this bulk collection initiative was indicated in the very "dirty word" that got it flagged on my system: STLW, an abbreviation of STELLARWIND. This turned out to be the single major component of the PSP that had continued, and even grown, in secret after the rest of the program had been made public in the press.

STELLARWIND was the classified report's deepest secret. It was, in fact, the NSA's deepest secret, and the one that the report's sensitive status had been designed to protect. The program's very existence was an indication that the agency's mission had been transformed, from using technology to defend America to using technology to control it by redefining citizens' private Internet communications as potential signals intelligence.

Such fraudulent redefinitions ran throughout the report, but perhaps the most fundamental and transparently desperate involved the government's vocabulary. STELLARWIND had been collecting communications since the PSP's inception in 2001, but in 2004—when Justice Department officials balked at the continuation of the initiative—the Bush administration attempted to legitimize it ex post facto by changing the meanings of basic English words, such as "acquire" and "obtain." According to the report, it was the government's position that the NSA could collect whatever communications records it wanted to, without having to get a warrant, because it could only be said to have *acquired* or *obtained* them, in the legal sense, if and when the agency "searched for and retrieved" them from its database.

This lexical sophistry was particularly galling to me, as I was well aware that the agency's goal was to be able to retain as much data as it could for as long as it could—for perpetuity. If communications records would only be considered definitively "obtained" once they were used, they could remain "unobtained" but collected in storage forever, raw data awaiting its future manipulation. By redefining the terms "acquire" and "obtain"—from describing the act of data being entered into a database, to describing the act of a person (or, more likely, an algorithm) querying that database and getting a "hit" or "return" at any conceivable point in the future—the US government was developing the capacity of an eternal law-enforcement agency. At any time, the government could dig through the past communications of anyone it wanted to victimize in search of a crime (and everybody's communications contain evidence of something). At any point, for all perpetuity, any new administration—any future rogue head of the NSA—could just show up to work and, as easily as flicking a switch, instantly track everybody with a phone or a computer, know who they were, where they were, what they were doing with whom, and what they had ever done in the past.

THE TERM "MASS surveillance" is more clear to me, and I think to most people, than the government's preferred "bulk collection," which to my mind threatens to give a falsely fuzzy impression of the agency's work. "Bulk collection" makes it sound like a particularly busy post office or sanitation department, as opposed to a historic effort to achieve total access to—and clandestinely take possession of—the records of all digital communications in existence.

But even once a common ground of terminology is established, misperceptions can still abound. Most people, even today, tend to think of mass surveillance in terms of content—the actual words they use when they make a phone call or write an email. When they find out that the government actually cares comparatively little about that content, they tend to care comparatively little about government surveillance. This relief is understandable, to a degree, due to what each of us must regard as the uniquely revealing and intimate nature of our communications: the sound of our voice, almost as personal as a thumbprint; the inimitable facial expression we put on in a selfie sent by text. The unfortunate truth, however, is that the content of our communications is rarely as revealing as its other elements—the unwritten, unspoken information that can expose the broader context and patterns of behavior.

The NSA calls this "metadata." The term's prefix, "meta," which traditionally is translated as "above" or "beyond," is here used in the sense of "about": metadata is data about data. It is, more accurately, data that is made by data—a cluster of tags and markers that allow data to be useful. The most direct way of thinking about metadata, however, is as "activity data," all the records of all the things you do on your devices and all the things your devices do on their own. Take a phone call, for example: its metadata might include the date and time of the call, the call's duration, the number from which the call was made, the number being called, and their locations. An email's metadata might include information about what type of computer it was generated on, where, and when, who the computer belonged to, who sent the email, who received it, where and when it was sent and received, and who if anyone besides the sender and recipient accessed it, and where and when. Metadata can tell your surveillant the address you slept at last night and what time you got up this morning. It reveals every place you visited during your day and how long you spent there. It shows who you were in touch with and who was in touch with you.

It's this fact that obliterates any government claim that metadata is somehow not a direct window into the substance of a communication. With the dizzying volume of digital communications in the world, there is simply no way that every phone call could be listened to or email could be read. Even if it were feasible, however, it still wouldn't be useful, and anyway, metadata makes this unnecessary by winnowing the field. This is why it's best to regard metadata not as some benign abstraction, but as the very essence of content: it is precisely the first line of information that the party surveilling you requires.

There's another thing, too: content is usually defined as something that you knowingly produce. You know what you're saying during a phone call, or what you're writing in an email. But you have hardly any control over the metadata you produce, because it is generated automatically. Just as it's collected, stored, and analyzed by machine, it's made by machine, too, without your participation or even consent. Your devices are constantly communicating for you whether you want them to or not. And, unlike the humans you communicate with of your own volition, your devices don't withhold private information or use code words in an attempt to be discreet. They merely ping the nearest cell phone towers with signals that never lie.

One major irony here is that law, which always lags behind technological innovation by at least a generation, gives substantially more protections to a communication's content than to its metadata—and yet intelligence agencies are far more interested in the metadata—the activity records that allow them both the "big picture" ability to analyze data at scale, and the "little picture" ability to make perfect maps, chronologies, and associative synopses of an individual person's life, from which they presume to extrapolate predictions of behavior. In sum, metadata can tell your surveillant virtually everything they'd ever want or need to know about you, except what's actually going on inside your head.

After reading this classified report, I spent the next weeks, even months, in a daze. I was sad and low, trying to deny everything I was thinking and feeling—that's what was going on in my head, toward the end of my stint in Japan.

I felt far from home, but monitored. I felt more adult than ever, but also cursed with the knowledge that all of us had been reduced to something like children, who'd be forced to live the rest of our lives under omniscient parental supervision. I felt like a fraud, making excuses to Lindsay to explain my sullenness. I felt like a fool, as someone of supposedly serious technical skills who'd somehow helped to build an essential component of this system without realizing its purpose. I felt used, as an employee of the IC who only now was realizing that all along I'd been protecting not my country but the state. I felt, above all, violated. Being in Japan only accentuated the sense of betrayal.

I'll explain.

The Japanese that I'd managed to pick up through community college and my interests in anime and manga was enough for me to speak and get through basic conversations, but reading was a different matter. In Japanese, each word can be represented by its own unique character, or a combination of characters, called kanji, so there were tens of thousands of them—far too many for me to memorize. Often, I was only able to decode particular kanji if they were written with their phonetic gloss, the *furigana*, which are most commonly meant for foreigners and young readers and so are typically absent from public texts like street signs. The result of all this was that I walked around functionally illiterate. I'd get confused and end up going right when I should have gone left, or left when I should have gone right. I'd wander down the wrong streets and misorder from menus. I was a stranger, is what I'm saying, and often lost, in more ways than one. There were times when I'd accompany Lindsay out on one of her photography trips into the countryside and I'd suddenly stop and realize, in the midst of a village or in the middle of a forest, that I knew nothing whatsoever about my surroundings.

And yet: everything was known about me. I now understood that I was totally transparent to my government. The phone that gave me directions, and corrected me when I went the wrong way, and helped me translate the traffic signs, and told me the times of the buses and trains, was also making sure that all of my doings were legible to my employers. It was telling my bosses where I was and when, even if I never touched the thing and just left it in my pocket.

I remember forcing myself to laugh about this once when Lindsay and I got lost on a hike and Lindsay—to whom I'd told nothing—just spontaneously said, "Why don't you text Fort Meade and have them find us?" She kept the joke going, and I tried to find it funny but couldn't. "Hello," she mimicked me, "can you help us with directions?"

Later I would live in Hawaii, near Pearl Harbor, where America was attacked and dragged into what might have been its last just war. Here, in Japan, I was closer to Hiroshima and Nagasaki, where that war ignominiously ended. Lindsay and I had always hoped to visit those cities, but every time we planned to go we wound up having to cancel. On one of my first days off, we were all set to head down Honshu to Hiroshima, but I was called in to work and told to go in the opposite direction—to Misawa Air Base in the frozen north. On the day of our next scheduled attempt, Lindsay got sick, and then I got sick, too. Finally, the night before we intended to go to Nagasaki, Lindsay and I were woken by our first major earthquake, jumped up from our futon, ran down seven flights of stairs, and spent the rest of the night out on the street with our neighbors, shivering in our pajamas.

To my true regret, we never went. Those places are holy places, whose memorials honor the two hundred thousand incinerated and the countless poisoned by fallout while reminding us of technology's amorality.

I think often of what's called the "atomic moment"—a phrase that in physics describes the moment when a nucleus coheres the protons and neutrons spinning around it into an atom, but that's popularly understood to mean the advent of the nuclear age, whose isotopes enabled advances in energy production, agriculture, water potability, and the diagnosis and treatment of deadly disease. It also created the atomic bomb.

Technology doesn't have a Hippocratic oath. So many decisions that have been made by technologists in academia, industry, the military, and government since at least the Industrial Revolution have been made on the basis of "can we," not "should we." And the intention driving a technology's invention rarely, if ever, limits its application and use.

I do not mean, of course, to compare nuclear weapons with cybersurveillance in terms of human cost. But there is a commonality when it comes to the concepts of proliferation and disarmament.

The only two countries I knew of that had previously prac-ticed mass surveillance were those two other major combatants of World War II—one America's enemy, the other America's ally. In both Nazi Germany and Soviet Russia, the earliest public indica-tions of that surveillance took the superficially innocuous form of a census, the official enumeration and statistical recording of a pop-ulation. The First All-Union Census of the Soviet Union, in 1926, had a secondary agenda beyond a simple count: it overtly queried Soviet citizens about their nationality. Its findings convinced the ethnic Russians who comprised the Soviet elite that they were in the minority when compared to the aggregated masses of citizens who claimed a Central Asian heritage, such as Uzbeks, Kazakhs, Tajiks, Turkmen, Georgians, and Armenians. These findings sig-nificantly strengthened Stalin's resolve to erad-icate these cultures, by "reeducating" their populations in the deracinating ideology of Marxism-Leninism.

The Nazi German census of 1939 took on a similar statistical project, but with the assistance of computer technology. It set out to count the Reich's population in order to control it and to purge it—mainly of Jews and Roma—before exerting its murderous efforts on populations beyond its borders. To effect this, the Reich partnered with Dehomag, a German subsidiary of the American IBM, which owned the patent to the punch card tabulator, a sort of analog computer that counted holes punched into cards. Each citizen was represented by a card, and certain holes on the cards represented certain markers of identity. Column 22 addressed the religion rubic: hole 1 was Protestant, hole 2 Catholic, and hole 3 Jewish. Shortly thereafter, this census information was used to identify and deport Europe's Jewish population to the death camps.

A single current-model smartphone commands more computing power than all of the wartime machinery of the Reich and the Soviet Union combined. Recalling this is the surest way to contextualize not just the modern American IC's technological dominance, but also the threat it poses to democratic governance. In the century or so since those census efforts, technology has made astounding progress, but the same could not be said for the law or human scruples that could restrain it.

The United States has a census, too, of course. The Constitution established the American census and enshrined it as the official federal count of each state's population in order to determine its proportional delegation to the House of Representatives. That was something of a revisionist principle, in that authoritarian governments, including the British monarchy that ruled the colonies, had traditionally used the census as a method of assessing taxes and ascertaining the number of young men eligible for military conscription. It was the Constitution's genius to repurpose what had been a mechanism of oppression into one of democracy. The census, which is officially under the jurisdiction of the Senate, was ordered to be performed every ten years, which was roughly the amount of time it took to process the data of most American censuses following the first census of 1790. This decade-long lag was shortened by the census of 1890, which was the world's first census to make use of computers (the prototypes of the models that IBM later sold to Nazi Germany). With computing technology, the processing time was cut in half.

Digital technology didn't just further streamline such accounting—it is rendering it obsolete. Mass surveillance is now a never-ending census, substantially more dangerous than any questionnaire sent through the mail. All our devices, from our phones to our computers, are basically miniature census-takers we carry in our backpacks and in our pockets—census-takers that remember everything and forgive nothing.

Japan was my atomic moment. It was then that I realized where these new technologies were headed, and that if my generation didn't intervene the escalation would only continue. It would be a tragedy if, by the time we'd finally resolved to resist, such resistance were futile. The generations to come would have to get used to a world in which surveillance wasn't something occasional and directed in legally justified circumstances, but a constant and indiscriminate presence: the ear that always hears, the eye that always sees, a memory that is sleepless and permanent.

Once the ubiquity of collection was combined with the permanency of storage, all any government had to do was select a person or a group to scapegoat and go searching—as I'd gone searching through the agency's files—for evidence of a suitable crime.

17

Home on the Cloud

In 2011, I was back in the States, working for the same nominal employer, Dell, but now attached to my old agency, the CIA. One mild spring day, I came home from my first day at the new job and was amused to notice: the house I'd moved into had a mailbox. It was nothing fancy, just one of those subdivided rectangles common to town house communities, but still, it made me smile. I hadn't had a mailbox in years, and hadn't ever checked this one. I might not even have registered its existence had it not been overflowing—stuffed to bursting with heaps of junk mail addressed to "Mr. Edward J. Snowden or Current Resident." The envelopes contained coupons and ad circulars for household products. Someone knew that I'd just moved in.

A memory surfaced from my childhood, a memory of checking the mail and finding a letter to my sister. Although I wanted to open it, my mother wouldn't let me.

I remember asking why. "Because," she said, "it's not addressed to you." She explained that opening mail intended for someone else, even if it was just a birthday card or a chain letter, wasn't a very nice thing to do. In fact, it was a crime.

I wanted to know what kind of crime. "A big one, buddy," my mother said. "A federal crime."

I stood in the parking lot, tore the envelopes in half, and carried them to the trash.

I had a new iPhone in the pocket of my new Ralph Lauren suit. I had new Burberry glasses. A new haircut. Keys to this new town house in Columbia, Maryland, the largest place I'd ever lived in, and the first place that really felt like mine. I was rich, or at least my friends thought so. I barely recognized myself.

I'd decided it was best to live in denial and just make some money, make life better for the people I loved—after all, wasn't that what everybody else did? But it was easier said than done. The denial, I mean. The money—that came easy. So easy that I felt guilty.

Counting Geneva, and not counting periodic trips home, I'd been away for nearly four years. The America I returned to felt like a changed country. I won't go as far as to say that I felt like a foreigner, but I did find myself mired in way too many conversations I didn't understand. Every other word was the name of some TV show or movie I didn't know, or a celebrity scandal I didn't care about, and I couldn't respond—I had nothing to respond with.

Contradictory thoughts rained down like *Tetris* blocks, and I struggled to sort them out—to make them disappear. I thought, pity these poor, sweet, innocent people—they're victims, watched by the government, watched by the very screens they worship. Then I thought: Shut up, stop being so dramatic—they're happy, they don't care, and you don't have to, either. Grow up, do your work, pay your bills. That's life.

A normal life was what Lindsay and I were hoping for. We were ready for the next stage and had decided to settle down. We had a nice backyard with a cherry tree that reminded me of a sweeter Japan, a spot on the Tama River where Lindsay and I had laughed and rolled around atop the fragrant carpet of Tokyo blossoms as we watched the *sakura* fall.

Lindsay was getting certified as a yoga instructor. I, meanwhile, was getting used to my new position—in sales.

One of the external vendors I'd worked with on EPICSHEL-TER ended up working for Dell, and convinced me that I was wasting my time with getting paid by the hour. I should get into the sales side of Dell's business, he said, where I could earn a fortune—for more ideas like EPICSHELTER. I'd be making an astronomical leap up the corporate ladder, and he'd be getting a substantial referral bonus. I was ready to be convinced, especially since it meant distracting myself from my growing sense of unease, which could only get me into trouble. The official job title was solutions consultant. It meant, in essence, that I had to solve the problems created by my new partner, whom I'm going to call Cliff, the account manager.

Cliff was supposed to be the face, and I was to be the brain. When we sat down with the CIA's technical royalty and purchasing agents, his job was to sell Dell's equipment and expertise by any means necessary. This meant reaching deep into the seat of his pants for unlimited slick promises as to how we'd do things for the agency, things that were definitely, definitely not possible for our competitors (and, in reality, not possible for us, either). My job was to lead a team of experts in building something that reduced the degree to which Cliff had lied by just enough that, when the person who signed the check pressed the Power button, we wouldn't all be sent to jail.

No pressure.

Our main project was to help the CIA catch up with the bleeding edge—or just with the technical standards of the NSA—by building it the buzziest of new technologies, a "private cloud." The aim was to unite the agency's processing and storage while distributing the ways by which data could be accessed. In plain American, we wanted to make it so that someone in a tent in Afghanistan could do exactly the same work in exactly the same way as someone at CIA headquarters. The agency—and indeed the whole IC's technical leadership—was constantly complaining about "silos":

the problem of having a billion buckets of data spread all over the world that they couldn't keep track of or access. So I was leading a team of some of the smartest people at Dell to come up with a way that anyone, anywhere, could reach anything.

During the proof of concept stage, the working name of our cloud became "Frankie." Don't blame me: on the tech side, we just called it "The Private Cloud." It was Cliff who named it, in the middle of a demo with the CIA, saying they were going to love our little Frankenstein "because it's a real monster."

The more promises Cliff made, the busier I became, leaving Lindsay and me only the weekends to catch up with our parents and old friends. We tried to furnish and equip our new home. The three-story place had come empty, so we had to get everything, or everything that our parents hadn't generously handed down to us. This felt very mature, but was at the same time very telling about our priorities: we bought dishes, cutlery, a desk, and a chair, but we still slept on a mattress on the floor. I'd become allergic to credit cards, with all their tracking, so we bought everything outright, with hard currency. When we needed a car, I bought a '98 Acura Integra from a classified ad for $3,000 cash. Earning money was one thing, but neither Lindsay nor I liked to spend it, unless it was for computer equipment—or a special occasion. For Valentine's Day, I bought Lindsay the revolver she always wanted.

Our new condo was a twenty-minute drive from nearly a dozen malls, including the Columbia Mall, which has nearly 1.5 million square feet of shopping, occupied by some two hundred stores, a fourteen-screen AMC multiplex, a P.F. Chang's, and a Cheesecake Factory. As we drove the familiar roads in the beat-up Integra, I was impressed, but also slightly taken aback, by all the development that had occurred in my absence. The post-9/11 government spending spree had certainly put a lot of money into a lot of local pockets. It was an unsettling and even overwhelming experience to come back to America after having been away for a while and to realize anew just how wealthy this part of the country was, and how many consumer options it offered—how many big-box retailers and high-end interior design showrooms. And all of them had sales. For Presidents' Day, Memorial Day, Independence Day, Labor Day, Columbus Day, Veterans' Day. Festive banners announced the latest discounts, just below all the flags.

Our mission was pretty much appliance-based on this one afternoon I'm recalling—we were at Best Buy. Having settled on a new microwave, we were checking out, on Lindsay's healthful insistence, a display of blenders. She had her phone out and was in the midst of researching which of the ten or so devices had the best reviews, when I found myself wandering over to the computer department at the far end of the store.

But along the way, I stopped. There, at the edge of the kitchenware section, ensconced atop a brightly decorated and lit elevated platform, was a shiny new refrigerator. Rather, it was a "Smartfridge," which was being advertised as "Internet-equipped."

This, plain and simple, blew my mind.

A salesperson approached, interpreting my stupefaction as interest—"It's amazing, isn't it?"—and proceeded to demonstrate a few of the features. A screen was embedded in the door of the fridge, and next to the screen was a holder for a tiny stylus, which allowed you to scribble messages. If you didn't want to scribble, you could record audio and video memos. You could also use the screen as you would your regular computer, because the refrigerator had Wi-Fi. You could check your email, or check your calendar. You could watch YouTube clips, or listen to MP3s. You could even make phone calls. I had to restrain myself from keying in Lindsay's number and saying, from across the floor, "I'm calling from a fridge."

Beyond that, the salesperson continued, the fridge's computer kept track of internal temperature, and, through scanning barcodes, the freshness of your food. It also provided nutritional information and suggested recipes. I think the price was over $9,000. "Delivery included," the salesperson said.

I remember driving home in a confused silence. This wasn't quite the stunning moonshot tech-future we'd been promised. I was convinced the only reason that thing was Internet-equipped was so that it could report back to its manufacturer about its owner's usage and about any other household data that was obtainable. The manufacturer, in turn, would monetize that data by selling it. And we were supposed to pay for the privilege.

I wondered what the point was of my getting so worked up over government surveillance if my friends, neighbors, and fellow citizens were more than happy to invite corporate surveillance into their homes, allowing themselves to be tracked while browsing in their pantries as efficiently as if they were browsing the Web. It would still be another half decade before the domotics revolution, before "virtual assistants" like Amazon Echo and Google Home were welcomed into the bedroom and placed proudly on nightstands to record and transmit all activity within range, to log all habits and preferences (not to mention fetishes and kinks), which would then be developed into advertising algorithms and converted into cash. The data we generate just by living—or just by letting ourselves be surveilled while living—would enrich private enterprise and impoverish our private existence in equal measure. If government surveillance was having the effect of turning the citizen into a subject, at the mercy of state power, then corporate surveillance was turning the consumer into a product, which corporations sold to other corporations, data brokers, and advertisers.

Meanwhile, it felt as if every major tech company, including Dell, was rolling out new civilian versions of what I was working on for the CIA: a cloud. (In fact, Dell had even tried four years previously to trademark the term "cloud computing" but was denied.) I was amazed at how willingly people were signing up, so excited at the prospect of their photos and videos and music and e-books being universally backed up and available that they never gave much thought as to why such an uber-sophisticated and convenient storage solution was being offered to them for "free" or for "cheap" in the first place.

I don't think I'd ever seen such a concept be so uniformly

bought into, on every side. "The cloud" was as effective a sales term for Dell to sell to the CIA as it was for Amazon and Apple and Google to sell to their users. I can still close my eyes and hear Cliff schmoozing some CIA suit about how "with the cloud, you'll be able to push security updates across agency computers worldwide," or "when the cloud's up and running, the agency will be able to track who has read what file worldwide." The cloud was white and fluffy and peaceful, floating high above the fray. Though many clouds make a stormy sky, a single cloud provided a benevolent bit of shade. It was protective. I think it made everyone think of heaven.

Dell—along with the largest cloud-based private companies, Amazon, Apple, and Google—regarded the rise of the cloud as a new age of computing. But in concept, at least, it was something of a regression to the old mainframe architecture of computing's earliest history, where many users all depended upon a single powerful central core that could only be maintained by an elite cadre of professionals. The world had abandoned this "impersonal" mainframe model only a generation before, once businesses like Dell developed "personal" computers cheap enough, and simple enough, to appeal to mortals. The renaissance that followed produced desktops, laptops, tablets, and smartphones—all devices that allowed people the freedom to make an immense amount of creative work. The only issue was—how to store it?

This was the genesis of "cloud computing." Now it didn't really matter what kind of personal computer you had, because the real computers that you relied upon were warehoused in the enormous data centers that the cloud companies built throughout the world. These were, in a sense, the new mainframes, row after row of racked, identical servers linked together in such a way that each individual machine acted together within a collective computing system. The loss of a single server or even of an entire data center no longer mattered, because they were mere droplets in the larger, global cloud.

From the standpoint of a regular user, a cloud is just a storage mechanism that ensures that your data is being processed or stored not on your personal device, but on a range of different servers, which can ultimately be owned and operated by different companies. The result is that your data is no longer truly yours. It's controlled by companies, which can use it for virtually any purpose.

Read your terms of service agreements for cloud storage, which get longer and longer by the year—current ones are over six thousand words, twice the average length of one of these book chapters. When we choose to store our data online, we're often ceding our claim to it. Companies can decide what type of data they will hold for us, and can willfully delete any data they object to. Unless we've kept a separate copy on our own machines or drives, this data will be lost to us forever. If any of our data is found to be particularly objectionable or otherwise in violation of the terms of service, the companies can unilaterally delete our accounts, deny us our own data, and yet retain a copy for their own records, which they can turn over to the authorities without our knowledge or consent. Ultimately, the privacy of our data depends on the ownership of our data. There is no property less protected, and yet no property more private.

THE INTERNET I'D grown up with, the Internet that had raised me, was disappearing. And with it, so was my youth. The very act of going online, which had once seemed like a marvelous adventure, now seemed like a fraught ordeal. Self-expression now required such strong self-protection as to obviate its liberties and nullify its pleasures. Every communication was a matter not of creativity but of safety. Every transaction was a potential danger.

Meanwhile, the private sector was busy leveraging our reliance on technology into market consolidation. The majority of American Internet users lived their entire digital lives on email, social media, and e-commerce platforms owned by an imperial triumvirate of companies (Google, Facebook, and Amazon), and the American IC was seeking to take advantage of that fact by obtaining access to their networks—both through direct orders that were kept secret from the public, and clandestine subversion efforts that were kept secret from the companies themselves. Our user data was turning vast profits for the companies, and the government pilfered it for free. I don't think I'd ever felt so powerless.

Then there was this other emotion that I felt, a curious sense of being adrift and yet, at the same time, of having my privacy violated. It was as if I were dispersed—with parts of my life scattered across servers all over the globe—and yet intruded or imposed upon. Every morning when I left our town house, I found myself nodding at the security cameras dotted throughout our development. Previously I'd never paid them any attention, but now, when a light turned red on my commute, I couldn't help but think of its leering sensor, keeping tabs on me whether I blew through the intersection or stopped. License-plate readers were recording my comings and goings, even if I maintained a speed of 35 miles per hour.

America's fundamental laws exist to make the job of law enforcement not easier but harder. This isn't a bug, it's a core feature of democracy. In the American system, law enforcement is expected to protect citizens from one another. In turn, the courts are expected to restrain that power when it's abused, and to provide redress against the only members of society with the domestic authority to detain, arrest, and use force—including lethal force. Among the most important of these restraints are the prohibitions against law enforcement surveilling private citizens on their property and taking possession of their private recordings without a warrant. There are few laws, however, that restrain the surveillance of public property, which includes the vast majority of America's streets and sidewalks.

Law enforcement's use of surveillance cameras on public property was originally conceived of as a crime deterrent and an aid to investigators after a crime had occurred. But as the cost of these devices continued to fall, they became ubiquitous, and their role became preemptive—with law enforcement using them to track people who had not committed, or were not even suspected of, any crime. And the greatest danger still lies ahead, with the refinement of artificial intelligence capabilities such as facial and pattern recognition. An AI-equipped surveillance camera would be no mere recording device, but could be made into something closer to an automated police officer—a true robo-cop actively seeking out "suspicious" activity, such as apparent drug deals (that is, people embracing or shaking hands) and apparent gang affiliation (such as people wearing specific colors and brands of clothing). Even in 2011, it was clear to me that this was where technology was leading us, without any substantive public debate.

Potential monitoring abuses piled up in my mind to cumulatively produce a vision of an appalling future. A world in which all people were totally surveilled would logically become a world in which all laws were totally enforced, automatically, by computers. After all, it's difficult to imagine an AI device that's capable of noticing a person breaking the law not holding that person accountable. No policing algorithm would ever be programmed, even if it could be, toward leniency or forgiveness.

I wondered whether this would be the final but grotesque fulfillment of the original American promise that all citizens would be equal before the law: an equality of oppression through total automated law enforcement. I imagined the future SmartFridge stationed in my kitchen, monitoring my conduct and habits, and using my tendency to drink straight from the carton or not wash my hands to evaluate the probability of my being a felon.

Such a world of total automated law enforcement—of, say, all pet-ownership laws, or all zoning laws regulating home businesses—would be intolerable. Extreme justice can turn out to be extreme injustice, not just in terms of the severity of punishment for an infraction, but also in terms of how consistently and thoroughly the law is applied and prosecuted. Nearly every large and long-lived society is full of unwritten laws that everyone is expected to follow, along with vast libraries of written laws that no one is expected to follow, or even know about. According to Maryland Criminal Law Section 10-501, adultery is illegal and punishable by a $10 fine. In North Carolina, statute 14-309.8 makes it illegal for a bingo game to last more than five hours. Both of these laws come from a more prudish past and yet, for one reason or another, were never repealed. Most of our lives, even if we don't realize it, occur not in black and white but in a gray area, where we jaywalk, put trash in the recycling bin and recyclables in the trash, ride our bicycles in the improper lane, and borrow a stranger's Wi-Fi to download a book that we didn't pay for. Put simply, a world in which every law is always enforced would be a world in which everyone was a criminal.

I tried to talk to Lindsay about all this. But though she was generally sympathetic to my concerns, she wasn't so sympathetic that she was ready to go off the grid, or even off Facebook or Instagram. "If I did that," she said, "I'd be giving up my art and abandoning my friends. You used to like being in touch with other people."

She was right. And she was right to be worried about me. She thought I was too tense, and under too much stress. I was—not because of my work, but because of my desire to tell her a truth that I wasn't allowed to. I couldn't tell her that my former coworkers at the NSA could target her for surveillance and read the love poems she texted me. I couldn't tell her that they could access all the photos she took—not just her public photos, but the intimate ones. I couldn't tell her that her information was being collected, that everyone's information was being collected, which was tantamount to a government threat: If you ever get out of line, we'll use your private life against you.

I tried to explain it to her, obliquely, through an analogy. I told her to imagine opening up her laptop one day and finding a spreadsheet on her desktop.

"Why?" she said. "I don't like spreadsheets."

I wasn't prepared for this response, so I just said the first thing that came to mind. "Nobody does, but this one's called *The End*."

"Ooh, mysterious."

"You don't remember having created this spreadsheet, but once you open it up, you recognize its contents. Because inside it is everything, absolutely everything, that could ruin you. Every speck of information that could destroy your life."

Lindsay smiled. "Can I see the one for you?"

She was joking, but I wasn't. A spreadsheet containing every scrap of data about you would pose a mortal hazard. Imagine it: all the secrets big and small that could end your marriage, end your career, poison even your closest relationships, and leave you broke, friendless, and in prison. Maybe the spreadsheet would include the joint you smoked last weekend at a friend's house, or the one line of cocaine you snorted off the screen of your phone in a bar in college. Or the drunken one-night stand you had with your friend's girlfriend, who's now your friend's wife, which you both regret and have agreed never to mention to anyone. Or an abortion you got when you were a teenager, which you kept hidden from your parents and that you'd like to keep hidden from your spouse. Or maybe it's just information about a petition you signed, or a protest you attended. Everyone has something, some compromising information buried among their bytes—if not in their files then in their email, if not in their email then in their browsing history. And now this information was being stored by the US government.

Some time after our exchange, Lindsay came up to me and said, "I figured out what would be on my Spreadsheet of Total Destruction—the secret that would ruin me."

"What?"

"I'm not going to tell you."

I tried to chill, but I kept having strange physical symptoms. I'd become weirdly clumsy, falling off ladders—more than once—or bumping into door frames. Sometimes I'd trip, or drop spoons I was holding, or fail to gauge distances accurately and miss what I was reaching for. I'd spill water over myself, or choke on it. Lindsay and I would be in the middle of a conversation when I'd miss what she'd said, and she'd ask where I'd gone to—it was like I'd been frozen in another world.

One day when I went to meet Lindsay after her pole-fitness class, I started feeling dizzy. This was the most disturbing of the symptoms I'd had thus far. It scared me, and scared Lindsay, too, especially when it led to a gradual diminishing of my senses. I had too many explanations for these incidents: poor diet, lack of exercise, lack of sleep. I had too many rationalizations: the plate was too close to the edge of the counter, the stairs were slippery. I couldn't make up my mind whether it was worse if what I was experiencing was psychosomatic or genuine. I decided to go to the doctor, but the only appointment wasn't for weeks.

A day or so later, I was home around noon, trying my best to keep up with work remotely. I was on the phone with a security officer at Dell when the dizziness hit me hard. I immediately excused myself from the call, slurring my words, and as I struggled to hang up the phone, I was sure: I was going to die.

For those who've experienced it, this sense of impending doom needs no description, and for those who haven't, there is no explanation. It strikes so suddenly and primally that it wipes out all other feeling, all thought besides helpless resignation. My life was over. I slumped in my chair, a big black padded Aeron that tilted underneath me as I fell into a void and lost consciousness.

I came to still seated, with the clock on my desk reading just shy of 1:00 p.m. I'd been out less than an hour, but I was exhausted. It was as if I'd been awake since the beginning of time.

I reached for the phone in a panic, but my hand kept missing it and grabbing the air. Once I managed to grab ahold of it and get a dial tone, I found I couldn't remember Lindsay's number, or could only remember the digits but not their order.

Somehow I managed to get myself downstairs, taking each step deliberately, palm against the wall. I got some juice out of the fridge and chugged it, keeping both hands on the carton and dribbling a fair amount on my chin. Then I lay down on the floor, pressed my cheek to the cool linoleum, and fell asleep, which was how Lindsay found me.

I'd just had an epileptic seizure.

My mother had epilepsy, and for a time at least was prone to grand mal seizures: the foaming at the mouth, her limbs thrashing, her body rolling around until it stilled into a horrible unconscious rigidity. I couldn't believe I hadn't previously associated my symptoms with hers, though that was the very same denial she herself had been in for decades, attributing her frequent falls to "clumsiness" and "lack of coordination." She hadn't been diagnosed until her first grand mal in her late thirties, and, after a brief spell on medication, her seizures stopped. She'd always told me and my sister that epilepsy wasn't hereditary and to this day I'm still not sure if that's what her doctor had told her or if she was just trying to reassure us that her fate wouldn't be ours.

There is no diagnostic test for epilepsy. The clinical diagnosis is just two or more unexplained seizures—that's it. Very little is known about the condition. Medicine tends to treat epilepsy phenomenologically. Doctors don't talk about "epilepsy," they talk about "seizures." They tend to divide seizures into two types: localized and generalized, the former being an electrical misfire in a certain section of your brain that doesn't spread, the latter being an electrical misfire that creates a chain reaction. Basically, a wave of misfiring synapses rolls across your brain, causing you to lose motor function and, ultimately, consciousness.

Epilepsy is such a strange syndrome. Its sufferers feel different things, depending on which part of their brain has the initial electrical cascade failure. Those who have this failure in their auditory center famously hear bells. Those who have it in their visual center either have their vision go dark or see sparkles. If the failure happens in the deeper core areas of the brain—which was where mine occurred—it can cause severe vertigo. In time, I came to know the warning signs, so I could prepare for an oncoming seizure. These signs are called "auras," in the popular language of epilepsy, though in scientific fact these auras are the seizure itself. They are the proprioceptive experience of the misfire.

I consulted with as many epilepsy specialists as I could find—the best part of working for Dell was the insurance: I had CAT scans, MRIs, the works. Meanwhile, Lindsay, who was my stalwart angel throughout all this, driving me back and forth from appointments, went about researching all the information that was available about the syndrome. She Googled both allopathic and homeopathic treatments so intensely that basically all her Gmail ads were for epilepsy pharmaceuticals.

I felt defeated. The two great institutions of my life had been betrayed and were betraying me: my country and the Internet. And now my body was following suit.

My brain had, quite literally, short-circuited.

18

On the Couch

It was late at night on May 1, 2011, when I noticed the news alert on my phone: Osama bin Laden had been tracked down to Abbottabad, Pakistan, and killed by a team of Navy SEALs.

So there it was. The man who'd masterminded the attacks that had propelled me into the army, and from there into the Intelligence Community, was now dead, a dialysis patient shot point-blank in the embrace of his multiple wives in their lavish compound just down the road from Pakistan's major military academy. Site after site showed maps indicating where the hell Abbottabad was, alternating with street scenes from cities throughout America, where people were fist-pumping, chest-bumping, yelling, getting wasted. Even New York was celebrating, which almost never happens.

I turned off the phone. I just didn't have it in me to join in. Don't get me wrong: I was glad the motherfucker was dead. I was just having a pensive moment and felt a circle closing.

Ten years. That's how long it had been since those two planes flew into the Twin Towers, and what did we have to show for it? What had the last decade actually accomplished? I sat on the couch I'd inherited from my mother's condo and gazed through the window into the street beyond as a neighbor honked the horn of his parked car. I couldn't shake the idea that I'd wasted the last decade of my life.

The previous ten years had been a cavalcade of American-made tragedy: the forever war in Afghanistan, catastrophic regime change in Iraq, indefinite detentions at Guantánamo Bay, extraordinary renditions, torture, targeted killings of civilians—even of American civilians—via drone strikes. Domestically, there was the Homeland Securitization of everything, which assigned a threat rating to every waking day (Red–Severe, Orange–High, Yellow–Elevated), and, from the Patriot Act on, the steady erosion of civil liberties, the very liberties we were allegedly fighting to protect. The cumulative damage—the malfeasance in aggregate—was staggering to contemplate and felt entirely irreversible, and yet we were still honking our horns and flashing our lights in jubilation.

The biggest terrorist attack on American soil happened concurrently with the development of digital technology, which made much of the earth American soil—whether we liked it or not. Terrorism, of course, was the stated reason why most of my country's surveillance programs were implemented, at a time of great fear and opportunism. But it turned out that fear was the true terrorism, perpetrated by a political system that was increasingly willing to use practically any justification to authorize the use of force. American politicians weren't as afraid of terror as they were of seeming weak, or of being disloyal to their party, or of being disloyal to their campaign donors, who had ample appetites for government contracts and petroleum products from the Middle East. The politics of terror became more powerful than the terror itself, resulting in "counterterror": the panicked actions of a country unmatched in capability, unrestrained by policy, and blatantly unconcerned about upholding the rule of law. After 9/11, the IC's orders had been "never again," a mission that could never be accomplished. A decade later, it had become clear, to me at least, that the repeated evocations of terror by the political class were not a response to any specific threat or concern but a cynical attempt to turn terror into a permanent danger that required permanent vigilance enforced by unquestionable authority.

After a decade of mass surveillance, the technology had proved itself to be a potent weapon less against terror and more against liberty itself. By continuing these programs, by continuing these lies, America was protecting little, winning nothing, and losing much—until there would be few distinctions left between those post-9/11 polarities of "Us" and "Them."

THE LATTER HALF of 2011 passed in a succession of seizures, and in countless doctors' offices and hospitals. I was imaged, tested, and prescribed medications that stabilized my body but clouded my mind, turning me depressed, lethargic, and unable to focus.

I wasn't sure how I was going to live with what Lindsay was now calling my "condition" without losing my job. Being the top technologist for Dell's CIA account meant I had tremendous flexibility: my office was my phone, and I could work from home. But meetings were an issue. They were always in Virginia, and I lived in Maryland, a state whose laws prevented people diagnosed with epilepsy from driving. If I were caught behind the wheel, I could lose my driver's license, and with it my ability to attend the meetings that were the single nonnegotiable requirement of my position.

I finally gave in to the inevitable, took a short-term disability leave from Dell, and decamped to my mother's secondhand couch. It was as blue as my mood, but comfortable. For weeks and weeks it was the center of my existence—the place where I slept and ate and read and slept some more, the place where I just generally wallowed bleakly as time mocked me.

I don't remember what books I tried to read, but I do remember never managing much more than a page before closing my eyes and sinking back again into the cushions. I couldn't concentrate on anything except my own weakness, the uncooperative lump that used to be me spread across the upholstery, motionless but for a lone finger atop the screen of the phone that was the only light in the room.

I'd scroll through the news, then nap, then scroll again, then nap—while protesters in Tunisia, Libya, Egypt, Yemen, Algeria, Morocco, Iraq, Lebanon, and Syria were being imprisoned and tortured or just shot in the streets by the secret state agents of thuggish regimes, many of which America had helped keep in power. The suffering of that season was immense, spiraling out of the regular news cycle. What I was witnessing was desperation, compared with which my own struggles seemed cheap. They seemed small—morally and ethically small—and privileged.

Throughout the Middle East, innocent civilians were living under the constant threat of violence, with work and school suspended, no electricity, no sewage. In many regions, they didn't have access to even the most rudimentary medical care. But if at any moment I doubted that my anxieties about surveillance and privacy were relevant, or even appropriate, in the face of such immediate danger and privation, I only had to pay a bit more attention to the crowds on the street and the proclamations they were making—in Cairo and Sanaa, in Beirut and Damascus, in Ahvaz, Khuzestan, and in every other city of the Arab Spring and Iranian Green Movement. The crowds were calling for an end to oppression, censorship, and precarity. They were declaring that in a truly just society the people were not answerable to the government, the government was answerable to the people. Although each crowd in each city, even on each day, seemed to have its own specific motivation and its own specific goals, they all had one thing in common: a rejection of authoritarianism, a recommitment to the humanitarian principle that an individual's rights are inborn and inalienable.

In an authoritarian state, rights derive from the state and are granted to the people. In a free state, rights derive from the people and are granted to the state. In the former, people are subjects, who are only allowed to own property, pursue an education, work, pray, and speak because their government permits them to.

In the latter, people are citizens, who agree to be governed in a covenant of consent that must be periodically renewed and is constitutionally revocable. It's this clash, between the authoritarian and the liberal democratic, that I believe to be the major ideological conflict of my time—not some concocted, prejudiced notion of an East-West divide, or of a resurrected crusade against Christendom or Islam.

Authoritarian states are typically not governments of laws, but governments of leaders, who demand loyalty from their subjects and are hostile to dissent. Liberal-democratic states, by contrast, make no or few such demands, but depend almost solely on each citizen voluntarily assuming the responsibility of protecting the freedoms of everyone else around them, regardless of their race, ethnicity, creed, ability, sexuality, or gender. Any collective guarantee, predicated not on blood but on assent, will wind up favoring egalitarianism—and though democracy has often fallen far short of its ideal, I still believe it to be the one form of governance that most fully enables people of different backgrounds to live together, equal before the law.

This equality consists not only of rights but also of freedoms. In fact, many of the rights most cherished by citizens of democracies aren't even provided for in law except by implication. They exist in that open-ended empty space created through the restriction of government power. For example, Americans only have a "right" to free speech because the government is forbidden from making any law restricting that freedom, and a "right" to a free press because the government is forbidden from making any law to abridge it. They only have a "right" to worship freely because the government is forbidden from making any law respecting an establishment of religion, and a "right" to peaceably assemble and protest because the government is forbidden from making any law that says they can't.

In contemporary life, we have a single concept that encompasses all this negative or potential space that's off-limits to the government. That concept is "privacy." It is an empty zone that lies beyond the reach of the state, a void into which the law is only permitted to venture with a warrant—and not a warrant "for everybody," such as the one the US government has arrogated to itself in pursuit of mass surveillance, but a warrant for a specific person or purpose supported by a specific probable cause.

The word "privacy" itself is somewhat empty, because it is essentially indefinable, or over-definable. Each of us has our own idea of what it is. "Privacy" means something to everyone. There is no one to whom it means nothing.

It's because of this lack of common definition that citizens of pluralistic, technologically sophisticated democracies feel that they have to justify their desire for privacy and frame it as a right. But citizens of democracies don't have to justify that desire—the state, instead, must justify its violation. To refuse to claim your privacy is actually to cede it, either to a state trespassing its constitutional restraints or to a "private" business.

There is, simply, no way to ignore privacy. Because a citizenry's freedoms are interdependent, to surrender your own privacy is really to surrender everyone's. You might choose to give it up out of convenience, or under the popular pretext that privacy is only required by those who have something to hide. But saying that you don't need or want privacy because you have nothing to hide is to assume that no one should have, or could have, to hide anything—including their immigration status, unemployment history, financial history, and health records. You're assuming that no one, including yourself, might object to revealing to anyone information about their religious beliefs, political affiliations, and sexual activities, as casually as some choose to reveal their movie and music tastes and reading preferences.

Ultimately, saying that you don't care about privacy because you have nothing to hide is no different from saying you don't care about freedom of speech because you have nothing to say. Or that you don't care about freedom of the press because you don't like to read. Or that you don't care about freedom of religion because you don't believe in God. Or that you don't care about the freedom to peaceably assemble because you're a lazy, antisocial agoraphobe. Just because this or that freedom might not have meaning to you today doesn't mean that it doesn't or won't have meaning tomorrow, to you, or to your neighbor—or to the crowds of principled dissidents I was following on my phone who were protesting halfway across the planet, hoping to gain just a fraction of the freedoms that my country was busily dismantling.

I wanted to help, but I didn't know how. I'd had enough of feeling helpless, of being just an asshole in flannel lying around on a shabby couch eating Cool Ranch Doritos and drinking Diet Coke while the world went up in flames.

The young people of the Middle East were agitating for higher wages, lower prices, and better pensions, but I couldn't give them any of that, and no one could give them a better shot at self-governance than the one they were taking themselves. They were, however, also agitating for a freer Internet. They were decrying Iran's Ayatollah Khamenei, who had been increasingly censoring and blocking threatening Web content, tracking and hacking traffic to offending platforms and services, and shutting down certain foreign ISPs entirely. They were protesting Egypt's president, Hosni Mubarak, who'd cut off Internet access for his whole country—which had merely succeeded in making every young person in the country even more furious and bored, luring them out into the streets.

Ever since I'd been introduced to the Tor Project in Geneva, I'd used its browser and run my own Tor server, wanting to do my professional work from home and my personal Web browsing unmonitored. Now, I shook off my despair, propelled myself off the couch, and staggered over to my home office to set up a bridge relay that would bypass the Iranian Internet blockades. I then distributed its encrypted configuration identity to the Tor core developers.

This was the least I could do. If there was just the slightest chance that even one young kid from Iran who hadn't been able to get online could now bypass the imposed filters and restrictions and connect to me—connect through me—protected by the Tor system and my server's anonymity, then it was certainly worth my minimal effort.

I imagined this person reading their email, or checking their social media accounts to make sure that their friends and family had not been arrested. I had no way of knowing whether this was what they did, or whether anyone at all linked to my server from Iran. And that was the point: the aid I offered was private.

The guy who started the Arab Spring was almost exactly my age. He was a produce peddler in Tunisia, selling fruits and vegetables out of a cart. In protest against repeated harassment and extortion by the authorities, he stood in the square and set fire to his life, dying a martyr. If burning himself to death was the last free act he could manage in defiance of an illegitimate regime, I could certainly get up off the couch and press a few buttons.

PART THREE

19

The Tunnel

Imagine you're entering a tunnel. Imagine the perspective: as you look down the length that stretches ahead of you, notice how the walls seem to narrow to the tiny dot of light at the other end. The light at the end of the tunnel is a symbol of hope, and it's also what people say they see in near-death experiences. They have to go to it, they say. They're drawn to it. But then where else is there to go in a tunnel, except through it? Hasn't everything led up to this point?

My tunnel was the Tunnel: an enormous Pearl Harbor–era airplane factory turned NSA facility located under a pineapple field in Kunia, on the island of Oahu, Hawaii. The facility was built out of reinforced concrete, its eponymous tunnel a kilometer-long tube in the side of a hill opening up into three cavernous floors of server vaults and offices. At the time the Tunnel was built, the hill was covered over with huge amounts of sand, soil, desiccated pineapple plant leaves, and patches of sun-parched grass to camouflage it from Japanese bombers. Sixty years later it resembled the vast burial mound of a lost civilization, or some gigantic arid pile that a weird god had heaped up in the middle of a god-size sandbox. Its official name was the Kunia Regional Security Operations Center.

I went to work there, still on a Dell contract, but now for the NSA again, early in 2012. One day that summer—actually, it was my birthday—as I passed through the security checks and proceeded down the tunnel, it struck me: this, in front of me, was my future.

I'm not saying that I made any decisions at that instant. The most important decisions in life are never made that way. They're made subconsciously and only express themselves consciously once fully formed—once you're finally strong enough to admit to yourself that this is what your conscience has already chosen for you, this is the course that your beliefs have decreed. That was my twenty-ninth birthday present to myself: the awareness that I had entered a tunnel that would narrow my life down toward a single, still-indistinct act.

Just as Hawaii has always been an important waystation—historically, the US military treated the island chain as little more than a mid-Pacific refueling depot for boats and planes—it had also become an important switchpoint for American communications. These include the intelligence that flowed between the contiguous forty-eight states and my former place of employment, Japan, as well as other sites in Asia.

The job I'd taken was a significant step down the career ladder, with duties I could at this point perform in my sleep. It was supposed to mean less stress, a lighter burden. I was the sole employee of the aptly named Office of Information Sharing, where I worked as a SharePoint systems administrator. SharePoint is a Microsoft product, a dopey poky program, or rather a grab-bag of programs, focused on internal document management: who can read what, who can edit what, who can send and receive what, and so on. By making me Hawaii's SharePoint systems administrator, the NSA had made me the manager of document management. I was, in effect, the reader in chief at one of the agency's most significant facilities. As was my typical practice in any new technical position,

I spent the earliest days automating my tasks—meaning writing scripts to do my work for me—so as to free up my time for something more interesting.

Before I go any further, I want to emphasize this: my active searching out of NSA abuses began not with the copying of documents, but with the reading of them. My initial intention was just to confirm the suspicions that I'd first had back in 2009 in Tokyo. Three years later, I was determined to find out if an American system of mass surveillance existed and, if it did, how it functioned. Though I was uncertain about how to conduct this investigation, I was at least sure of this: I had to understand exactly how the system worked before I could decide what, if anything, to do about it.

THIS, OF COURSE, was not why Lindsay and I had come to Hawaii. We hadn't hauled all the way out to paradise just so I could throw our lives away for a principle.

We'd come to start over. To start over yet again.

My doctors told me that the climate and more relaxed lifestyle in Hawaii might be beneficial for my epilepsy, since lack of sleep was thought to be the leading trigger of the seizures. Also, the move eliminated the driving problem: the Tunnel was within bicycling distance of a number of communities in Kunia, the quiet heart of the island's dry, red interior. It was a pleasant, twenty-minute ride to work, through sugarcane fields in brilliant sunshine. With the mountains rising calm and high in the clear blue distance, the gloomy mood of the last few months lifted like the morning fog.

Lindsay and I found a decent-size bungalow-type house on Eleu Street in Waipahu's Royal Kunia, which we furnished with our stuff from Columbia, Maryland, since Dell paid relocation expenses. The furniture didn't get much use, though, since the sun and heat would often cause us to walk in the door, strip off our clothes, and lie naked on the carpet beneath the overworked air conditioner. Eventually, Lindsay turned the garage into a fitness studio, filling it with yoga mats and the spinning pole she'd brought from Columbia. I set up a new Tor server. Soon, traffic from around the world was reaching the Internet via the laptop sitting in our entertainment center, which had the ancillary benefit of hiding my own Internet activity in the noise.

One night during the summer I turned twenty-nine, Lindsay finally prevailed on me to go out with her to a luau. She'd been after me to go for a while, because a few of her pole-fitness friends had been involved in some hula-girl capacity, but I'd been resistant. It had seemed like such a cheesy touristy thing to do, and had felt, somehow, disrespectful. Hawaiian culture is ancient, although its traditions are very much alive; the last thing I wanted was to disturb someone's sacred ritual.

Finally, however, I capitulated. I'm very glad I did. What impressed me the most was not the luau itself—though it was very much a fire-twirling spectacle—but the old man who was holding court nearby in a little amphitheater down by the sea. He was a native Hawaiian, an erudite man with that soft but nasal island voice, who was telling a group of people gathered around a fire the creation stories of the islands' indigenous peoples.

The one story that stuck with me concerned the twelve sacred islands of the gods. Apparently, there had existed a dozen islands in the Pacific that were so beautiful and pure and blessed with freshwater that they had to be kept secret from humanity, who would spoil them. Three of them were especially revered: Kane-huna-moku, Kahiki, and Pali-uli. The lucky gods who inhabited these islands decided to keep them hidden, because they believed that a glimpse of their bounty would drive people mad. After considering numerous ingenious schemes by which these islands might be concealed, including dyeing them the color of the sea, or sinking them to the bottom of the ocean, they finally decided to make them float in the air.

Once the islands were airborne, they were blown from place to place, staying constantly in motion. At sunrise and sunset, especially, you might think that you'd noticed one, hovering far at the horizon. But the moment you pointed it out to anyone, it would suddenly drift away or assume another form entirely, such as a pumice raft, a hunk of rock ejected by a volcanic eruption—or a cloud.

I thought about that legend a lot while I went about my search. The revelations I was pursuing were exactly like those islands: exotic preserves that a pantheon of self-important, self-appointed rulers were convinced had to be kept secret and hidden from humanity. I wanted to know what the NSA's surveillance capabilities were exactly; whether and how they extended beyond the agency's actual surveillance activities; who approved them; who knew about them; and, last but surely not least, how these systems—both technical and institutional—really operated.

The moment I'd think that I spotted one of these "islands"—some capitalized code name I didn't understand, some program referenced in a note buried at the end of a report—I'd go chasing after further mentions of it in other documents, but find none. It was as if the program I was searching for had floated away from me and was lost. Then, days later, or weeks later, it might surface again under a different designation, in a document from a different department.

Sometimes I'd find a program with a recognizable name, but without an explanation of what it did. Other times I'd just find a nameless explanation, with no indication as to whether the capability it described was an active program or an aspirational desire. I was running up against compartments within compartments, caveats within caveats, suites within suites, programs within programs. This was the nature of the NSA—by design, the left hand rarely knew what the right hand was doing.

In a way, what I was doing reminded me of a documentary I once watched about map-making—specifically, about the way that nautical charts were created in the days before imaging and GPS. Ship captains would keep logs and note their coordinates, which landbound mapmakers would then try to interpret. It was through the gradual accretion of this data, over hundreds of years, that the full extent of the Pacific became known, and all its islands identified.

But I didn't have hundreds of years or hundreds of ships. I was alone, one man hunched over a blank blue ocean, trying to find where this one speck of dry land, this one data point, belonged in relation to all the others.

20

Heartbeat

Back in 2009 in Japan, when I went to that fateful China conference as a substitute briefer, I guess I'd made some friends, especially at the Joint Counterintelligence Training Academy (JCITA) and its parent agency, the Defense Intelligence Agency (DIA). In the three years since, JCITA had invited me a half-dozen or so times to give seminars and lectures at DIA facilities. Essentially, I was teaching classes in how the American Intelligence Community could protect itself from Chinese hackers and exploit the information gained from analyzing their hacks to hack them in return.

I always enjoyed teaching—certainly more than I ever enjoyed being a student—and in the early days of my disillusionment, toward the end of Japan and through my time at Dell, I had the sense that were I to stay in intelligence work for the rest of my career, the positions in which my principles would be least compromised, and my mind most challenged, would almost certainly be academic. Teaching with JCITA was a way of keeping that door open. It was also a way of keeping up to date—when you're teaching, you can't let your students get ahead of you, especially in technology.

This put me in the regular habit of perusing what the NSA

called "readboards." These are digital bulletin boards that function
something like news blogs, only the "news" here is the product of
classified intelligence activities. Each major NSA site maintains its
own, which its local staff updates daily with what they regard as
the day's most important and interesting documents—everything
an employee has to read to keep current.

As a holdover from my JCITA lecture preparation, and also,
frankly, because I was bored in Hawaii, I got into the habit of
checking a number of these boards every day: my own site's readboard in Hawaii, the readboard of my former posting in Tokyo,
and various readboards from Fort Meade. This new low-pressure
position gave me as much time to read as I wanted. The scope of
my curiosity might have raised a few questions at a prior stage of
my career, but now I was the only employee of the Office of Information Sharing—I *was* the Office of Information Sharing—so my
very job was to know what sharable information was out there.
Meanwhile, most of my colleagues at the Tunnel spent their breaks
streaming Fox News.

In the hopes of organizing all the documents I wanted to read
from these various readboards, I put together a personal best-of-
the-readboards queue. The files quickly began to pile up, until the
nice lady who managed the digital storage quotas complained to
me about the folder size. I realized that my personal readboard
had become less a daily digest than an archive of sensitive information with relevance far beyond the day's immediacy. Not
wanting to erase it or stop adding to it, which would've been a
waste, I decided instead to share it with others. This was the best
justification for what I was doing that I could think of, especially
because it allowed me to more or less legitimately collect material
from a wider range of sources. So, with my boss's approval, I set
about creating an automated readboard—one that didn't rely on
anybody posting things to it, but edited itself.

Like EPICSHELTER, my automated readboard platform was
designed to perpetually scan for new and unique documents. It did
so in a far more comprehensive manner, however, peering beyond

NSAnet, the NSA's network, into the networks of the CIA and the FBI as well as into the Joint Worldwide Intelligence Communications System (JWICS), the Department of Defense's top-secret intranet. The idea was that its findings would be made available to every NSA officer by comparing their digital identity badges—called PKI certificates—to the classification of the documents, generating a personal readboard customized to their clearances, interests, and office affiliations. Essentially, it would be a readboard of readboards, an individually tailored newsfeed aggregator, bringing each officer all the newest information pertinent to their work, all the documents they had to read to stay current. It would be run from a server that I alone managed, located just down the hall from me. That server would also store a copy of every document it sourced, making it easy for me to perform the kind of deep interagency searches that the heads of most agencies could only dream of.

I called this system Heartbeat, because it took the pulse of the NSA and of the wider IC. The volume of information that crashed through its veins was simply enormous, as it pulled documents from internal sites dedicated to every specialty from updates on the latest cryptographic research projects to minutes of the meetings of the National Security Council. I'd carefully configured it to ingest materials at a slow, constant pace, so as not to monopolize the undersea fiber-optic cable tying Hawaii to Fort Meade, but it still pulled so many more documents than any human ever could that it immediately became the NSAnet's most comprehensive readboard.

Early on in its operation I got an email that almost stopped Heartbeat forever. A faraway administrator—apparently the only one in the entire IC who actually bothered to look at his access logs—wanted to know why a system in Hawaii was copying, one by one, every record in his database. He had immediately blocked me as a precaution, which effectively locked me out, and was demanding an explanation. I told him what I was doing and showed him how to use the internal website that would let him read

Heartbeat for himself. His response reminded me of an unusual characteristic of the technologists' side of the security state: once I gave him access, his wariness instantly turned into curiosity. He might have doubted a person, but he'd never doubt a machine. He could now see that Heartbeat was just doing what it'd been meant to do, and was doing it perfectly. He was fascinated. He unblocked me from his repository of records, and even offered to help me by circulating information about Heartbeat to his colleagues.

Nearly all of the documents that I later disclosed to journalists came to me through Heartbeat. It showed me not just the aims but the abilities of the IC's mass surveillance system. This is something I want to emphasize: in mid-2012, I was just trying to get a handle on how mass surveillance actually worked. Almost every journalist who later reported on the disclosures was primarily concerned with the targets of surveillance—the efforts to spy on American citizens, for instance, or on the leaders of America's allies. That is to say, they were more interested in the topics of the surveillance reports than in the system that produced them. I respect that interest, of course, having shared it myself, but my own primary curiosity was still technical in nature. It's all well and good to read a document or to click through the slides of a PowerPoint presentation to find out what a program is *intended* to do, but the better you can understand a program's mechanics, the better you can understand its potential for abuse.

This meant that I wasn't much interested in the briefing materials—like, for example, what has become perhaps the best-known file I disclosed, a slide deck from a 2011 PowerPoint presentation that delineated the NSA's new surveillance posture as a matter of six protocols: "Sniff It All, Know It All, Collect It All, Process It All, Exploit It All, Partner It All." This was just PR speak, marketing jargon. It was intended to impress America's allies: Australia, Canada, New Zealand, and the UK, the primary countries with which the United States shares intelligence. (Together with the United States, these countries are known as the Five Eyes.) "Sniff It All" meant finding a data source; "Know It All" meant finding out what that data was; "Collect It All" meant capturing that data; "Process It All" meant analyzing that data for usable intelligence; "Exploit It All" meant using that intelligence to further the agency's aims; and "Partner It All" meant sharing the new data source with allies. While this six-pronged taxonomy was easy to remember, easy to sell, and an accurate measure of the scale of the agency's ambition and the degree of its collusion with foreign governments, it gave me no insight into how exactly that ambition was realized in technological terms.

Much more revealing was an order I found from the FISA Court, a legal demand for a private company to turn over its customers' private information to the federal government. Orders such as these were notionally issued on the authority of public legislation; however, their contents, even their existence, were classified Top Secret. According to Section 215 of the Patriot Act, aka the "business records" provision, the government was authorized to obtain orders from the FISA Court that compelled third parties to produce "any tangible thing" that was "relevant" to foreign intelligence or terrorism investigations. But as the court order I found made clear, the NSA had secretly interpreted this authorization as a license to collect all of the "business records," or metadata, of telephone communications coming through American telecoms, such as Verizon and AT&T, on "an ongoing daily basis." This included, of course, records of telephone communications between American citizens, the practice of which was unconstitutional.

Additionally, Section 702 of the FISA Amendments Act allows the IC to target any foreigner outside the United States deemed likely to communicate "foreign intelligence information"—a broad category of potential targets that includes journalists, corporate employees, academics, aid workers, and countless others innocent of any wrongdoing whatsoever. This legislation was being used by the NSA to justify its two most prominent Internet surveillance methods: the PRISM program and upstream collection.

PRISM enabled the NSA to routinely collect data from Microsoft, Yahoo!, Google, Facebook, Paltalk, YouTube, Skype,

AOL, and Apple, including email, photos, video and audio chats, Web-browsing content, search engine queries, and all other data stored on their clouds, transforming the companies into witting coconspirators. Upstream collection, meanwhile, was arguably even more invasive. It enabled the routine capturing of data directly from private-sector Internet infrastructure—the switches and routers that shunt Internet traffic worldwide, via the satellites in orbit and the high-capacity fiber-optic cables that run under the ocean. This collection was managed by the NSA's Special Sources Operations unit, which built secret wiretapping equipment and embedded it inside the corporate facilities of obliging Internet service providers around the world. Together, PRISM (collection from the servers of service providers) and upstream collection (direct collection from Internet infrastructure) ensured that the world's information, both stored and in transit, was surveillable.

The next stage of my investigation was to figure out how this collection was actually accomplished—that is to say, to examine the documents that explained which tools supported this program and how they selected from among the vast mass of dragneted communications those that were thought worthy of closer inspection. The difficulty was that this information did not exist in any presentation, no matter the level of classification, but only in engineering diagrams and raw schematics. These were the most important materials for me to find. Unlike the Five Eyes' pitch-deck cant, they would be concrete proof that the capacities I was reading about weren't merely the fantasies of an overcaffeinated project manager. As a systems guy who was always being prodded to build faster and deliver more, I was all too aware that the agencies would sometimes announce technologies before they even existed—sometimes because a Cliff-type salesperson had made one too many promises, and sometimes just out of unalloyed ambition.

In this case, the technologies behind upstream collection did exist. As I came to realize, these tools are the most invasive elements of the NSA's mass surveillance system, if only because they're the closest to the user—that is, the closest to the person being surveilled. Imagine yourself sitting at a computer, about to visit a website. You open a Web browser, type in a URL, and hit Enter. The URL is, in effect, a request, and this request goes out in search of its destination server. Somewhere in the midst of its travels, however, before your request gets to that server, it will have to pass through TURBULENCE, one of the NSA's most powerful weapons.

Specifically, your request passes through a few black servers stacked on top of one another, together about the size of a four-shelf bookcase. These are installed in special rooms at major private telecommunications buildings throughout allied countries, as well as in US embassies and on US military bases, and contain two critical tools. The first, TURMOIL, handles "passive collection," making a copy of the data coming through. The second, TURBINE, is in charge of "active collection"—that is, actively tampering with the users.

You can think of TURMOIL as a guard positioned at an invisible firewall through which Internet traffic must pass. Seeing your request, it checks its metadata for selectors, or criteria, that mark it as deserving of more scrutiny. Those selectors can be whatever the NSA chooses, whatever the NSA finds suspicious: a particular email address, credit card, or phone number; the geographic origin or destination of your Internet activity; or just certain keywords such as "anonymous Internet proxy" or "protest."

If TURMOIL flags your traffic as suspicious, it tips it over to TURBINE, which diverts your request to the NSA's servers. There, algorithms decide which of the agency's exploits—malware programs—to use against you. This choice is based on the type of website you're trying to visit as much as on your computer's software and Internet connection. These chosen exploits are sent back to TURBINE (by programs of the QUANTUM suite, if you're wondering), which injects them into the traffic channel and delivers them to you along with whatever website you requested.

The end result: you get all the content you want, along with all the surveillance you don't, and it all happens in less than 686 milliseconds. Completely unbeknownst to you.

Once the exploits are on your computer, the NSA can access not just your metadata, but your data as well. Your entire digital life now belongs to them.

21

Whistleblowing

If any NSA employee who didn't work with the SharePoint software I managed knew anything at all about SharePoint, they knew the calendars. These were pretty much the same as any normal nongovernment group calendars, just way more expensive, providing the basic when-and-where-do-I-have-to-be-at-a-meeting scheduling interface for NSA personnel in Hawaii. This was about as exciting for me to manage as you might imagine. That's why I tried to spice it up by making sure the calendar always had reminders of all the holidays, and I mean all of them: not just the federal holidays, but Rosh Hashanah, Eid al-Fitr, Eid al-Adha, Diwali.

Then there was my favorite, the seventeenth of September. Constitution Day and Citizenship Day, which is the holiday's formal name, commemorates the moment in 1787 when the delegates to the Constitutional Convention officially ratified, or signed, the document. Technically, Constitution Day is not a federal holiday, just a federal observance, meaning that Congress didn't think our country's founding document and the oldest national constitution still in use in the world were important enough to justify giving people a paid day off.

The Intelligence Community had always had an uncomfortable relationship with Constitution Day, which meant its involvement was typically limited to circulating a bland email drafted by its agencies' press shops and signed by Director So-and-So, and setting up a sad little table in a forgotten corner of the cafeteria. On the table would be some free copies of the Constitution printed, bound, and donated to the government by the kind and generous rabble-rousers at places like the Cato Institute or the Heritage Foundation, since the IC was rarely interested in spending some of its own billions on promoting civil liberties through stapled paper.

I suppose the staff got the message, or didn't: over the seven Constitution Days I spent in the IC, I don't think I'd ever known anyone but myself to actually take a copy off the table. Because I love irony almost as much as I love freebies, I'd always take a few—one for myself, and the others to salt across my friends' workstations. I kept my copy propped against the Rubik's Cube on my desk, and for a time made a habit of reading it over lunch, trying not to drip grease on "We the People" from one of the cafeteria's grim slices of elementary-school pizza.

I liked reading the Constitution partially because its ideas are great, partially because its prose is good, but really because it freaked out my coworkers. In an office where everything you printed had to be thrown into a shredder after you were done with it, someone would always be intrigued by the presence of hardcopy pages lying on a desk. They'd amble over to ask, "What have you got there?"

"The Constitution."

Then they'd make a face and back away slowly.

On Constitution Day 2012, I picked up the document in earnest. I hadn't really read the whole thing in quite a few years, though I was glad to note that I still knew the preamble by heart. Now, however, I read through it in its entirety, from the Articles to the Amendments. I was surprised to be reminded that fully 50 percent of the Bill of Rights, the document's first ten amendments, were intended to make the job of law enforcement harder. The

Fourth, Fifth, Sixth, Seventh, and Eighth Amendments were all deliberately, carefully designed to create inefficiencies and hamper the government's ability to exercise its power and conduct surveillance.

This is especially true of the Fourth, which protects people and their property from government scrutiny: *The right of the people to be secure in their persons, houses, papers, and effects, against unreasonable searches and seizures, shall not be violated, and no Warrants shall issue, but upon probable cause, supported by Oath or affirmation, and particularly describing the place to be searched, and the persons or things to be seized.*

Translation: If officers of the law want to go rooting through your life, they first have to go before a judge and show probable cause under oath. This means they have to explain to a judge why they have reason to believe that you might have committed a specific crime or that specific evidence of a specific crime might be found on or in a specific part of your property. Then they have to swear that this reason has been given honestly and in good faith. Only if the judge approves a warrant will they be allowed to go searching—and even then, only for a limited time.

The Constitution was written in the eighteenth century, back when the only computers were abacuses, gear calculators, and looms, and it could take weeks or months for a communication to cross the ocean by ship. It stands to reason that computer files, whatever their contents, are our version of the Constitution's "papers." We certainly use them like "papers," particularly our word-processing documents and spreadsheets, our messages and histories of inquiry. Data, meanwhile, is our version of "effects," a catchall term for all the stuff that we own, produce, sell, and buy online. That includes, by default, metadata, which is the record of all the stuff that we own, produce, sell, and buy online—a perfect ledger of our private lives.

In the centuries since the original Constitution Day, our clouds, computers, and phones have become our homes, just as personal and intimate as our actual houses nowadays. If you don't agree, then answer me this: Would you rather let your coworkers hang out at your home alone for an hour, or let them spend even just ten minutes alone with your unlocked phone?

The NSA's surveillance programs, its domestic surveillance programs in particular, flouted the Fourth Amendment completely. The agency was essentially making a claim that the amendment's protections didn't apply to modern-day lives. The agency's internal policies neither regarded your data as your legally protected personal property, nor regarded their collection of that data as a "search" or "seizure." Instead, the NSA maintained that because you had already "shared" your phone records with a "third party"—your telephone service provider—you had forfeited any constitutional privacy interest you may once have had. And it insisted that "search" and "seizure" occurred only when its analysts, not its algorithms, actively queried what had already been automatically collected.

Had constitutional oversight mechanisms been functioning properly, this extremist interpretation of the Fourth Amendment— effectively holding that the very act of using modern technologies is tantamount to a surrender of your privacy rights—would have been rejected by Congress and the courts. America's Founders were skilled engineers of political power, particularly attuned to the perils posed by legal subterfuge and the temptations of the presidency toward exercising monarchical authority. To forestall such eventualities, they designed a system, laid out in the Constitution's first three articles, that established the US government in three coequal branches, each supposed to provide checks and balances to the others. But when it came to protecting the privacy of American citizens in the digital age, each of these branches failed in its own way, causing the entire system to halt and catch fire.

The legislative branch, the two houses of Congress, willingly abandoned its supervisory role: even as the number of IC government employees and private contractors was exploding, the number of congresspeople who were kept informed about the IC's capabilities and activities kept dwindling, until only a few special committee members were apprised in closed-door hearings. Even then they were only informed of some, but not all, of the IC's activities. When rare public hearings on the IC were held, the NSA's position was made strikingly clear: The agency would not cooperate, it would not be honest, and, what was worse, through classification and claims of secrecy it would force America's federal legislatures to collaborate in its deception. In early 2013, for instance, James Clapper, then the director of National Intelligence, testified under oath to the US Senate Select Committee on Intelligence that the NSA did not engage in bulk collection of the communications of American citizens. To the question, "Does the NSA collect any type of data at all on millions or hundreds of millions of Americans?" Clapper replied, "No, sir," and then added, "There are cases where they could inadvertently perhaps collect, but not wittingly." That was a witting, bald-faced lie, of course, not just to Congress but to the American people. More than a few of the congresspeople to whom Clapper was testifying knew very well that what he was saying was untrue, yet they refused, or felt legally powerless, to call him out on it.

The failure of the judiciary was, if anything, even more disappointing. The Foreign Intelligence Surveillance Court (FISC), which oversees intelligence surveillance within the United States, is a specialized body that meets in secret and hears only from the government. It was designed to grant individual warrants for foreign intelligence collection, and has always been especially accommodating to the NSA, approving well over 99 percent of the agency's requests—a rate more suggestive of a ministerial rubber stamp than a deliberative judicial process. After 9/11, the court expanded its role from authorizing the surveillance of specific individuals to ruling on the legality and constitutionality of broad programmatic surveillance, without any adversarial scrutiny. A body that previously had been tasked with approving the surveillance of Foreign Terrorist #1 or Foreign Spy #2 was now being used to legitimize the whole combined infrastructure of PRISM and upstream collection. Judicial review of that infrastructure was reduced, in the words of the ACLU to a secret court upholding secret programs by secretly reinterpreting federal law.

When civil society groups like the ACLU tried to challenge the NSA's activities in ordinary, open federal courts, a curious thing happened. The government didn't defend itself on the ground that the surveillance activities were legal or constitutional. It declared, instead, that the ACLU and its clients had no right to be in court at all, because the ACLU could not prove that its clients had in fact been surveilled. Moreover, the ACLU could not use the litigation to seek evidence of surveillance, because the existence (or nonexistence) of that evidence was "a state secret," and leaks to journalists didn't count. In other words, the court couldn't recognize the information that was publicly known from having been published in the media; it could only recognize the information that the government officially confirmed as being publicly known. This invocation of classification meant that neither the ACLU, nor anyone else, could ever establish standing to raise a legal challenge in open court. To my disgust, in February 2013 the US Supreme Court decided 5 to 4 to accept the government's reasoning and dismissed an ACLU and Amnesty International lawsuit challenging mass surveillance without even considering the legality of the NSA's activities.

Finally, there was the executive branch, the primary cause of this constitutional breach. The president's office, through the Justice Department, had committed the original sin of secretly issuing directives that authorized mass surveillance in the wake of 9/11. Executive overreach has only continued in the decades since, with administrations of both parties seeking to act unilaterally and establish policy directives that circumvent law—policy directives that cannot be challenged, since their classification keeps them from being publicly known.

The constitutional system only functions as a whole if and when each of its three branches works as intended. When all three don't just fail, but fail deliberately and with coordination, the result is a culture of impunity. I realized that I was crazy to have imagined that the Supreme Court, or Congress, or President Obama, seeking to distance his administration from President George W. Bush's, would ever hold the IC legally responsible—for anything. It was time to face the fact that the IC believed themselves above the law, and given how broken the process was, they were right. The IC had come to understand the rules of our system better than the people who had created it, and they used that knowledge to their advantage.

They'd hacked the Constitution.

AMERICA WAS BORN from an act of treason. The Declaration of Independence was an outrageous violation of the laws of England and yet the fullest expression of what the Founders called the "Laws of Nature," among which was the right to defy the powers of the day and rebel on point of principle, according to the dictates of one's conscience. The first Americans to exercise this right, the first "whistleblowers" in American history, appeared one year later—in 1777.

These men, like so many of the men in my family, were sailors, officers of the Continental Navy who, in defense of their new land, had taken to the sea. During the Revolution, they served on the USS *Warren*, a thirty-two-gun frigate under the command of Commodore Esek Hopkins, the commander in chief of the Continental Navy. Hopkins was a lazy and intractable leader who refused to bring his vessel into combat. His officers also claimed to have witnessed him beating and starving British prisoners of war. Ten of the *Warren*'s officers—after consulting their consciences, and with barely a thought for their careers—reported all of this up the chain of command, writing to the Marine Committee:

Much Respected Gentlemen,

We who present this petition are engaged on board the ship Warren with an earnest desire and fixed expectation of doing our country some service. We are still anxious for the Weal of America & wish nothing more earnestly than to see her in peace & prosperity. We are ready to hazard every thing that is dear & if necessary sacrifice our lives for the welfare of our country. We are desirous of being active in the defence of our constitutional liberties and privileges against the unjust cruel claims of tyranny & oppression; but as things are now circumstanced on board this frigate, there seems to be no prospect of our being serviceable in our present station. We have been in this situation for a considerable space of time. We are personally well acquainted with the real character & conduct of our commander, Commodore Hopkins, & we take this method not having a more convenient opportunity of sincerely & humbly petitioning the honorable Marine Committee that they would inquire into his character & conduct, for we suppose that his character is such & that he has been guilty of such crimes as render him quite unfit for the public department he now occupies, which crimes, we the subscribers can sufficiently attest.

After receiving this letter, the Marine Committee investigated Commodore Hopkins. He reacted by dismissing his officers and crew, and in a fit of rage filed a criminal libel suit against Midshipman Samuel Shaw and Third Lieutenant Richard Marven, the two officers who admitted to having authored the petition. The suit was filed in the courts of Rhode Island, whose last colonial governor had been Stephen Hopkins, a signatory to the Declaration of Independence and the commodore's brother.

The case was assigned to a judge appointed by Governor Hopkins, but before the trial commenced Shaw and Marven were saved by a fellow naval officer, John Grannis, who broke ranks and presented their case directly to the Continental Congress. The Continental Congress was so alarmed by the precedent being set by allowing military complaints regarding dereliction of duty to be subject to the criminal charge of libel that it intervened. On July 30, 1778, it terminated the command of Commodore Hopkins, ordered the Treasury Office to pay Shaw and Marven's legal fees, and by unanimous consent enacted America's first whistleblower protection law. This law declared it "the duty of all persons in the service of the United States, as well as all other inhabitants thereof, to give the earliest information to Congress or any other proper authority of any misconduct, frauds, or misdemeanors committed by any officers or persons in the service of these states, which may come to their knowledge."

The law gave me hope—and it still does. Even at the darkest hour of the Revolution, with the very existence of the country at stake, Congress didn't just welcome an act of principled dissent, it enshrined such acts as duties. By the latter half of 2012, I was resolved to perform this duty myself, though I knew I'd be making my disclosures at a very different time—a time both more comfortable and more cynical. Few if any of my IC superiors would have sacrificed their careers for the same American principles for which military personnel regularly sacrifice their lives. And in my case, going up "the chain of command," which the IC prefers to call "the proper channels," wasn't an option as it was for the ten men who crewed on the *Warren*. My superiors were not only aware of what the agency was doing, they were actively directing it—they were complicit.

In organizations like the NSA—in which malfeasance has become so structural as to be a matter not of any particular initiative, but of an ideology—proper channels can only become a trap, to catch the heretics and disfavorables. I'd already experienced the failure of command back in Warrenton, and then again in Geneva, where in the regular course of my duties I had discovered a security vulnerability in a critical program. I'd reported the vulnerability, and when nothing was done about it I reported that, too. My supervisors weren't happy that I'd done so, because their supervisors weren't happy, either. The chain of command is truly a chain that binds, and the lower links can only be lifted by the higher.

Coming from a Coast Guard family, I've always been fascinated by how much of the English language vocabulary of disclosure has a nautical undercurrent. Even before the days of the USS *Warren*, organizations, like ships, sprang leaks. When steam replaced wind for propulsion, whistles were blown at sea to signal intentions and emergencies: one whistle to pass by port, two whistles to pass by starboard, five for a warning.

The same terms in European languages, meanwhile, often have fraught political valences conditioned by historical context. French used *dénonciateur* throughout much of the twentieth century, until the word's WWII-era association with being a "denouncer" or "informant" for the Germans led to a preference for *lanceur d'alerte* ("one who launches a warning"). German, a language that has struggled with its culture's Nazi and Stasi past, evolved beyond its own *Denunziant* and *Informant* to settle on the unsatisfactory *Hinweisgeber* (a "hint- or tip-giver"), *Enthueller* ("revealer"), *Skandalaufdecker* ("scandal-uncoverer"), and even the pointedly political *ethische Dissidenten* ("ethical dissident"). German uses few of these words online, however; with respect to today's Internet-based disclosures, it has simply borrowed the noun *Whistleblower* and the verb *leaken*. The languages of regimes like Russia and China, for their part, employ terms that bear the pejorative sense of "snitch" and "traitor." It would take the existence of a strong free press in those societies to imbue those words with a more positive coloration, or to coin new ones that would frame disclosure not as a betrayal but as an honorable duty.

Ultimately, every language, including English, demonstrates its culture's relationship to power by how it chooses to define the act of disclosure. Even the nautically derived English words that seem neutral and benign frame the act from the perspective of the institution that perceives itself wronged, not of the public that the institution has failed. When an institution decries "a leak," it is implying that the "leaker" damaged or sabotaged something.

Today, "leaking" and "whistleblowing" are often treated as interchangeable. But to my mind, the term "leaking" should be used differently than it commonly is. It should be used to describe acts of disclosure done not out of public interest but out of self-interest, or in pursuit of institutional or political aims. To be more precise, I understand a leak as something closer to a "plant," or an incidence of "propaganda-seeding": the selective release of protected information in order to sway popular opinion or affect the course of decision making. It is rare for even a day to go by in which some "unnamed" or "anonymous" senior government official does not leak, by way of a hint or tip to a journalist, some classified item that advances their own agenda or the efforts of their agency or party.

This dynamic is perhaps most brazenly exemplified by a 2013 incident in which IC officials, likely seeking to inflate the threat of terrorism and deflect criticism of mass surveillance, leaked to a few news websites extraordinarily detailed accounts of a conference call between al-Qaeda leader Ayman al-Zawahiri and his global affiliates. In this so-called conference call of doom, al-Zawahiri purportedly discussed organizational cooperation with Nasser al-Wuhayshi, the leader of al-Qaeda in Yemen, and representatives of the Taliban and Boko Haram. By disclosing the ability to intercept this conference call—that is, if we're to believe this leak, which consisted of a description of the call, not a recording—the IC irrevocably burned an extraordinary means of apprising itself of the plans and intentions of the highest ranks of terrorist leadership, purely for the sake of a momentary political advantage in the news cycle. Not a single person was prosecuted as a result of this stunt, though it was most certainly illegal, and cost America the ability to keep wiretapping the alleged al-Qaeda hotline.

Time and again, America's political class has proven itself willing to tolerate, even generate leaks that serve its own ends. The IC often announces its "successes," regardless of their classification and regardless of the consequences. Nowhere in recent memory has that been more apparent than in the leaks relating to the extrajudicial killing of the American-born extremist cleric Anwar al-Aulaqi in Yemen. By breathlessly publicizing its drone attack on al-Aulaqi to the *Washington Post* and the *New York Times*, the Obama administration was tacitly admitting the existence of the CIA's drone program and its "disposition matrix," or kill list, both of which are officially top secret. Additionally, the government was implicitly confirming that it engaged not just in targeted assassinations, but in targeted assassinations of American citizens. These leaks, accomplished in the coordinated fashion of a media campaign, were shocking demonstrations of the state's situational approach to secrecy: a seal that must be maintained for the government to act with impunity, but that can be broken whenever the government seeks to claim credit.

It's only in this context that the US government's latitudinal relationship to leaking can be fully understood. It has forgiven "unauthorized" leaks when they've resulted in unexpected benefits, and forgotten "authorized" leaks when they've caused harm. But if a leak's harmfulness and lack of authorization, not to mention its essential illegality, make scant difference to the government's reaction, what does? What makes one disclosure permissible, and another not?

The answer is power. The answer is control. A disclosure is deemed acceptable only if it doesn't challenge the fundamental prerogatives of an institution. If all the disparate components of an organization, from its mailroom to its executive suite, can be assumed to have the same power to discuss internal matters, then its executives have surrendered their information control, and the organization's continued functioning is put in jeopardy. Seizing this equality of voice, independent of an organization's managerial or decision-making hierarchy, is what is properly meant by the term "whistleblowing"—an act that's particularly threatening to the IC, which operates by strict compartmentalization under a legally codified veil of secrecy.

A "whistleblower," in my definition, is a person who through hard experience has concluded that their life inside an institution has become incompatible with the principles developed in—and the loyalty owed to—the greater society outside it, to which that institution should be accountable. This person knows that they can't remain inside the institution, and knows that the institution can't or won't be dismantled. Reforming the institution might be possible, however, so they blow the whistle and disclose the information to bring public pressure to bear.

This is an adequate description of my situation, with one crucial addition: all the information I intended to disclose was classified top secret. To blow the whistle on secret programs, I'd also have to blow the whistle on the larger system of secrecy, to expose it not as the absolute prerogative of state that the IC claimed it was but rather as an occasional privilege that the IC abused to subvert democratic oversight. Without bringing to light the full scope of this systemic secrecy, there would be no hope of restoring a balance of power between citizens and their governance. This motive of restoration I take to be essential to whistleblowing: it marks the disclosure not as a radical act of dissent or resistance, but a conventional act of return—signaling the ship to return back to port, where it'll be stripped, refitted, and patched of its leaks before being given the chance to start over.

A total exposure of the total apparatus of mass surveillance—not by me, but by the media, the de facto fourth branch of the US government, protected by the Bill of Rights: that was the only response appropriate to the scale of the crime. It wouldn't be enough, after all, to merely reveal a particular abuse or set of abuses, which the agency could stop (or pretend to stop) while preserving the rest of the shadowy apparatus intact. Instead, I was resolved to bring to light a single, all-encompassing fact: that my government had developed and deployed a global system of mass surveillance without the knowledge or consent of its citizenry.

Whistleblowers can be elected by circumstance at any working level of an institution. But digital technology has brought us to an age in which, for the first time in recorded history, the most effective will come up from the bottom, from the ranks traditionally least incentivized to maintain the status quo. In the IC, as in virtually every other outsize decentralized institution that relies on computers, these lower ranks are rife with technologists like myself, whose legitimate access to vital infrastructure is grossly out of proportion to their formal authority to influence institutional decisions. In other words, there is usually an imbalance that obtains between what people like me are intended to know and what we are able to know, and between the slight power we have to change the institutional culture and the vast power we have to address our concerns to the culture at large. Though such technological privileges can certainly be abused—after all, most systems-level technologists have access to everything—the highest exercise of that privilege is in cases involving the technology itself. Specialist abilities incur weightier responsibilities. Technologists seeking to report on the systemic misuse of technology must do more than just bring their findings to the public, if the significance of those findings is to be understood. They have a duty to contextualize and explain—to demystify.

A few dozen or so of the people best positioned to do this in the whole entire world were here—they were sitting all around me in the Tunnel. My fellow technologists came in every day and sat at their terminals and furthered the work of the state. They weren't merely oblivious to its abuses, but incurious about them, and that lack of curiosity made them not evil but tragic. It didn't matter whether they'd come to the IC out of patriotism or opportunism: once they'd gotten inside the machine, they became machines themselves.

22

Fourth Estate

Nothing is harder than living with a secret that can't be spoken. Lying to strangers about a cover identity or concealing the fact that your office is under the world's most top-secret pineapple field might sound like it qualifies, but at least you're part of a team: though your work may be secret, it's a shared secret, and therefore a shared burden. There is misery but also laughter.

When you have a real secret, though, that you can't share with anyone, even the laughter is a lie. I could talk about my concerns, but never about where they were leading me. To the day I die I'll remember explaining to my colleagues how our work was being applied to violate the oaths we had sworn to uphold and their verbal shrug in response: "What can you do about it?" I hated that question, its sense of resignation, its sense of defeat, but it still felt valid enough that I had to ask myself, "Well, what?"

When the answer presented itself, I decided to become a whistleblower. Yet to breathe to Lindsay, the love of my life, even a word about that decision would have put our relationship to an even crueler test than saying nothing. Not wishing to cause her any more harm than I was already resigned to causing, I kept silent, and in my silence I was alone.

I thought that solitude and isolation would be easy for me, or at least easier than it had been for my predecessors in the whistleblowing world. Hadn't each step of my life served as a kind of preparation? Hadn't I gotten used to being alone, after all those years spent hushed and spellbound in front of a screen? I'd been the solo hacker, the night-shift harbormaster, the keeper of the keys in an empty office. But I was human, too, and the lack of companionship was hard. Each day was haunted by struggle, as I tried and failed to reconcile the moral and the legal, my duties and my desires. I had everything I'd ever wanted—love, family, and success far beyond what I ever deserved—and I lived in Eden amid plentiful trees, only one of which was forbidden to me. The easiest thing should have been to follow the rules.

And even if I was already reconciled to the dangers of my decision, I wasn't yet adjusted to the role. After all, who was I to put this information in front of the American public? Who'd elected me the president of secrets?

The information I intended to disclose about my country's secret regime of mass surveillance was so explosive, and yet so technical, that I was as scared of being doubted as I was of being misunderstood. That was why my first decision, after resolving to go public, was to go public with documentation. The way to reveal a secret program might have been merely to describe its existence, but the way to reveal programmatic secrecy was to describe its workings. This required documents, the agency's actual files—as many as necessary to expose the scope of the abuse though I knew that disclosing even one PDF would be enough to earn me prison.

The threat of government retribution against any entity or platform to which I made the disclosure led me to briefly consider self-publishing. That would've been the most convenient and safest method: just collecting the documents that best communicated my concerns and posting them online, as they were, then circulating a link. Ultimately, one of my reasons for not pursuing this course had to do with authentication. Scores of people post "classified secrets" to the Internet every day—many of them about time-travel technologies and aliens. I didn't want my own revelations, which were fairly incredible already, to get lumped in with the outlandish and lost among the crazy.

It was clear to me then, from the earliest stage of the process, that I required, and that the public deserved, some person or institution to vouch for the veracity of the documents. I also wanted a partner to vet the potential hazards posed by the revelation of classified information, and to help explain that information by putting it in technological and legal context. I trusted myself to present the problems with surveillance, and even to analyze them, but I'd have to trust others to solve them. Regardless of how wary of institutions I might have been by this point, I was far warier of trying to act like one myself. Cooperating with some type of media organization would defend me against the worst accusations of rogue activity, and correct for whatever biases I had, whether they were conscious or unconscious, personal or professional. I didn't want any political opinion of mine to prejudice anything with regard to the presentation, or reception, of the disclosures. After all, in a country in which everyone was being surveilled, no issue was less partisan than surveillance.

In retrospect, I have to credit at least some of my desire to find ideological filters to Lindsay's improving influence. Lindsay had spent years patiently instilling in me the lesson that my interests and concerns weren't always hers, and certainly weren't always the world's, and that just because I shared my knowledge didn't mean that anyone had to share my opinion. Not everybody who was opposed to invasions of privacy might be ready to adopt 256-bit encryption standards or drop off the Internet entirely. An illegal act that disturbed one person as a violation of the Constitution might upset another person as a violation of their privacy, or of that of their spouse or children. Lindsay was my key to unlocking this truth—that diverse motives and approaches can only improve the chances of achieving common goals. She, without even knowing it, gave me the confidence to conquer my qualms and reach out to other people.

But which people? Who? It might be hard to remember, or even to imagine, but at the time when I first considered coming forward, the whistleblower's forum of choice was WikiLeaks. Back then, it operated in many respects like a traditional publisher, albeit one that was radically skeptical of state power. WikiLeaks regularly joined up with leading international publications like the *Guardian*, the *New York Times*, *Der Spiegel*, *Le Monde*, and *El País* to publish the documents provided by its sources. The work that these partner news organizations accomplished over the course of 2010 and 2011 suggested to me that WikiLeaks was most valuable as a go-between that connected sources with journalists, and as a firewall that preserved sources' anonymity.

WikiLeaks' practices changed following its publication of disclosures by US Army private Chelsea Manning—huge caches of US military field logs pertaining to the Iraq and Afghan wars, information about detainees at Guantanamo Bay, along with US diplomatic cables. Due to the governmental backlash and media controversy surrounding the site's redaction of the Manning materials, WikiLeaks decided to change course and publish future leaks as they received them: pristine and unredacted. This switch to a policy of total transparency meant that publishing with WikiLeaks would not meet my needs. Effectually, it would have been the same for me as self-publishing, a route I'd already rejected as insufficient. I knew that the story the NSA documents told about a global system of mass surveillance deployed in the deepest secrecy was a difficult one to understand—a story so tangled and technical that I was increasingly convinced it could not be presented all at once in a "document dump," but only by the patient and careful work of journalists, undertaken, in the best scenario I could conceive of, with the support of multiple independent press institutions.

Though I felt some relief once I'd resolved to disclose directly to journalists, I still had some lingering reservations. Most of them involved my country's most prestigious publications—particularly

America's newspaper of record, the *New York Times*. Whenever I thought about contacting the *Times*, I found myself hesitating. While the paper had shown some willingness to displease the US government with its WikiLeaks reporting, I couldn't stop reminding myself of its earlier conduct involving an important article on the government's warrantless wiretapping program by Eric Lichtblau and James Risen.

Those two journalists, by combining information from Justice Department whistleblowers with their own reporting, had managed to uncover one aspect of STELLARWIND—the NSA's original-recipe post-9/11 surveillance initiative—and had produced a fully written, edited, and fact-checked article about it, ready to go to press by mid-2004. It was at this point that the paper's editor in chief, Bill Keller, ran the article past the government, as part of a courtesy process whose typical purpose is for a publication's editorial staff to have a chance to assess the government's arguments as to why the publication of certain information might endanger national security. In this case, as in most cases, the government refused to provide a specific reason, but implied that one existed and that it was classified, too. The Bush administration told Keller and the paper's publisher, Arthur Sulzberger, without providing any evidence, that the *Times* would be emboldening America's enemies and enabling terror if it went public with the information that the government was wiretapping American citizens without a warrant. Unfortunately, the paper allowed itself to be convinced and spiked the article. Lichtblau and Risen's reporting finally ran, but over a year later, in December 2005, and only after Risen pressured the paper by announcing that the material was included in a book of his that was about to be released. Had that article run when it was originally written, it might well have changed the course of the 2004 election.

If the *Times*, or any paper, did something similar to me—if it took my revelations, reported on them, submitted the reporting for review, and then suppressed its publication—I'd be sunk. Given the likelihood of my identification as the source, it would be tantamount to turning me in before any revelations were brought to the public.

If I couldn't trust a legacy newspaper, could I trust any institution? Why even bother? I hadn't signed up for any of this. I had just wanted to screw around with computers and maybe do some good for my country along the way. I had a lease and a lover and my health was improved. Every STOP sign on my commute I took as advice to stop this voluntary madness. My head and heart were in conflict, with the only constant being the desperate hope that somebody else, somewhere else, would figure it out on their own. After all, wasn't journalism about following the bread crumbs and connecting the dots? What else did reporters do all day, besides tweet?

I knew at least two things about the denizens of the Fourth Estate: they competed for scoops, and they knew very little about technology. It was this lack of expertise or even interest in tech that largely caused journalists to miss two events that stunned me during the course of my fact-gathering about mass surveillance.

The first was the NSA's announcement of the construction of a vast new data facility in Bluffdale, Utah. The agency called it the Massive Data Repository, until somebody with a knack for PR realized the name might be tough to explain if it ever got out, so it was renamed the Mission Data Repository—because as long as you don't change the acronym, you don't have to change all the briefing slides. The MDR was projected to contain a total of four twenty-five-thousand-square-foot halls, filled with servers. It could hold an immense amount of data, basically a rolling history of the entire planet's pattern of life, insofar as life can be understood through the connection of payments to people, people to phones, phones to calls, calls to networks, and the synoptic array of Internet activity moving along those networks' lines.

The only prominent journalist who seemed to notice the announcement was James Bamford, who wrote about it for *Wired* in March 2012. There were a few follow-ups in the nontech press, but none of them furthered the reporting. No one asked what, to

me at least, were the most basic questions: Why does any government agency, let alone an intelligence agency, need that much
space? What data, and how much of it, do they really intend to
store there, and for how long? Because there was simply no reason to build something to those specs unless you were planning
on storing absolutely everything, forever. Here was, to my mind,
the corpus delicti—the plain-as-day corroboration of a crime, in
a gigantic concrete bunker surrounded by barbed wire and guard
towers, sucking up a city's worth of electricity from its own power
grid in the middle of the Utah desert. And no one was paying
attention.

The second event happened one year later, in March 2013—
one week after Clapper lied to Congress and Congress gave him
a pass. A few periodicals had covered that testimony, though they
merely regurgitated Clapper's denial that the NSA collected bulk
data on Americans. But no so-called mainstream publication at
all covered a rare public appearance by Ira "Gus" Hunt, the chief
technology officer of the CIA.

I'd known Gus slightly from my Dell stint with the CIA. He
was one of our top customers, and every vendor loved his apparent inability to be discreet: he'd always tell you more than he was
supposed to. For sales guys, he was like a bag of money with a
mouth. Now he was appearing as a special guest speaker at a civilian tech event in New York called the GigaOM Structure: Data
conference. Anyone with $40 could go to it. The major talks, such
as Gus's, were streamed for free live online.

The reason I'd made sure to catch his talk was that I'd just
read, through internal NSA channels, that the CIA had finally
decided on the disposition of its cloud contract. It had refused
my old team at Dell, and turned down HP, too, instead signing a
ten-year, $600 million cloud development and management deal
with Amazon. I had no negative feelings about this—actually, at
this juncture, I was pleased that my work wasn't going to be used
by the agency. I was just curious, from a professional standpoint,
whether Gus might obliquely address this announcement and of-

fer any insight into why Amazon had been chosen, since rumors were going around that the proposal process had been rigged in Amazon's favor.

I got insight, certainly, but of an unexpected kind. I had the opportunity of witnessing the highest-ranking technical officer at the CIA stand onstage in a rumpled suit and brief a crowd of uncleared normies—and, via the Internet, the uncleared world—about the agency's ambitions and capacities. As his presentation unfolded, and he alternated bad jokes with an even worse command of PowerPoint, I grew more and more incredulous.

"At the CIA," he said, "we fundamentally try to collect everything and hang on to it forever." As if that wasn't clear enough, he went on: "It is nearly within our grasp to compute on <u>all</u> human generated information." The underline was Gus's own. He was reading from his slide deck, ugly words in an ugly font illustrated with the government's signature four-color clip art.

There were a few journalists in the crowd, apparently, though it seemed as if almost all of them were from specialty tech-government publications like *Federal Computer Week*. It was telling that Gus stuck around for a Q & A toward the conclusion of his presentation. Rather, it wasn't quite a Q & A, but more like an auxiliary presentation, offered directly to the journalists. He must have been trying to get something off his chest, and it wasn't just his clown tie.

Gus told the journalists that the agency could track their smartphones, even when they were turned off—that the agency could surveil every single one of their communications. Remember: this was a crowd of domestic journalists. American journalists. And the way that Gus said "could" came off as "has," "does," and "will." He perorated in a distinctly disturbed, and disturbing, manner, at least for a CIA high priest: "Technology is moving faster than government or law can keep up. It's moving faster . . . than you can keep up: you should be asking the question of what are your rights and who owns your data." I was floored—anybody more junior than Gus who had given a presentation like this would've been wearing orange by the end of the day.

Coverage of Gus's confession ran only in the *Huffington Post*. But the performance itself lived on at YouTube, where it still remains, at least at the time of this writing six years later. The last time I checked, it had 313 views—a dozen of them mine.

The lesson I took from this was that for my disclosures to be effective, I had to do more than just hand some journalists some documents—more, even, than help them interpret the documents. I had to become their partner, to provide the technological training and tools to help them do their reporting accurately and safely. Taking this course of action would mean giving myself over totally to one of the capital crimes of intelligence work: whereas other spies have committed espionage, sedition, and treason, I would be aiding and abetting an act of journalism. The perverse fact is that legally, those crimes are virtually synonymous. American law makes no distinction between providing classified information to the press in the public interest and providing it, even selling it, to the enemy. The only opinion I've ever found to contradict this came from my first indoctrination into the IC: there, I was told that it was in fact slightly better to offer secrets for sale to the enemy than to offer them for free to a domestic reporter. A reporter will tell the public, whereas an enemy is unlikely to share its prize even with its allies.

Given the risks I was taking, I needed to identify people I could trust who were also trusted by the public. I needed reporters who were diligent yet discreet, independent yet reliable. They would need to be strong enough to challenge me on the distinctions between what I suspected and what the evidence proved, and to challenge the government when it falsely accused their work of endangering lives. Above all, I had to be sure that whoever I picked wouldn't ultimately cave to power when put under pressure that was certain to be like nothing they, or I, had ever experienced before.

I cast my net not so widely as to imperil the mission, but widely enough to avoid a single point of failure—the *New York Times* problem. One journalist, one publication, even one country of publication wouldn't be enough, because the US government had already demonstrated its willingness to stifle such reporting. Ideally, I'd give each journalist their own set of documents simultaneously, leaving me with none. This would shift the focus of scrutiny to them, and ensure that even if I were arrested the truth would still get out.

As I narrowed down my list of potential partners, I realized I'd been going about this all wrong, or just wastefully. Instead of trying to select the journalists on my own, I should have been letting the system that I was trying to expose select them for me. My best partners, I decided, would be journalists whom the national security state had already targeted.

Laura Poitras I knew as a documentarian, primarily concerned with America's post-9/11 foreign policy. Her film *My Country, My Country* depicted the 2005 Iraqi national elections that were conducted under (and frustrated by) the US occupation. She had also made *The Program*, about the NSA cryptanalyst William Binney—who had raised objections through proper channels about TRAILBLAZER, the predecessor of STELLARWIND, only to be accused of leaking classified information, subjected to repeated harassment, and arrested at gunpoint in his home, though never charged. Laura herself had been frequently harassed by the government because of her work, repeatedly detained and interrogated by border agents whenever she traveled in or out of the country.

Glenn Greenwald I knew as a civil liberties lawyer turned columnist, initially for *Salon*—where he was one of the few who wrote about the unclassified version of the NSA IG's Report back in 2009—and later for the US edition of the *Guardian*. I liked him because he was skeptical and argumentative, the kind of man who'd fight with the devil, and when the devil wasn't around fight with himself. Though Ewen MacAskill, of the British edition of the *Guardian*, and Bart Gellman of the *Washington Post* would later prove stalwart partners (and patient guides to the journalistic wilderness), I found my earliest affinity with Laura and Glenn, perhaps because they weren't merely interested in reporting on the IC but had personal stakes in understanding the institution.

The only hitch was getting in touch.

Unable to reveal my true name, I contacted the journalists under a variety of identities, disposable masks worn for a time and then discarded. The first of these was "Cincinnatus," after the legendary farmer who became a Roman consul and then voluntarily relinquished his power. That was followed by "Citizenfour," a handle that some journalists took to mean that I considered myself the fourth dissident-employee in the NSA's recent history, after Binney and his fellow TRAILBLAZER whistleblowers J. Kirk Wiebe and Ed Loomis—though the triumvirate I actually had in mind consisted of Thomas Drake, who disclosed the existence of TRAIL-BLAZER to journalists, and Daniel Ellsberg and Anthony Russo, whose disclosure of *The Pentagon Papers* helped expose the deceptions of the Vietnam War and bring it to an end. The final name I chose for my correspondence was "Verax," Latin for "speaker of truth," in the hopes of proposing an alternative to the model of a hacker called "Mendax" ("speaker of lies")—the pseudonym of the young man who'd grow up to become WikiLeaks' Julian Assange.

You can't really appreciate how hard it is to stay anonymous online until you've tried to operate as if your life depended on it. Most of the communications systems set up in the IC have a single basic aim: the observer of a communication must not be able to discern the identities of those involved, or in any way attribute them to an agency. This is why the IC calls these exchanges "non-attributable." The pre-Internet spycraft of anonymity is famous, mostly from TV and the movies: a safe-house address coded in bathroom-stall graffiti, for instance, or scrambled into the abbreviations of a classified ad. Or think of the Cold War's "dead drops," the chalk marks on mailboxes signaling that a secret package was waiting inside a particular hollowed-out tree in a public park. The modern version might be fake profiles trading fake chats on a dating site, or, more commonly, just a superficially innocuous app that leaves superficially innocuous messages on a superficially innocuous Amazon server secretly controlled by the CIA. What I wanted, however, was something even better than that—something that required none of that exposure, and none of that budget.

I decided to use somebody else's Internet connection. I wish that were simply a matter of going to a McDonald's or Starbucks and signing on to their Wi-Fi. But those places have CCTV, and receipts, and other people—memories with legs. Moreover, every wireless device, from a phone to a laptop, has a globally unique identifier called a MAC (Machine Address Code), which it leaves on record with every access point it connects to—a forensic marker of its user's movements.

So I didn't go to McDonald's or Starbucks—I went driving. Specifically, I went war-driving, which is when you convert your car into a roving Wi-Fi sensor. For this you need a laptop, a high-powered antenna, and a magnetic GPS sensor, which can be slapped atop the roof. Power is provided by the car or by a portable battery, or else by the laptop itself. Everything you need can fit into a backpack.

I took along a cheap laptop running TAILS, which is a Linux-based "amnesiac" operating system—meaning it forgets everything when you turn it off, and starts fresh when you boot it up again, with no logs or memory traces of anything ever done on it. TAILS allowed me to easily "spoof," or disguise, the laptop's MAC: whenever it connected to a network it left behind the record of some other machine, in no way associable with mine. Usefully enough, TAILS also had built-in support for connecting to the anonymizing Tor network.

At nights and on weekends, I drove around what seemed like

the entire island of Oahu, letting my antenna pick up the pulses of each Wi-Fi network. My GPS sensor tagged each access point with the location at which it was noticed, thanks to a mapping program I used called Kismet. What resulted was a map of the invisible networks we pass by every day without even noticing, a scandalously high percentage of which had either no security at all or security I could trivially bypass. Some of the networks required more sophisticated hacking. I'd briefly jam a network, causing its legitimate users to be booted off-line; in their attempt to reconnect, they'd automatically rebroadcast their "authentication packets," which I could intercept and effectively decipher into passwords that would let me log on just like any other "authorized" user.

With this network map in hand, I'd drive around Oahu like a madman, trying to check my email to see which of the journalists had replied to me. Having made contact with Laura Poitras, I'd spend much of the evening writing to her—sitting behind the wheel of my car at the beach, filching the Wi-Fi from a nearby resort. Some of the journalists I'd chosen needed convincing to use encrypted email, which back in 2012 was a pain. In some cases, I had to show them how, so I'd upload tutorials—sitting in my idling car in a parking lot, availing myself of the network of a library. Or of a school. Or of a gas station. Or of a bank—which had horrifyingly poor protections. The point was to not create any patterns.

Atop the parking garage of a mall, secure in the knowledge that the moment I closed the lid of my laptop, my secret was safe, I'd draft manifestos explaining why I'd gone public, but then delete them. And then I'd try writing emails to Lindsay, only to delete them, too. I just couldn't find the words.

23

Read, Write, Execute

Read, Write, Execute: in computing, these are called permissions. Functionally speaking, they determine the extent of your authority within a computer or computer network, defining what exactly you can and cannot do. The right to *read* a file allows you to access its contents, while the right to *write* a file allows you to modify it. *Execution*, meanwhile, means that you have the ability to run a file or program, to carry out the actions it was designed to do.

Read, Write, Execute: this was my simple three-step plan. I wanted to burrow into the heart of the world's most secure network to find the truth, make a copy of it, and get it out into the world. And I had to do all this without getting caught—without being read, written, and executed myself.

Almost everything you do on a computer, on any device, leaves a record. Nowhere is this more true than at the NSA. Each log-in and log-out creates a log entry. Each permission I used left its own forensic trace. Every time I opened a file, every time I copied a file, that action was recorded. Every time I downloaded, moved, or deleted a file, that was recorded, too, and security logs were updated to reflect the event. There were network flow records, public key infrastructure records—people even joked about cameras hidden in the bathrooms, in the bathroom stalls. The agency had a not inconsiderable number of counterintelligence programs spying on the people who were spying on people, and if even one caught me doing something I wasn't supposed to be doing, it wouldn't be a file that was getting deleted.

Luckily, the strength of these systems was also their weakness: their complexity meant that not even the people running them necessarily knew how they worked. Nobody actually understood where they overlapped and where their gaps were. Nobody, that is, except the systems administrators. After all, those sophisticated monitoring systems you're imagining, the ones with scary names like MIDNIGHTRIDER—somebody's got to install them in the first place. The NSA may have paid for the network, but sysadmins like myself were the ones who really owned it.

The Read phase would involve dancing through the digital grid of tripwires laid across the routes connecting the NSA to every other intelligence agency, domestic and foreign. (Among these was the NSA's UK partner, the Government Communications Headquarters, or GCHQ, which was setting up dragnets like OPTICNERVE, a program that saved a snapshot every five minutes from the cameras of people video-chatting on platforms like Yahoo Messenger, and PHOTONTORPEDO, which grabbed the IP addresses of MSN Messenger users.) By using Heartbeat to bring in the documents I wanted, I could turn "bulk collection" against those who'd turned it against the public, effectively Frankensteining the IC. The agency's security tools kept track of who read what, but it didn't matter: anyone who bothered to check their logs was used to seeing Heartbeat by now. It would sound no alarms. It was the perfect cover.

But while Heartbeat would work as a way of collecting the files—far too many files—it only brought them to the server in Hawaii, a server that kept logs even I couldn't get around. I needed a way to work with the files, search them, and discard the irrelevant and uninteresting, along with those containing legitimate secrets that I wouldn't be giving to journalists. At this point, still in my Read phase, the hazards were manifold, due mainly to the fact that the protocols I was up against were no longer geared to monitoring but to prevention. If I ran my searches on the Heartbeat server, it would light a massive electronic sign blinking ARREST ME.

I thought about this for a while. I couldn't just copy the files directly from the Heartbeat server onto a personal storage device and waltz out of the Tunnel without being caught. What I could do, though, was bring the files closer, directing them to an intermediate way station.

I couldn't send them to one of our regular computers, because by 2012 all of the Tunnel had been upgraded to new "thin client" machines: small helpless computers with crippled drives and CPUs that couldn't store or process data on their own, but did all of their storage and processing on the cloud. In a forgotten corner of the office, however, there was a pyramid of disused desktop computers—old, moldering legacy machines the agency had wiped clean and discarded. When I say old here, I mean young by the standards of anyone who doesn't live on a budget the size of the NSA's. They were Dell PCs from as recently as 2009 or 2010, large gray rectangles of comforting weight, which could store and process data on their own without being connected to the cloud. What I liked about them was that though they were still in the NSA system, they couldn't really be closely tracked as long as I kept them off the central networks.

I could easily justify needing to use these stolid, reliable boxes by claiming that I was trying to make sure Heartbeat worked with older operating systems. After all, not everybody at every NSA site had one of the new "thin clients" just yet. And what if Dell wanted to implement a civilian version of Heartbeat? Or what if the CIA, or FBI, or some similarly backward organization wanted to use it? Under the guise of compatibility testing, I could transfer the files to these old computers, where I could search, filter, and organize them as much as I wanted, as long as I was careful. I was carrying one of the big old hulks back to my desk when I passed one of the IT directors, who stopped me and asked me what I needed it for—he'd been a major proponent of getting rid of them. "Stealing secrets," I answered, and we laughed.

The Read phase ended with the files I wanted all neatly organized into folders. But they were still on a computer that wasn't mine, which was still in the Tunnel underground. Enter, then, the Write phase, which for my purposes meant the agonizingly slow, boring-but-also-cripplingly-scary process of copying the files from the legacy Dells to something that I could spirit out of the building.

The easiest and safest way to copy a file off any IC workstation is also the oldest: a camera. Smartphones, of course, are banned in NSA buildings, but workers accidentally bring them in all the time without anyone noticing. They leave them in their gym bags or in the pockets of their windbreakers. If they're caught with one in a random search and they act goofily abashed instead of screaming panicked Mandarin into their wristwatch, they're often merely warned, especially if it's their first offense. But getting a smartphone loaded with NSA secrets out of the Tunnel is a riskier gambit. Odds are that nobody would've noticed—or cared—if I walked out with a smartphone, and it might have been an adequate tool for a staffer trying to copy a single torture report, but I wasn't wild about the idea of taking thousands of pictures of my computer screen in the middle of a top secret facility. Also, the phone would have had to be configured in such a way that even the world's foremost forensic experts could seize and search it without finding anything on it that they shouldn't.

I'm going to refrain from publishing how exactly I went about my own writing—my own copying and encryption—so that the NSA will still be standing tomorrow. I will mention, however, what storage technology I used for the copied files. Forget thumb-drives; they're too bulky for the relatively small amount they store. I went, instead, for SD cards—the acronym stands for Secure Digital. Actually, I went for the mini- and micro-SD cards.

You'll recognize SD cards if you've ever used a digital camera or video camera, or needed more storage on a tablet. They're tiny little buggers, miracles of nonvolatile flash storage, and—at 20 x 21.5 mm for the mini, 15 x 11 mm for the micro, basically the size of your pinkie fingernail—eminently concealable. You can fit one inside the pried-off square of a Rubik's Cube, then stick the square back on, and nobody will notice. In other attempts I carried a card in my sock, or, at my most paranoid, in my cheek, so I could swallow it if I had to. Eventually, as I gained confidence, and certainty in my methods of encryption, I'd just keep a card at the bottom of my pocket. They hardly ever triggered metal detectors, and who wouldn't believe I'd simply forgotten something so small?

The size of SD cards, however, has one downside: they're extremely slow to write. Copying times for massive volumes of data are always long—at least always longer than you want—but the duration tends to stretch even more when you're copying not to a speedy hard drive but to a minuscule silicon wafer embedded in plastic. Also, I wasn't just copying. I was deduplicating, compressing, encrypting, none of which processes could be accomplished simultaneously with any other. I was using all the skills I'd ever acquired in my storage work, because that's what I was doing, essentially. I was storing the NSA's storage, making an off-site backup of evidence of the IC's abuses.

It could take eight hours or more—entire shifts—to fill a card. And though I switched to working nights again, those hours were terrifying. There was the old computer chugging, monitor off, with all but one fluorescent ceiling panel dimmed to save energy in the after-hours. And there I was, turning the monitor back on every once in a while to check the rate of progress and cringing. You know the feeling—the sheer hell of following the completion bar as it indicates 84 percent completed, 85 percent completed . . . 1:58:53 left . . . As it filled toward the sweet relief of 100 percent, all files copied, I'd be sweating, seeing shadows and hearing footsteps around every corner.

EXECUTE: THAT WAS the final step. As each card filled, I had to run my getaway routine. I had to get that vital archive out of the building, past the bosses and military uniforms, down the stairs and out the empty hall, past the badge scans and armed guards and mantraps—those two-doored security zones in which the next door doesn't open until the previous door shuts and your badge scan is approved, and if it isn't, or if anything else goes awry, the guards draw their weapons and the doors lock you in and you say, "Well, isn't this embarrassing?" This—per all the reports I'd been studying, and all the nightmares I'd been having—was where they'd catch me, I was sure of it. Each time I left, I was petrified. I'd have to force myself not to think about the SD card. When you think about it, you act differently, suspiciously.

One unexpected upshot of gaining a better understanding of NSA surveillance was that I'd also gained a better understanding of the dangers I faced. In other words, learning about the agency's systems had taught me how not to get caught by them. My guides in this regard were the indictments that the government had brought against former agents—mostly real bastards who, in IC jargon, had "exfiltrated" classified information for profit. I compiled, and studied, as many of these indictments as I could. The FBI—the agency that investigates all crime within the IC—took great pride in explaining exactly how they caught their suspects, and believe me, I didn't mind benefiting from their experience. It seemed that in almost every case, the FBI would wait to make its arrest until the suspect had finished their work and was about to go home. Sometimes they would let the suspect take the material out of a SCIF—a Sensitive Compartmented Information Facility, which is a type of building or room shielded against surveillance—and out into the public, where its very presence was a federal crime. I kept imagining a team of FBI agents lying in wait for me—there, out in the public light, just at the far end of the Tunnel.

I'd usually try to banter with the guards, and this was where my Rubik's Cube came in most handy. I was known to the guards and to everybody else at the Tunnel as the Rubik's Cube guy, because I was always working the cube as I walked down the halls. I got so adept I could even solve it one-handed. It became my totem, my spirit toy, and a distraction device as much for myself as for my coworkers. Most of them thought it was an affectation, or a nerdy conversation starter. And it was, but primarily it relieved my anxiety. It calmed me.

I bought a few cubes and handed them out. Anyone who took to it, I'd give them pointers. The more that people got used to them, the less they'd ever want a closer look at mine.

I got along with the guards, or I told myself I did, mostly because I knew where their minds were: elsewhere. I'd done something like their job before, back at CASL. I knew how mind-numbing it was to spend all night standing, feigning vigilance. Your feet hurt. After a while, all the rest of you hurts. And you can get so lonely that you'll talk to a wall.

I aimed to be more entertaining than the wall, developing my own patter for each human obstacle. There was the one guard I talked to about insomnia and the difficulties of day-sleeping (remember, I was on nights, so this would've been around two in the morning). Another guy, we discussed politics. He called Democrats "Demon Rats," so I'd read Breitbart News in preparation for the conversation. What they all had in common was a reaction to my cube: it made them smile. Over the course of my employment at the Tunnel, pretty much all the guards said some variation of, "Oh man, I used to play with that when I was a kid," and then, invariably, "I tried to take the stickers off to solve it." Me too, buddy. Me too.

It was only once I got home that I was able to relax, even just slightly. I was still worried about the house being wired—that was another one of those charming methods the FBI used against those it suspected of inadequate loyalty. I'd rebuff Lindsay's concerns about my insomniac ways until she hated me and I hated myself. She'd go to bed and I'd go to the couch, hiding with my laptop under a blanket like a child because cotton beats cameras. With the threat of immediate arrest out of the way, I could focus on transferring the files to a larger external storage device via my laptop—only somebody who didn't understand technology very well would think I'd keep them on the laptop forever—and locking them down under multiple layers of encryption algorithms using differing implementations, so that even if one failed the others would keep them safe.

I'd been careful not to leave any traces at my work, and I took care that my encryption left no traces of the documents at home. Still, I knew the documents could lead back to me once I'd sent them to the journalists and they'd been decrypted. Any investigator looking at which agency employees had accessed, or could access, all these materials would come up with a list with probably only a single name on it: mine. I could provide the journalists with fewer materials, of course, but then they wouldn't be able to most effectively do their work. Ultimately, I had to contend with the fact that even one briefing slide or PDF left me vulnerable, because all digital files contain metadata, invisible tags that can be used to identify their origins.

I struggled with how to handle this metadata situation. I worried that if I didn't strip the identifying information from the documents, they might incriminate me the moment the journalists decrypted and opened them. But I also worried that by thoroughly stripping the metadata, I risked altering the files—if they were changed in any way, that could cast doubt on their authenticity. Which was more important: personal safety, or the public good? It might sound like an easy choice, but it took me quite a while to bite the bullet. I owned the risk, and left the metadata intact.

Part of what convinced me was my fear that even if I had stripped away the metadata I knew about, there could be other digital watermarks I wasn't aware of and couldn't scan for. Another part had to do with the difficulty of scrubbing single-user documents. A single-user document is a document marked with a user-specific code, so that if any publication's editorial staff decided to run it by the government, the government would know its source. Sometimes the unique identifier was hidden in the date and time-stamp coding, sometimes it involved the pattern of microdots in a graphic or logo. But it might also be embedded in something, in some way, I hadn't even thought of. This phenomenon should have discouraged me, but instead it emboldened me. The technological difficulty forced me, for the first time, to confront the prospect of discarding my lifetime practice of anonymity and coming forward to identify myself as the source. I would embrace my principles by signing my name to them and let myself be condemned.

Altogether, the documents I selected fit on a single drive, which I left out in the open on my desk at home. I knew that the materials were just as secure now as they had ever been at the office. Actually, they were more secure, thanks to multiple levels and methods of encryption. That's the incomparable beauty of the cryptological art. A little bit of math can accomplish what all the guns and barbed wire can't: a little bit of math can keep a secret.

24

Encrypt

Most people who use computers, and that includes members of the Fourth Estate, think there's a fourth basic permission besides Read, Write, and Execute, called "Delete."

Delete is everywhere on the user side of computing. It's in the hardware as a key on the keyboard, and it's in the software as an option that can be chosen from a drop-down menu. There's a certain finality that comes with choosing Delete, and a certain sense of responsibility. Sometimes a box even pops up to double-check: "Are you sure?" If the computer is second-guessing you by requiring confirmation—click "Yes"—it makes sense that Delete would be a consequential, perhaps even the ultimate decision.

Undoubtedly, that's true in the world outside of computing, where the powers of deletion have historically been vast. Even so, as countless despots have been reminded, to truly get rid of a document you can't just destroy every copy of it. You also have to destroy every memory of it, which is to say you have to destroy all the people who remember it, along with every copy of all the other documents that mention it and all the people who remember all those other documents. And then, maybe, just maybe, it's gone.

Delete functions appeared from the very start of digital computing. Engineers understood that in a world of effectively unlimited
options, some choices would inevitably turn out to be mistakes.
Users, regardless of whether or not they were really in control at
the technical level, had to *feel* in control, especially with regard
to anything that they themselves had created. If they made a file,
they should be able to unmake it at will. The ability to destroy
what they created and start over afresh was a primary function
that imparted a sense of agency to the user, despite the fact that
they might be dependent on proprietary hardware they couldn't
repair and software they couldn't modify, and bound by the rules
of third-party platforms.

Think about the reasons that you yourself press Delete. On
your personal computer, you might want to get rid of some document you screwed up, or some file you downloaded but no longer need—or some file you don't want anyone to know you ever
needed. On your email, you might delete an email from a former
lover that you don't want to remember or don't want your spouse
to find, or an RSVP for that protest you went to. On your phone,
you might delete the history of everywhere that phone has traveled, or some of the pictures, videos, and private records it automatically uploaded to the cloud. In every instance, you delete, and
the thing—the file—appears to be gone.

The truth, though, is that deletion has never existed technologically in the way that we conceive of it. Deletion is just a ruse,
a figment, a public fiction, a not-quite-noble lie that computing
tells you to reassure you and give you comfort. Although the deleted file disappears from view, it is rarely gone. In technical terms,
deletion is really just a form of the middle permission, a kind of
Write. Normally, when you press Delete for one of your files, its
data—which has been stashed deep down on a disk somewhere—
is not actually touched. Efficient modern operating systems are
not designed to go all the way into the bowels of a disk purely
for the purposes of erasure. Instead, only the computer's map of
where each file is stored—a map called the "file table"—is rewrit-

ten to say "I'm no longer using this space for anything important." What this means is that, like a neglected book in a vast library, the supposedly erased file can still be read by anyone who looks hard enough for it. If you only erase the reference to it, the book itself still remains.

This can be confirmed through experience, actually. Next time you copy a file, ask yourself why it takes so long when compared with the instantaneous act of deletion. The answer is that deletion doesn't really do anything to a file besides conceal it. Put simply, computers were not designed to correct mistakes, but to hide them—and to hide them only from those parties who don't know where to look.

THE WANING DAYS of 2012 brought grim news: the few remaining legal protections that prohibited mass surveillance by some of the most prominent members of the Five Eyes network were being dismantled. The governments of both Australia and the UK were proposing legislation for the mandatory recording of telephony and Internet metadata. This was the first time that notionally democratic governments publicly avowed the ambition to establish a sort of surveillance time machine, which would enable them to technologically rewind the events of any person's life for a period going back months and even years. These attempts definitively marked, to my mind at least, the so-called Western world's transformation from the creator and defender of the free Internet to its opponent and prospective destroyer. Though these laws were justified as public safety measures, they represented such a breathtaking intrusion into the daily lives of the innocent that they terrified—quite rightly—even the citizens of other countries who didn't think themselves affected (perhaps because their own governments chose to surveil them in secret).

These public initiatives of mass surveillance proved, once and for all, that there could be no natural alliance between technology and government. The rift between my two strangely interrelated communities, the American IC and the global online tribe of technologists, became pretty much definitive. In my earliest years in the IC, I could still reconcile the two cultures, transitioning smoothly between my spy work and my relationships with civilian Internet privacy folks—everyone from the anarchist hackers to the more sober academic Tor types who kept me current about computing research and inspired me politically. For years, I was able to fool myself that we were all, ultimately, on the same side of history: we were all trying to protect the Internet, to keep it free for speech and free of fear. But my ability to sustain that delusion was gone. Now the government, my employer, was definitively the adversary. What my technologist peers had always suspected, I'd only recently confirmed, and I couldn't tell them. Or I couldn't tell them yet.

What I could do, however, was help them out, so long as that didn't imperil my plans. This was how I found myself in Honolulu, a beautiful city in which I'd never had much interest, as one of the hosts and teachers of a CryptoParty. This was a new type of gathering invented by an international grassroots cryptological movement, at which technologists volunteered their time to teach free classes to the public on the topic of digital self-defense— essentially, showing anyone who was interested how to protect the security of their communications. In many ways, this was the same topic I taught for JCITA, so I jumped at the chance to participate.

Though this might strike you as a dangerous thing for me to have done, given the other activities I was involved with at the time, it should instead just reaffirm how much faith I had in the encryption methods I taught—the very methods that protected that drive full of IC abuses sitting back at my house, with locks that couldn't be cracked even by the NSA. I knew that no number of documents, and no amount of journalism, would ever be enough to address the threat the world was facing. People needed tools to protect themselves, and they needed to know how to use them. Given that I was also trying to provide these tools to journalists,

I was worried that my approach had become too technical. After so many sessions spent lecturing colleagues, this opportunity to simplify my treatment of the subject for a general audience would benefit me as much as anyone. Also, I honestly missed teaching: it had been a year since I'd stood at the front of a class, and the moment I was back in that position I realized I'd been teaching the right things to the wrong people all along.

When I say class, I don't mean anything like the IC's schools or briefing rooms. The CryptoParty was held in a one-room art gallery behind a furniture store and coworking space. While I was setting up the projector so I could share slides showing how easy it was to run a Tor server to help, for example, the citizens of Iran—but also the citizens of Australia, the UK, and the States— my students drifted in, a diverse crew of strangers and a few new friends I'd only met online. All in all, I'd say about twenty people showed up that December night to learn from me and my co-lecturer, Runa Sandvik, a bright young Norwegian woman from the Tor Project. (Runa would go on to work as the senior director of information security for the *New York Times*, which would sponsor her later CryptoParties.) What united our audience wasn't an interest in Tor, or even a fear of being spied on as much as a desire to re-establish a sense of control over the private spaces in their lives. There were some grandparent types who'd wandered in off the street, a local journalist covering the Hawaiian "Occupy!" movement, and a woman who'd been victimized by revenge porn. I'd also invited some of my NSA colleagues, hoping to interest them in the movement and wanting to show that I wasn't concealing my involvement from the agency. Only one of them showed up, though, and sat in the back, legs spread, arms crossed, smirking throughout.

I began my presentation by discussing the illusory nature of deletion, whose objective of total erasure could never be accomplished. The crowd understood this instantly. I went on to explain that, at best, the data they wanted no one to see couldn't be unwritten so much as overwritten: scribbled over, in a sense, with random or pseudo-random data until the original was rendered unreadable. But, I cautioned, even this approach had its drawbacks. There was always a chance that their operating system had silently hidden away a copy of the file they were hoping to delete in some temporary storage nook they weren't privy to.

That's when I pivoted to encryption.

Deletion is a dream for the surveillant and a nightmare for the surveilled, but encryption is, or should be, a reality for all. It is the only true protection against surveillance. If the whole of your storage drive is encrypted to begin with, your adversaries can't rummage through it for deleted files, or for anything else—unless they have the encryption key. If all the emails in your inbox are encrypted, Google can't read them to profile you—unless they have the encryption key. If all your communications that pass through hostile Australian or British or American or Chinese or Russian networks are encrypted, spies can't read them—unless they have the encryption key. This is the ordering principle of encryption: all power to the key holder.

Encryption works, I explained, by way of algorithms. An encryption algorithm sounds intimidating, and certainly looks intimidating when written out, but its concept is quite elementary. It's a mathematical method of reversibly transforming information—such as your emails, phone calls, photos, videos, and files—in such a way that it becomes incomprehensible to anyone who doesn't have a copy of the encryption key. You can think of a modern encryption algorithm as a magic wand that you can wave over a document to change each letter into a language that only you and those you trust can read, and the encryption key as the unique magic words that complete the incantation and put the wand to work. It doesn't matter how many people know that you used the wand, so long as you can keep your personal magic words from the people you don't trust.

Encryption algorithms are basically just sets of math problems designed to be incredibly difficult even for computers to solve. The encryption key is the one clue that allows a computer to solve the particular set of math problems being used. You push your readable data, called plaintext, into one end of an encryption algorithm, and incomprehensible gibberish, called ciphertext, comes out the other end. When somebody wants to read the ciphertext, they feed it back into the algorithm along with—crucially—the correct key, and out comes the plaintext again. While different algorithms provide different degrees of protection, the security of an encryption key is often based on its length, which indicates the level of difficulty involved in solving a specific algorithm's underlying math problem. In algorithms that correlate longer keys with better security, the improvement is exponential. If we presume that an attacker takes one day to crack a 64-bit key—which scrambles your data in one of 2^{64} possible ways (18,446,744,073,709,551,616 unique permutations)—then it would take double that amount of time, two days, to break a 65-bit key, and four days to break a 66-bit key. Breaking a 128-bit key would take 2^{64} times longer than a day, or fifty million billion years. By that time, I might even be pardoned.

In my communications with journalists, I used 4096- and 8192-bit keys. This meant that absent major innovations in computing technology or a fundamental redefining of the principles by which numbers are factored, not even all of the NSA's cryptanalysts using all of the world's computing power put together would be able to get into my drive. For this reason, encryption is the single best hope for fighting surveillance of any kind. If all of our data, including our communications, were enciphered in this fashion, from end to end (from the sender end to the recipient end), then no government—no entity conceivable under our current knowledge of physics, for that matter—would be able to understand them. A government could still intercept and collect the signals, but it would be intercepting and collecting pure noise. Encrypting our communications would essentially delete them from the memories of every entity we deal with. It would effectively withdraw permission from those to whom it was never granted to begin with.

Any government hoping to access encrypted communications has only two options: it can either go after the keymasters or go after the keys. For the former, they can pressure device manufacturers into intentionally selling products that perform faulty encryption, or mislead international standards organizations into accepting flawed encryption algorithms that contain secret access points known as "back doors." For the latter, they can launch targeted attacks against the endpoints of the communications, the hardware and software that perform the process of encryption. Often, that means exploiting a vulnerability that they weren't responsible for creating but merely found, and using it to hack you and steal your keys—a technique pioneered by criminals but today embraced by major state powers, even though it means knowingly preserving devastating holes in the cybersecurity of critical international infrastructure.

The best means we have for keeping our keys safe is called "zero knowledge," a method that ensures that any data you try to store externally—say, for instance, on a company's cloud platform—is encrypted by an algorithm running on your device before it is uploaded, and the key is never shared. In the zero knowledge scheme, the keys are in the users' hands—and only in the users' hands. No company, no agency, no enemy can touch them.

My key to the NSA's secrets went beyond zero knowledge: it was a zero-knowledge key consisting of multiple zero-knowledge keys.

Imagine it like this: Let's say that at the conclusion of my CryptoParty lecture, I stood by the exit as each of the twenty audience members shuffled out. Now, imagine that as each of them passed through the door and into the Honolulu night, I whispered a word into their ear—a single word that no one else could hear, and that they were only allowed to repeat if they were all together, once again, in the same room. Only by bringing back all twenty of these folks and having them repeat their words in the same order in which I'd originally distributed them could anyone reassemble the complete twenty-word incantation. If just one person forgot their word, or if the order of recitation was in any way different from the order of distribution, no spell would be cast, no magic would happen.

My keys to the drive containing the disclosures resembled this arrangement, with a twist: while I distributed most of the pieces of the incantation, I retained one for myself. Pieces of my magic spell were hidden everywhere, but if I destroyed just the single lone piece that I kept on my person, I would destroy all access to the NSA's secrets forever.

25

The Boy

It's only in hindsight that I'm able to appreciate just how high my star had risen. I'd gone from being the student who couldn't speak in class to being the teacher of the language of a new age, from the child of modest, middle-class Beltway parents to the man living the island life and making so much money that it had lost its meaning. In just the seven short years of my career, I'd climbed from maintaining local servers to crafting and implementing globally deployed systems—from graveyard-shift security guard to key master of the puzzle palace.

But there's always a danger in letting even the most qualified person rise too far, too fast, before they've had enough time to get cynical and abandon their idealism. I occupied one of the most unexpectedly omniscient positions in the Intelligence Community—toward the bottom rung of the managerial ladder, but high atop heaven in terms of access. And while this gave me the phenomenal, and frankly undeserved, ability to observe the IC in its grim fullness, it also left me more curious than ever about the one fact I was still finding elusive: the absolute limit of who the agency could turn its gaze against. It was a limit set less in policy or law than in the ruthless, unyielding capabilities of what I now knew to be a world-spanning machine. Was there anyone this machine could not surveil? Was there anywhere this machine could not go?

The only way to discover the answer was to descend, abandoning my panoptic perch for the narrow vision of an operational role. The NSA employees with the freest access to the rawest forms of intelligence were those who sat in the operator's chair and typed into their computers the names of the individuals who'd fallen under suspicion, foreigners and US citizens alike. For one reason or another, or for no reason at all, these individuals had become targets of the agency's closest scrutiny, with the NSA interested in finding out everything about them and their communications. My ultimate destination, I knew, was the exact point of this interface—the exact point where the state cast its eye on the human and the human remained unaware.

The program that enabled this access was called XKEYSCORE, which is perhaps best understood as a search engine that lets an analyst search through all the records of your life. Imagine a kind of Google that instead of showing pages from the public Internet returns results from your private email, your private chats, your private files, everything. Though I'd read enough about the program to understand how it worked, I hadn't yet used it, and I realized I ought to know more about it. By pursuing XKEYSCORE, I was looking for a personal confirmation of the depths of the NSA's surveillance intrusions—the kind of confirmation you don't get from documents but only from direct experience.

One of the few offices in Hawaii with truly unfettered access to XKEYSCORE was the National Threat Operations Center. NTOC worked out of the sparkling but soulless new open-plan office the NSA had formally named the Rochefort Building, after Joseph Rochefort, a legendary World War II–era Naval cryptanalyst who broke Japanese codes. Most employees had taken to calling it the Roach Fort, or simply "the Roach." At the time I applied for a job there, parts of the Roach were still under construction, and I was immediately reminded of my first cleared job, with CASL: it was my fate to begin and end my IC career in unfinished buildings.

In addition to housing almost all of the agency's Hawaii-based translators and analysts, the Roach also accommodated the local branch of the Tailored Access Operations (TAO) division. This was the NSA unit responsible for remotely hacking into the computers of people whom analysts had selected as targets—the agency's equivalent of the old burglary teams that once snuck into enemies' homes to plant bugs and find compromising material. NTOC's main job, by contrast, was to monitor and frustrate the activity of the TAO's foreign equivalents. As luck would have it, NTOC had a position open through a contractor job at Booz Allen Hamilton, a job they euphemistically described as "infrastructure analyst." The role involved using the complete spectrum of the NSA's mass surveillance tools, including XKEYSCORE, to monitor activity on the "infrastructure" of interest, the Internet.

Though I'd be making slightly more money at Booz, around $120,000 a year, I considered it a demotion—the first of many as I began my final descent, jettisoning my accesses, my clearances, and my agency privileges. I was an engineer who was becoming an analyst who would ultimately become an exile, a target of the very technologies I'd once controlled. From that perspective, this particular fall in prestige seemed pretty minor. From that perspective, everything seemed pretty minor, as the arc of my life bent back toward earth, accelerating toward the point of impact that would end my career, my relationship, my freedom, and possibly my life.

I'D DECIDED TO bring my archives out of the country and pass them to the journalists I'd contacted, but before I could even begin to contemplate the logistics of that act I had to go shake some hands. I had to fly east to DC and spend a few weeks meeting and greeting my new bosses and colleagues, who had high hopes for how they might apply my keen understanding of online anonymization to unmask their more clever targets. This was what brought me back home to the Beltway for the very last time, and back to the site of my first encounter with an institution that had lost control: Fort Meade. This time I was arriving as an insider.

The day that marked my coming of age, just over ten tumultuous years earlier, had profoundly changed not just the people who worked at NSA headquarters but the place itself. I first noticed this fact when I got stopped in my rental car trying to turn off Canine Road into one of the agency's parking lots, which in my memory still howled with panic, ringtones, car horns, and sirens. Since 9/11, all the roads that led to NSA headquarters had been permanently closed to anyone who didn't possess one of the special IC badges now hanging around my neck.

Whenever I wasn't glad-handing NTOC leadership at headquarters, I spent my time learning everything I could—"hot-desking" with analysts who worked different programs and different types of targets, so as to be able to teach my fellow team members back in Hawaii the newest ways the agency's tools might be used. That, at least, was the official explanation of my curiosity, which as always exceeded the requirements and earned the gratitude of the technologically inclined. They, in turn, were as eager as ever to demonstrate the power of the machinery they'd developed, without expressing a single qualm about how that power was applied. While at headquarters, I was also put through a series of tests on the proper use of the system, which were more like regulatory compliance exercises or procedural shields than meaningful instruction. The other analysts told me that since I could take these tests as many times as I had to, I shouldn't bother learning the rules: "Just click the boxes until you pass."

The NSA described XKEYSCORE, in the documents I'd later pass on to journalists, as its "widest-ranging" tool, used to search "nearly everything a user does on the Internet." The technical specs I studied went into more detail as to how exactly this was accomplished—by "packetizing" and "sessionizing," or cutting up the data of a user's online sessions into manageable packets for analysis—but nothing could prepare me for seeing it in action.

It was, simply put, the closest thing to science fiction I've ever seen in science fact: an interface that allows you to type in pretty much anyone's address, telephone number, or IP address, and then basically go through the recent history of their online activity. In some cases you could even play back recordings of their online sessions, so that the screen you'd be looking at was their screen, whatever was on their desktop. You could read their emails, their browser history, their search history, their social media postings, everything. You could set up notifications that would pop up when some person or some device you were interested in became active on the Internet for the day. And you could look through the packets of Internet data to see a person's search queries appear letter by letter, since so many sites transmitted each character as it was typed. It was like watching an autocomplete, as letters and words flashed across the screen. But the intelligence behind that typing wasn't artificial but human: this was a humancomplete.

My weeks at Fort Meade, and the short stint I put in at Booz back in Hawaii, were the only times I saw, firsthand, the abuses actually being committed that I'd previously read about in internal documentation. Seeing them made me realize how insulated my position at the systems level had been from the ground zero of immediate damage. I could only imagine the level of insulation of the agency's directorship or, for that matter, of the US president.

I didn't type the names of the agency director or the president into XKEYSCORE, but after enough time with the system I realized I could have. Everyone's communications were in the system—everyone's. I was initially fearful that if I searched those in the uppermost echelons of state, I'd be caught and fired, or worse. But it was surpassingly simple to disguise a query regarding even the most prominent figure by encoding my search terms in a machine format that looked like gibberish to humans but would be perfectly understandable to XKEYSCORE. If any of the auditors who were responsible for reviewing the searches ever bothered to look more closely, they would see only a snippet of obfuscated code, while I would be able to scroll through the most personal activities of a Supreme Court justice or a congressperson.

As far as I could tell, none of my new colleagues intended to abuse their powers so grandly, although if they had it's not like they'd ever mention it. Anyway, when analysts thought about abusing the system, they were far less interested in what it could do for them professionally than in what it could do for them personally. This led to the practice known as LOVEINT, a gross joke on HUMINT and SIGINT and a travesty of intelligence, in which analysts used the agency's programs to surveil their current and former lovers along with objects of more casual affection—reading their emails, listening in on their phone calls, and stalking them online. NSA employees knew that only the dumbest analysts were ever caught red-handed, and though the law stated that anyone engaging in any type of surveillance for personal use could be locked up for at least a decade, no one in the agency's history had been sentenced to even a day in prison for the crime. Analysts understood that the government would never publicly prosecute them, because you can't exactly convict someone of abusing your secret system of mass surveillance if you refuse to admit the existence of the system itself. The obvious costs of such a policy became apparent to me as I sat along the back wall of vault V22 at NSA headquarters with two of the more talented infrastructure analysts, whose work-space was decorated with a seven-foot-tall picture of *Star Wars*' famous wookie, Chewbacca. I realized, as one of them was explaining to me the details of his targets' security routines, that intercepted nudes were a kind of informal office currency, because his buddy kept spinning in his chair to interrupt us with a smile, saying, "Check *her* out," to which my instructor would invariably reply "Bonus!" or "Nice!" The unspoken transactional rule seemed to be that if you found a naked photo or video of an attractive target—or someone in communication with a target—you had to show the rest of the boys, at least as long as there weren't any women around. That was how you knew you could trust each other: you had shared in one another's crimes.

One thing you come to understand very quickly while using XKEYSCORE is that nearly everyone in the world who's online has at least two things in common: they have all watched porn at one time or another, and they all store photos and videos of their family. This was true for virtually everyone of every gender, ethnicity, race, and age—from the meanest terrorist to the nicest senior citizen, who might be the meanest terrorist's grandparent, or parent, or cousin.

It's the family stuff that got to me the most. I remember this one child in particular, a little boy in Indonesia. Technically, I shouldn't have been interested in this little boy, but I was, because my employers were interested in his father. I had been reading through the shared targeting folders of a "persona" analyst, meaning someone who typically spent most of their day sifting through artifacts like chat logs and Gmail inboxes and Facebook messages, rather than the more obscure and difficult, typically hacker-generated traffic of the infrastructure analysts.

The boy's father, like my own father, was an engineer—but unlike my father, this guy wasn't government- or military-affiliated. He was just a regular academic who'd been caught up in a surveillance dragnet. I can't even remember how or why he'd come to the agency's attention, beyond sending a job application to a research university in Iran. The grounds for suspicion were often poorly documented, if they were documented at all, and the connections could be incredibly tenuous—"believed to be potentially associated with" and then the name of some international organization that could be anything from a telecommunications standards body to UNICEF to something you might actually agree is menacing.

Selections from the man's communications had been sieved out of the stream of Internet traffic and assembled into folders—here was the fatal copy of the résumé sent to the suspect university;

here were his texts; here was his Web browser history; here was the last week or so of his correspondence both sent and received, tagged to IP addresses. Here were the coordinates of a "geo-fence" the analyst had placed around him to track whether he strayed too far from home, or perhaps traveled to the university for his interview.

Then there were his pictures, and a video. He was sitting in front of his computer, as I was sitting in front of mine. Except that in his lap he had a toddler, a boy in a diaper.

The father was trying to read something, but the kid kept shifting around, smacking the keys and giggling. The computer's internal mic picked up his giggling and there I was, listening to it on my headphones. The father held the boy tighter, and the boy straightened up, and, with his dark crescent eyes, looked directly into the computer's camera—I couldn't escape the feeling that he was looking directly at me. Suddenly I realized that I'd been holding my breath. I shut the session, got up from the computer, and left the office for the bathroom in the hall, head down, headphones still on with the cord trailing.

Everything about that kid, everything about his father, reminded me of my own father, whom I met for dinner one evening during my stint at Fort Meade. I hadn't seen him in a while, but there in the midst of dinner, over bites of Caesar salad and a pink lemonade, I had the thought: *I'll never see my family again.* My eyes were dry—I was exerting as much control as I could—but inside, I was devastated. I knew that if I told him what I was about to do, he would've called the cops. Or else he would've called me crazy and had me committed to a mental hospital. He would've done anything he thought he had to do to prevent me from making the gravest of mistakes.

I could only hope that his hurt would in time be healed by pride.

Back in Hawaii between March and May 2013, a sense of finality suffused nearly every experience for me, and though the experiences themselves might seem trivial, they eased my path. It was far less painful to think that this was the last time I'd ever stop at the curry place in Mililani or drop by the art-gallery hacker space in Honolulu or just sit on the roof of my car and scan the nighttime sky for falling stars than to think that I only had another month left with Lindsay, or another week left of sleeping next to her and waking up next to her and yet trying to keep my distance from her, for fear of breaking down.

The preparations I was making were those of a man about to die. I emptied my bank accounts, putting cash into an old steel ammo box for Lindsay to find so that the government couldn't seize it. I went around the house doing oft-procrastinated chores, like fixing windows and changing lightbulbs. I erased and encrypted my old computers, reducing them to the silent husks of better times. In sum, I was putting my affairs in order to try to make everything easier for Lindsay, or just for my conscience, which periodically would switch allegiance from a world that hadn't earned it to the woman who had and the family I loved.

Everything was imbued with this sense of an ending, and yet there were moments when it seemed that no end was in sight and that the plan I'd developed was collapsing. It was difficult to get the journalists to commit to a meeting, mostly because I couldn't tell them who they were meeting with, or even, for a while at least, where and when it was happening. I had to reckon with the prospect of them never showing up, or of them showing up but then dropping out. Ultimately I decided that if either of those happened, I'd just abandon the plan and return to work and to Lindsay as if everything was normal, to wait for my next chance.

In my wardrives back and forth from Kunia—a twenty-minute ride that could become a two-hour Wi-Fi scavenger hunt—I'd been researching various countries, trying to find a location for my meeting with the journalists. It felt like I was picking out my prison, or rather my grave. All of the Five Eyes countries were obviously off-limits. In fact, all of Europe was out, because its countries couldn't be counted upon to uphold international law against the extradition of those charged with political crimes in the face of what was sure to be significant American pressure. Africa and Latin America were no-go zones too—the United States had a history of acting there with impunity. Russia was out because it was Russia, and China was China: both were totally out of bounds. The US government wouldn't have to do anything to discredit me other than point at the map. The optics would only be worse in the Middle East. It sometimes seemed as if the most challenging hack of my life wasn't going to be plundering the NSA but rather trying to find a meeting venue independent enough to hold off the White House and free enough not to interfere with my activities.

The process of elimination left me with Hong Kong. In geopolitical terms, it was the closest I could get to no-man's-land, but with a vibrant media and protest culture, not to mention largely unfiltered Internet. It was an oddity, a reasonably liberal world city whose nominal autonomy would distance me from China and restrain Beijing's ability to take public action against me or the journalists—at least immediately—but whose de facto existence in Beijing's sphere of influence would reduce the possibility of unilateral US intervention. In a situation with no promise of safety, it was enough to have the guarantee of time. Chances were that things weren't going to end well for me, anyway: the best I could hope for was getting the disclosures out before I was caught.

The last morning I woke up with Lindsay, she was leaving on a camping trip to Kauai—a brief getaway with friends that I'd encouraged. We lay in bed and I held her too tightly, and when she asked with sleepy bewilderment why I was suddenly being so affectionate, I apologized. I told her how sorry I was for how busy I'd been, and that I was going to miss her—she was the best person I'd ever met in my life. She smiled, pecked me on the cheek, and then got up to pack.

The moment she was out the door, I started crying, for the first time in years. I felt guilty about everything except what my government would accuse me of, and especially guilty about my tears, because I knew that my pain would be nothing compared to the pain I'd cause to the woman I loved, or to the hurt and confusion I'd cause my family.

At least I had the benefit of knowing what was coming. Lindsay would return from her camping trip to find me gone, ostensibly on a work assignment, and my mother basically waiting on our doorstep. I'd invited my mother to visit, in a move so uncharacteristic that she must have expected another type of surprise—like an announcement that Lindsay and I were engaged. I felt horrible about the false pretenses and winced at the thought of her disappointment, but I kept telling myself I was justified. My mother would take care of Lindsay and Lindsay would take care of her. Each would need the other's strength to weather the coming storm.

The day after Lindsay left, I took an emergency medical leave of absence from work, citing epilepsy, and packed scant luggage and four laptops: secure communications, normal communications, a decoy, and an "airgap" (a computer that had never gone and would never go online). I left my smartphone on the kitchen counter alongside a notepad on which I scribbled in pen: *Got called away for work. I love you.* I signed it with my call-letter nickname, Echo. Then I went to the airport and bought a ticket in cash for the next flight to Tokyo. In Tokyo, I bought another ticket in cash, and on May 20 arrived in Hong Kong, the city where the world first met me.

26

Hong Kong

The deep psychological appeal of games, which are really just a series of increasingly difficult challenges, is the belief that they can be won. Nowhere is this more clear to me than in the case of the Rubik's Cube, which satisfies a universal fantasy: that if you just work hard enough and twist yourself through all of the possibilities, everything in the world that appears scrambled and incoherent will finally click into position and become perfectly aligned; that human ingenuity is enough to transform the most broken and chaotic system into something logical and orderly where every face of three-dimensional space shines with perfect uniformity.

I'd had a plan—I'd had multiple plans—in which a single mistake would have meant getting caught, and yet I hadn't been: I'd made it out of the NSA, I'd made it out of the country. I had beaten the game. By every standard I could imagine, the hard part was over. But my imagination hadn't been good enough, because the journalists I'd asked to come meet me weren't showing up. They kept postponing, giving excuses, apologizing.

I knew that Laura Poitras—to whom I'd already sent a few documents and the promise of many more—was ready to fly anywhere from New York City at a moment's notice, but she wasn't going to come alone. She was busy trying to get Glenn Greenwald to commit, trying to get him to buy a new laptop that he wouldn't put online. Trying to get him to install encryption programs so we could better communicate. And there I was, in Hong Kong, watching the clock tick away the hours, watching the calendar tick off the days, beseeching, begging: *please come before the NSA realizes I've been gone from work too long.* It was tough to think about all the lengths I'd gone to only to face the prospect of being left in Hong Kong high and dry. I tried to work up some sympathy for these journalists who seemed too busy or too nervous to lock down their travel plans, but then I'd recall just how little of the material for which I was risking everything would actually make it to the public if the police arrived first. I thought about my family and Lindsay and how foolish it was to have put my life in the hands of people who didn't even know my name.

I barricaded myself in my room at the Mira Hotel, which I chose because of its central location in a crowded shopping and business district. I put the "Privacy Please—Do Not Disturb" sign on the door handle to keep housekeeping out. For ten days, I didn't leave the room for fear of giving a foreign spy the chance to sneak in and bug the place. With the stakes so high, the only move I had was to wait. I converted the room into a poor man's operations center, the invisible heart of the network of encrypted Internet tunnels from which I'd send increasingly shrill pleas to the absent emissaries of our free press. Then I'd stand at the window hoping for a reply, looking out onto the beautiful park I'd never visit. By the time Laura and Glenn finally arrived, I'd eaten every item on the room service menu.

That isn't to say that I just sat around during that week and a half writing wheedling messages. I also tried to organize the last briefing I'd ever give—going through the archive, figuring out how best to explain its contents to the journalists in the surely limited time we'd have together. It was an interesting problem: how to most cogently express to nontechnical people who were almost certainly inclined to be skeptical of me the fact that the US government was surveilling the world and the methods by which it was doing so. I put together dictionaries of terms of art like "metadata" and "communications bearer." I put together glossaries of acronyms and abbreviations: CCE, CSS, DNI, NOFORN. I made the decision to explain not through technologies, or systems, but through surveillance programs—in essence, through stories—in an attempt to speak their language. But I couldn't decide which stories to give them first, and I kept shuffling them around, trying to put the worst crimes in the best order.

I had to find a way to help at least Laura and Glenn understand something in the span of a few days that it had taken me years to puzzle out. Then there was another thing: I had to help them understand who I was and why I'd decided to do this.

AT LONG LAST, Glenn and Laura showed up in Hong Kong on June 2. When they came to meet me at the Mira, I think I disappointed them, at least initially. They even told me as much, or Glenn did: He'd been expecting someone older, some chain-smoking, tipsy depressive with terminal cancer and a guilty conscience. He didn't understand how a person as young as I was—he kept asking me my age—not only had access to such sensitive documents, but was also so willing to throw his life away. For my part, I didn't know how they could have expected some graybeard, given my instructions to them about how to meet: Go to a certain quiet alcove by the hotel restaurant, furnished with an alligator-skin-looking pleather couch, and wait around for a guy holding a Rubik's Cube. The funny thing was that I'd originally been wary of using that bit of tradecraft, but the cube was the only thing I'd brought with me that was likely to be unique and identifiable from a distance. It also helped me hide the stress of waiting for what I feared might be the surprise of handcuffs.

That stress would reach its visible peak just ten or so minutes later, when I'd brought Laura and Glenn up to my room—#1014, on the tenth floor. Glenn had barely had the chance to stow his smartphone in my minibar fridge at my request when Laura started rearranging and adjusting the lights in the room. Then she unpacked her digital video camera. Though we'd agreed, over encrypted email, that she could film our encounter, I wasn't ready for the reality.

Nothing could have prepared me for the moment when she pointed her camera at me, sprawled out on my unmade bed in a cramped, messy room that I hadn't left for the past ten days. I think everybody has had this kind of experience: the more conscious you are of being recorded, the more self-conscious you become. Merely the awareness that there is, or might be, somebody pressing Record on their smartphone and pointing it at you can cause awkwardness, even if that somebody is a friend. Though today nearly all of my interactions take place via camera, I'm still not sure which experience I find more alienating: seeing myself on film or being filmed. I try to avoid the former, but avoiding the latter is now difficult for everyone.

In a situation that was already high-intensity, I stiffened. The red light of Laura's camera, like a sniper's sight, kept reminding me that at any moment the door might be smashed in and I'd be dragged off forever. And whenever I wasn't having that thought, I kept thinking about how this footage was going to look when it was played back in court. I realized there were so many things I should have done, like putting on nicer clothes and shaving. Room-service plates and trash had accumulated throughout the room. There were noodle containers and half-eaten burgers, piles of dirty laundry and damp towels on the floor.

It was a surreal dynamic. Not only had I never met any filmmakers before being filmed by one, I had never met any journalists before serving as their source. The first time I ever spoke aloud to anyone about the US government's system of mass surveillance, I was speaking to everyone in the world with an Internet connection. In the end, though, regardless of how rumpled I looked and stilted I sounded, Laura's filming was indispensable, because it showed the world exactly what happened in that hotel room in a way that newsprint never could. The footage she shot over the course of our days together in Hong Kong can't be distorted. Its existence is a tribute not just to her professionalism as a documentarian but to her foresight.

I spent the week between June 3 and June 9 cloistered in that room with Glenn and his colleague from the *Guardian*, Ewen MacAskill, who joined us a bit later that first day. We talked and talked, going through the NSA's programs, while Laura hovered and filmed. In contrast to the frenetic days, the nights were empty and desolate. Glenn and Ewen would retreat to their own hotel, the nearby W, to write up their findings into articles. Laura would disappear to edit her footage and do her own reporting with Bart Gellman of the *Washington Post*, who never made it to Hong Kong but worked remotely with the documents he received from her.

I'd sleep, or try to—or else I'd put on the TV, find an English-language channel like the BBC or CNN, and watch the international reaction. On June 5, the *Guardian* broke Glenn's first story, the FISA court order that authorized the NSA to collect information from the American telecom Verizon about every phone call it handled. On June 6, it ran Glenn's PRISM story, pretty much simultaneously with a similar account in the *Washington Post* by Laura and Bart. I knew, and I think we all knew, that the more pieces came out the more likely it was that I'd be identified, particularly because my office had begun emailing me asking for status updates and I wasn't answering. But though Glenn and Ewen and Laura were unfailingly sympathetic to my ticking time-bomb situation, they never let their desire to serve the truth be tempered by that knowledge. And following their example, neither did I.

Journalism, like documentary film, can only reveal so much. It's interesting to think about what a medium is forced to omit, both by convention and technology. In Glenn's prose, especially in the *Guardian*, you got a laser-focused statement of fact, stripped of the dogged passion that defines his personality. Ewen's prose more fully reflected his character: sincere, gracious, patient, and fair. Meanwhile, Laura, who saw all but was rarely seen, had an omniscient reserve and a sardonic wit—half master spy, half master artist.

As the revelations ran wall to wall on every TV channel and website, it became clear that the US government had thrown the whole of its machinery into identifying the source. It was also clear that when they did, they would use the face they found—my face—to evade accountability: instead of addressing the revelations, they'd impugn the credibility and motives of "the leaker." Given the stakes, I had to seize the initiative before it was too late. If I didn't explain my actions and intentions, the government would, in a way that would swing the focus away from its misdeeds.

The only hope I had of fighting back was to come forward first and identify myself. I'd give the media just enough personal detail to satisfy their mounting curiosity, with a clear statement that what mattered wasn't me, but rather the subversion of American democracy. Then I'd vanish just as quickly as I'd appeared. That, at least, was the plan.

Ewen and I decided that he'd write a story about my IC career and Laura suggested filming a video statement to appear alongside it in the *Guardian*. In it, I'd claim direct and sole responsibility as the source behind the reporting on global mass surveillance. But even though Laura had been filming all week (a lot of that footage would make it into her feature documentary, *Citizenfour*), we just didn't have the time for her to go through everything she'd shot in search of snippets of me speaking coherently and making eye contact. What she proposed, instead, was my first recorded statement, which she started filming right there and then—the one that begins, "Uh, my name is Ed Snowden. I'm, ah, twenty-nine years old."

Hello, world.

WHILE I'VE NEVER once regretted tugging aside the curtain and revealing my identity, I do wish I had done it with better diction and a better plan in mind for what was next. In truth, I had no plan at all. I hadn't given much thought to answering the question of what to do once the game was over, mainly because a winning conclusion was always so unlikely. All I'd cared about was getting the facts out into the world: I figured that by putting the documents into the public record, I was essentially putting myself at the public's mercy. No exit strategy could be the only exit strategy, because any next step I might have premeditated taking would have run the risk of undermining the disclosures.

If I'd made preexisting arrangements to fly to a specific country and seek asylum, for example, I would've been called a foreign agent of that country. Meanwhile, if I returned to my own country, the best I could hope for was to be arrested upon landing and charged under the Espionage Act. That would've entitled me to a show trial deprived of any meaningful defense, a sham in which all discussion of the most important facts would be forbidden.

The major impediment to justice was a major flaw in the law, a purposeful flaw created by the government. Someone in my position would not even be allowed to argue in court that the disclosures I made to journalists were civically beneficial. Even now, years after the fact, I would not be allowed to argue that the reporting based on my disclosures had caused Congress to change certain laws regarding surveillance, or convinced the courts to strike down a certain mass surveillance program as illegal, or influenced the attorney general and the president of the United States to admit that the debate over mass surveillance was a crucial one for the public to have, one that would ultimately strengthen the country. All these claims would be deemed not just irrelevant but inadmissible in the kind of proceedings that I would face were I to head home. The only thing my government would have to prove in court is that I disclosed classified information to journalists, a fact that is not in dispute. This is why anyone who says I have to come back to the States for trial is essentially saying I have to come back to the States for sentencing, and the sentence would, now as then, surely be a cruel one. The penalty for disclosing top secret documents, whether to foreign spies or domestic journalists, is up to ten years per document.

From the moment that Laura's video of me was posted on the *Guardian* website on June 9, I was marked. There was a target on my back. I knew that the institutions I'd shamed would not relent until my head was bagged and my limbs were shackled. And until then—and perhaps even after then—they would harass my loved ones and disparage my character, prying into every aspect of my life and career, seeking information (or opportunities for disinformation) with which to smear me. I was familiar enough with how this process went, both from having read classified examples of it within the IC and from having studied the cases of other whistleblowers and leakers. I knew the stories of heroes like Daniel Ellsberg and Anthony Russo, and more recent opponents of government secrecy like Thomas Tamm, an attorney with the Justice Department's Office of Intelligence Policy and Review who served as a source for much of the warrantless wiretapping reporting of the mid-2000s. There were also Drake, Binney, Wiebe, and Loomis, the digital-age successors to Perry Fellwock, who back in 1971 had revealed the existence of the then-unacknowledged NSA in the press, which caused the Senate's Church Committee (the forerunner of today's Senate Select Committee on Intelligence) to try to ensure that the agency's brief was limited to the gathering of foreign rather than domestic signals intelligence. And then there was US Army Private Chelsea Manning, who for the crime of exposing America's war crimes was court-martialed and sentenced to thirty-five years in prison, of which she served seven, her sentence commuted only after an international outcry arose over the treatment she received during solitary confinement.

All of these people, whether they faced prison or not, encountered some sort of backlash, most often severe and derived from the very abuse that I'd just helped expose: surveillance. If ever they'd expressed anger in a private communication, they were "disgruntled." If they'd ever visited a psychiatrist or a psychologist, or just checked out books on related subjects from a library, they were "mentally unsound." If they'd been drunk even once, they were said to be alcoholics. If they'd had even one extramarital affair, they were said to be sexual deviants. Not a few lost their homes and were bankrupted. It's easier for an institution to tarnish a reputation than to substantively engage with principled dissent—for the IC, it's just a matter of consulting the files, amplifying the available evidence, and, where no evidence exists, simply fabricating it.

As sure as I was of my government's indignation, I was just as sure of the support of my family, and of Lindsay, who I was certain would understand—perhaps not forgive, but understand—the context of my recent behavior. I took comfort from recalling their love: it helped me cope with the fact that there was nothing left for me to do, no further plans in play. I could only extend the belief I had in my family and Lindsay into a perhaps idealistic belief in my fellow citizens, a hope that once they'd been made aware of the full scope of American mass surveillance they'd mobilize and call for justice. They'd be empowered to seek that justice for themselves, and, in the process, my own destiny would be decided. This was the ultimate leap of faith, in a way: I could hardly trust anyone, so I had to trust everyone.

WITHIN HOURS AFTER my *Guardian* video ran, one of Glenn's regular readers in Hong Kong contacted him and offered to put me in touch with Robert Tibbo and Jonathan Man, two local attorneys who then volunteered to take on my case. These were the men who helped get me out of the Mira when the press finally located me and besieged the hotel. As a diversion, Glenn went out the front lobby door, where he was immediately thronged by the cameras and mics. Meanwhile, I was bundled out of one of the Mira's myriad other exits, which connected via a skybridge to a mall.

I like Robert—to have been his client is to be his friend for life.

He's an idealist and a crusader, a tireless champion of lost causes. Even more impressive than his lawyering, however, was his creativity in finding safe houses. While journalists were scouring every five-star hotel in Hong Kong, he took me to one of the poorest neighborhoods of the city and introduced me to some of his other clients, a few of the nearly twelve thousand forgotten refugees in Hong Kong—under Chinese pressure, the city has maintained a dismal 1 percent approval rate for permanent residency status. I wouldn't usually name them, but since they have bravely identified themselves to the press, I will: Vanessa Mae Bondalian Rodel from the Philippines, and Ajith Pushpakumara, Supun Thilina Kellapatha, and Nadeeka Dilrukshi Nonis, all from Sri Lanka.

These unfailingly kind and generous people came through with charitable grace. The solidarity they showed me was not political. It was human, and I will be forever in their debt. They didn't care who I was, or what dangers they might face by helping me, only that there was a person in need. They knew all too well what it meant to be forced into a mad escape from mortal threat, having survived ordeals far in excess of anything I'd dealt with and hopefully ever will: torture by the military, rape, and sexual abuse. They let an exhausted stranger into their homes—and when they saw my face on TV, they didn't falter. Instead, they smiled, and took the opportunity to reassure me of their hospitality.

Though their resources were limited—Supun, Nadeeka, Vanessa, and two little girls lived in a crumbling, cramped apartment smaller than my room at the Mira—they shared everything they had with me, and they shared it unstintingly, refusing my offers to reimburse them for the cost of taking me in so vociferously that I had to hide money in the room to get them to accept it. They fed me, they let me bathe, they let me sleep, and they protected me. I will never be able to explain what it meant to be given so much by those with so little, to be accepted by them without judgment as I perched in corners like a stray street cat, skimming the Wi-Fi of distant hotels with a special antenna that delighted the children.

Their welcome and friendship was a gift, for the world to even have such people is a gift, and so it pains me that, all these years later, the cases of Ajith, Supun, Nadeeka, and Nadeeka's daughter are still pending. The admiration I feel for these folks is matched only by the resentment I feel toward the bureaucrats in Hong Kong, who continue to deny them the basic dignity of asylum. If folks as fundamentally decent and selfless as these aren't deemed worthy of the protection of the state, it's because the state itself is unworthy. What gives me hope, however, is that just as this book was going to press, Vanessa and her daughter received asylum in Canada. I look forward to the day when I can visit all of my old Hong Kong friends in their new homes, wherever those may be, and we can make happier memories together in freedom.

On June 14, the US government charged me under the Espionage Act in a sealed complaint, and on June 21 they formally requested my extradition. I knew it was time to go. It was also my thirtieth birthday.

Just as the US State Department sent its request, my lawyers received a reply to my appeal for assistance from the UN High Commissioner on Refugees: there was nothing that could be done for me. The Hong Kong government, under Chinese pressure or not, resisted any UN effort at affording me international protection on its territory, and furthermore asserted that it would first have to consider the claims of my country of citizenship. In other words, Hong Kong was telling me to go home and deal with the UN from prison. I wasn't just on my own—I was unwelcome. If I was going to leave freely, I had to leave now. I wiped my four laptops completely clean and destroyed the cryptographic key, which meant that I could no longer access any of the documents even if compelled. Then I packed the few clothes I had and headed out. There was no safety to be found in the "fragrant harbor."

27

Moscow

For a coastal country at the northwestern edge of South America, half a globe away from Hong Kong, Ecuador is in the middle of everything: not for nothing does its name translate to "The Republic of the Equator." Most of my fellow North Americans would correctly say that it's a small country, and some might even know enough to call it historically oppressed. But they are ignorant if they think it's a backwater. When Rafael Correa became president in 2007, as part of a tide of so-called democratic socialist leaders who swept elections in the late 1990s and early 2000s in Bolivia, Argentina, Brazil, Paraguay, and Venezuela, he initiated a spate of policies intended to oppose and reverse the effects of US imperialism in the region. One of these measures, reflecting President Correa's previous career as an economist, was an announcement that Ecuador would consider its national debt illegitimate—technically, it would be classified as "odious debt," which is national debt incurred by a despotic regime or through despotic imperialist trade policies. Repayment of odious debt is not enforceable. With this announcement, Correa freed his people from decades of economic serfdom, though he made not a few enemies among the class of financiers who direct much of US foreign policy.

Ecuador, at least in 2013, had a hard-earned belief in the institution of political asylum. Most famously, the Ecuadorean embassy in London had become, under Correa, the safe haven and redoubt of WikiLeaks' Julian Assange. I had no desire to live in an embassy, perhaps because I'd already worked in one. Still, my Hong Kong lawyers agreed that, given the circumstances, Ecuador seemed to be the most likely country to defend my right to political asylum and the least likely to be cowed by the ire of the hegemon that ruled its hemisphere. My growing but ad hoc team of lawyers, journalists, technologists, and activists concurred. My hope was to make it to Ecuador proper.

With my government having decided to charge me under the Espionage Act, I stood accused of a political crime, meaning a crime whose victim is the state itself rather than a person. Under international humanitarian law, those accused in this way are generally exempt from extradition, because the charge of political criminality is more often than not an authoritarian attempt at quashing legitimate dissent. In theory, this means that government whistleblowers should be protected against extradition almost everywhere. In practice, of course, this is rarely the case, especially when the government that perceives itself wronged is America's—which claims to foster democracy abroad yet secretly maintains fleets of privately contracted aircraft dedicated to that form of unlawful extradition known as rendition, or, as everyone else calls it, kidnapping.

The team supporting me had reached out to officials everywhere from Iceland to India, asking if they would respect the prohibition against extradition of those accused of political crimes and commit to noninterference in my potential travel. It soon became evident that even the most advanced democracies were afraid of incurring the wrath of the US government. They were happy to privately express their sympathies, but reluctant to offer even unofficial guarantees. The common denominator of the advice that filtered back to me was to land only in non-extradition countries, and avoid any route that crossed the airspace of any countries with a record of cooperation with or deference to the US military. One official, I think from France, suggested that the odds of my successful transit might be significantly increased if I were issued a *laissez-passer*, a UN-recognized one-way travel document typically issued to grant safe passage to refugees crossing borders—but obtaining one of those was easier said than done.

Enter Sarah Harrison, a journalist and an editor for WikiLeaks. The moment the news broke that an American had unmasked a global system of mass surveillance, she had immediately flown to Hong Kong. Through her experience with the website and particularly with the fate of Assange, she was poised to offer me the world's best asylum advice. It didn't hurt that she also had family connections with the legal community in Hong Kong.

People have long ascribed selfish motives to Assange's desire to give me aid, but I believe he was genuinely invested in one thing above all—helping me evade capture. That doing so involved tweaking the US government was just a bonus for him, an ancillary benefit, not the goal. It's true that Assange can be self-interested and vain, moody, and even bullying—after a sharp disagreement just a month after our first, text-based conversation, I never communicated with him again—but he also sincerely conceives of himself as a fighter in a historic battle for the public's right to know, a battle he will do anything to win. It's for this reason that I regard it as too reductive to interpret his assistance as merely an instance of scheming or self-promotion. More important to him, I believe, was the opportunity to establish a counterexample to the case of the organization's most famous source, US Army Private Chelsea Manning, whose thirty-five-year prison sentence was historically unprecedented and a monstrous deterrent to whistleblowers everywhere. Though I never was, and never would be, a source for Assange, my situation gave him a chance to right a wrong. There was nothing he could have done to save Manning, but he seemed, through Sarah, determined to do everything he could to save me.

That said, I was initially wary of Sarah's involvement. But Laura told me that she was serious, competent, and, most important, independent: one of the few at WikiLeaks who dared to openly disagree with Assange. Despite my caution, I was in a difficult position, and as Hemingway once wrote, the way to make people trustworthy is to trust them.

Laura informed me of Sarah's presence in Hong Kong only a day or so before she communicated with me on an encrypted channel, which itself was only a day or two before I actually met her in person—and if I'm somewhat loose on my dates here, you'll have to forgive me: one frenetic day bled into the next. Sarah had been a whirlwind, apparently, since the moment of her landing in Hong Kong. Though she wasn't a lawyer, she had deep expertise when it came to what I'll call the interpersonal or subofficial nuances of avoiding extradition. She met with local Hong Kong human rights attorneys to seek independent opinions, and I was deeply impressed by both her pace and her circumspection. Her connections through WikiLeaks and the extraordinary courage of the Ecuadorean consul in London, Fidel Narváez, together produced a *laissez-passer* in my name. This *laissez-passer*, which was meant to get me to Ecuador, had been issued by the consul on an emergency basis, since we didn't have time for his home government to formally approve it. The moment it was in hand, Sarah hired a van to take us to the airport.

That's how I met her—in motion. I'd like to say that I started off our acquaintance by offering my thanks, but instead the first thing I said was: "When was the last time you slept?" Sarah looked just as ragged and disheveled as I did. She stared out the window, as if trying to recall the answer, but then just shook her head: "I don't know."

We were both developing colds and our careful conversation was punctuated by sneezes and coughs. By her own account, she was motivated to support me out of loyalty to her conscience more than to the ideological demands of her employer. Certainly her politics seemed shaped less by Assange's feral opposition to central power than by her own conviction that too much of what passed for contemporary journalism served government interests rather than challenged them. As we hurtled to the airport, as we checked in, as we cleared passport control for the first of what should have been three flights, I kept waiting for her to ask me for something—anything, even just for me to make a statement on Assange's, or the organization's, behalf. But she never did, although she did cheerfully share her opinion that I was a fool for trusting media conglomerates to fairly guard the gate between the public and the truth. For that instance of straight talk, and for many others, I'll always admire Sarah's honesty.

We were traveling to Quito, Ecuador, via Moscow via Havana via Caracas for a simple reason: it was the only safe route available. There were no direct flights to Quito from Hong Kong, and all of the other connecting flights traveled through US airspace. While I was concerned about the massive layover in Russia—we'd have almost twenty hours before the Havana flight departed—my primary fear was actually the next leg of the journey, because traveling from Russia to Cuba meant passing through NATO airspace. I didn't particularly relish flying over a country like Poland, which during my lifetime has done everything to please the US government, including hosting CIA black sites where my former IC colleagues subjected prisoners to "enhanced interrogations," another Bush-era euphemism for "torture."

I wore my hat down over my eyes to avoid being recognized, and Sarah did the seeing for me. She took my arm and led me to the gate, where we waited until boarding. This was the last moment for her to back out, and I told her so. "You don't have to do this," I said.

"Do what?"

"Protect me like this."

Sarah stiffened. "Let's get one thing clear," she said as we boarded, "I'm not protecting you. No one can protect you. What I'm here for is to make it harder for anyone to interfere. To make sure everyone's on their best behavior."

"So you're my witness," I said.

She gave a slight wry smile. "Someone has to be the last person to ever see you alive. It might as well be me."

Though the three points where I'd thought we were most likely to get stopped were now behind us (check-in, passport control, and the gate), I didn't feel safe on the plane. I didn't want to get complacent. I took the window seat and Sarah sat next to me, to screen me from the other passengers across the row. After what felt like an eternity, the cabin doors were shut, the skybridge pulled away, and finally, we were moving. But just before the plane rolled from the tarmac onto the runway, it halted sharply. I was nervous. Pressing the brim of my hat up against the glass, I strained to catch the sound of sirens or the flashing of blue lights. It felt like I was playing the waiting game all over again—it was a wait that wouldn't end. Until, suddenly, the plane rolled into motion again and took a turn, and I realized that we were just far back in the line for takeoff.

My spirits rose with the wheels, but it was hard to believe I was out of the fire. Once we were airborne, I loosened my grip from my thighs and felt an urge to take my lucky Rubik's Cube out of my bag. But I knew I couldn't, because nothing would make me more conspicuous. Instead, I sat back, pulled my hat down again, and kept my half-open eyes on the map on the seatback screen just in front of me, tracking the pixelated route across China, Mongolia, and Russia—none of which would be especially amenable to doing any favors for the US State Department. However, there was no predicting what the Russian government would do once we landed, beyond hauling us into an inspection so they could search through my blank laptops and empty bag. What I hoped might spare us any more invasive treatment was that the world was watching and my lawyers and WikiLeaks' lawyers were aware of our itinerary.

It was only once we'd entered Chinese airspace that I realized I wouldn't be able to get any rest until I asked Sarah this question explicitly: "Why are you helping me?"

She flattened out her voice, as if trying to tamp down her passions, and told me that she wanted me to have a better outcome. She never said better than what outcome or whose, and I could only take that answer as a sign of her discretion and respect.

I was reassured, enough at least to finally get some sleep.

WE LANDED AT Sheremetyevo on June 23 for what we assumed would be a twenty-hour layover. It has now dragged on for over six years. Exile is an endless layover.

In the IC, and in the CIA in particular, you get a lot of training on how not to get into trouble at customs. You have to think about how you dress, how you act. You have to think about the things in your bag and the things in your pockets and the tales they tell about you. Your goal is to be the most boring person in line, with the most perfectly forgettable face. But none of that really matters when the name on your passport is all over the news.

I handed my little blue book to the bearish guy in the passport control booth, who scanned it and rifled through its pages. Sarah stood stalwart behind me. I'd made sure to take note of the time it took for the people ahead of us in line to clear the booth, and our turn was taking too long. Then the guy picked up his phone, grumbled some words in Russian, and almost immediately—far too quickly—two security officers in suits approached. They must have been waiting. The officer in front took my little blue book from the guy in the booth and leaned in close to me. "There is problem with passport," he said. "Please, come with."

Sarah immediately stepped to my side and unleashed a fast flurry of English: "I'm his legal adviser. Wherever he goes, I go. I'm coming with you. According to the—"

But before she could cite the relevant UN covenants and Genevan codicils, the officer held up his hand and glanced at the line. He said, "Okay, sure, okay. You come."

I don't know whether the officer had even understood what she said. He just clearly didn't want to make a scene.

The two security officers marched us briskly toward what I assumed was going to be a special room for secondary inspection, but instead turned out to be one of Sheremetyevo's plush business lounges—like a business-class or first-class area, with just a few passengers basking obliviously in their luxury seats. Sarah and I were directed past them and down a hall into a conference room of sorts, filled with men in gray sitting around a table. There were a half-dozen of them or so, with military haircuts. One guy sat separately, holding a pen. He was a notetaker, a kind of secretary, I guessed. He had a folder in front of him containing a pad of paper. On the cover of the folder was a monocolor insignia that I didn't need Russian in order to understand: it was a sword and shield, the symbol of Russia's foremost intelligence service, the Federal Security Service (FSB). Like the FBI in the United States, the FSB exists not only to spy and investigate but also to make arrests.

At the center of the table sat an older man in a finer suit than the others, the white of his hair shining like a halo of authority. He gestured for Sarah and me to sit opposite him, with an authoritative sweep of the hand and a smile that marked him as a seasoned case officer, or whatever the term is for a CO's Russian equivalent. Intelligence services the world over are full of such figures—dedicated actors who will try on different emotions until they get the response they want.

He cleared his throat and gave me, in decent English, what the CIA calls a cold pitch, which is basically an offer by a foreign intelligence service that can be summarized as "come and work for us." In return for cooperation, the foreigners dangle favors, which can be anything from stacks of cash to a get-out-of-jail-free card for pretty much anything from fraud to murder. The catch, of course, is that the foreigners always expect something of equal or better value in exchange. That clear and unambiguous transaction, however, is never how it starts. Come to think of it, it's funny that it's called a cold pitch, because the person making it always starts warm, with grins, levity, and words of sympathy.

I knew I had to cut him off. If you don't cut off a foreign in-

telligence officer right away, it might not matter whether you ultimately reject their offer, because they can destroy your reputation
simply by leaking a recording of you considering it. So as the man
apologized for inconveniencing us, I imagined the hidden devices
recording us, and tried to choose my words carefully.

"Listen, I understand who you are, and what this is," I said.
"Please let me be clear that I have no intention to cooperate with
you. I'm not going to cooperate with any intelligence service. I
mean no disrespect, but this isn't going to be that kind of meeting.
If you want to search my bag, it's right here," and I pointed to it
under my chair. "But I promise you, there's nothing in it that can
help you."

As I was speaking, the man's face changed. He started to act
wounded. "No, we would never do that," he said. "Please believe
me, we only want to help you."

Sarah cleared her throat and jumped in. "That's quite kind of
you, but I hope you can understand that all we'd like is to make
our connecting flight."

For the briefest instant, the man's feigned sorrow became irritation. "You are his lawyer?"

"I'm his legal adviser," Sarah answered.

The man asked me, "So you are not coming to Russia to be in
Russia?"

"No."

"And so may I ask where you are trying to go? What is your
final destination?"

I said, "Quito, Ecuador, via Caracas, via Havana," even though
I knew that he already knew the answer. He certainly had a copy
of our itinerary, since Sarah and I had traveled from Hong Kong
on Aeroflot, the Russian flagship airline.

Up until this point, he and I had been reading from the same intelligence script, but now the conversation swerved. "You haven't
heard?" he said. He stood and looked at me like he was delivering
the news of a death in the family. "I am afraid to inform you that
your passport is invalid."

I was so surprised, I just stuttered. "I'm sorry, but I—I don't believe that."

The man leaned over the table and said, "No, it is true. Believe me. It is the decision of your minister, John Kerry. Your passport has been canceled by your government, and the air services have been instructed not to allow you to travel."

I was sure it was a trick, but I wasn't quite sure to what purpose. "Give us a minute," I said, but even before I could ask, Sarah had snatched her laptop out of her bag and was getting onto the airport Wi-Fi.

"Of course, you will check," the man said, and he turned to his colleagues and chatted amiably to them in Russian, as if he had all the time in the world.

It was reported on every site Sarah looked at. After the news had broken that I'd left Hong Kong, the US State Department announced that it had canceled my passport. It had revoked my travel document while I was still in midair.

I was incredulous: my own government had trapped me in Russia. The State Department's move might merely have been the result of bureaucratic proceduralism—when you're trying to catch a fugitive, putting out an Interpol alert and canceling their passport is just standard operating procedure. But in the final accounting it was self-defeating, as it handed Russia a massive propaganda victory.

"It's true," said Sarah, with a shake of her head.

"So what will you do?" the man asked, and he walked around to our side of the table.

Before I could take the Ecuadorean safe conduct pass out of my pocket, Sarah said, "I'm so sorry, but I'm going to have to advise Mr. Snowden not to answer any more questions."

The man pointed at me, and said, "You will come."

He gestured me to follow him to the far end of the conference room, where there was a window. I went and stood next to him and looked. About three or four floors below was street level and the largest media scrum I've ever seen, scads of reporters wielding cameras and mics.

It was an impressive show, perhaps choreographed by the FSB, perhaps not, most likely half and half. Almost everything in Russia is half and half. But at least now I knew why Sarah and I had been brought to this conference room in this lounge.

I went back to my chair but didn't sit down again.

The man turned from the window to face me and said, "Life for a person in your situation can be very difficult without friends who can help." He let the words linger.

Here it comes, I thought—the direct solicitation.

He said, "If there is some information, perhaps, some small thing you could share with us?"

"We'll be okay on our own," I said. Sarah stood up next to me.

The man sighed. He turned to mumble in Russian, and his comrades rose and filed out. "I hope you will not regret your decision," he said to me. Then he gave a slight bow and made his own exit, just as a pair of officials from the airport administration entered.

I demanded to be allowed to go to the gate for the flight to Havana, but they ignored me. I finally reached into my pocket and brandished the Ecuadorean safe conduct pass, but they ignored that, too.

All told, we were trapped in the airport for a biblical forty days and forty nights. Over the course of those days, I applied to a total of twenty-seven countries for political asylum. Not a single one of them was willing to stand up to American pressure, with some countries refusing outright, and others declaring that they were unable to even consider my request until I arrived in their territory—a feat that was impossible. Ultimately, the only head of state that proved sympathetic to my cause was Burger King, who never denied me a Whopper (hold the tomato and onion).

Soon, my presence in the airport became a global spectacle. Eventually the Russians found it a nuisance. On July 1, the president of Bolivia, Evo Morales, left another airport in Moscow, Vnukovo, in his Bolivian state plane after attending the annual GECF, or Gas Exporting Countries Forum. The US government, suspecting that I was onboard due to President Morales's expressions of solidarity, pressured the governments of Italy, France, Spain, and Portugal to deny the plane access to their airspace, and succeeded in diverting it to Vienna, Austria. There it was grounded, searched, and only allowed to continue on its journey once no traces of me were found. This was a startling violation of sovereignty, which occasioned UN censure. The incident was an affront to Russia, which couldn't guarantee a visiting head of state safe passage home. And it confirmed to Russia and to me that any flight that America suspected me of stowing away on ran the same risk of being diverted and grounded.

The Russian government must have decided that it would be better off without me and the media swarm clogging up the country's major airport. On August 1 it granted me temporary asylum. Sarah and I were allowed to leave Sheremetyevo, but eventually only one of us would be heading home. Our time together served to bind us as friends for life. I will always be grateful for the weeks she spent by my side, for her integrity and her fortitude.

28

From the Diaries of Lindsay Mills

As far away from home as I was, my thoughts were consumed with Lindsay. I've been wary of telling her story—the story of what happened to her once I was gone: the FBI interrogations, the surveillance, the press attention, the online harassment, the confusion and pain, the anger and sadness. Finally, I realized that only Lindsay herself should be the person to recount that period. No one else has the experience, but more than that: no one else has the right. Luckily, Lindsay has kept a diary since adolescence, using it to record her life and draft her art. She has graciously agreed to let me include a few pages here. In the entries that follow, all names have been changed (except those of family), some typos fixed, and a few redactions made. Otherwise, this is how it was, from the moment that I left Hawaii.

5.22.2013

Stopped in at K-Mart to get a lei. Trying to welcome Wendy with proper aloha spirit, but I'm pissed. Ed's been planning his mother's visit for weeks. He's the one who invited her. I was hoping he'd be there when I woke up this morning. On the drive back to Waipahu from the airport Wendy was worried. She's not used to him having to go away on a moment's notice. I tried to tell her this was usual. But it was usual when we lived overseas, not in Hawaii, and I can't remember any other time that Ed was away and wasn't in touch. We went to a nice dinner to distract ourselves and Wendy talked about how she thought Ed was on medical leave. It didn't make any sense to her that he'd be called away for work while on medical leave. The moment we got home Wendy went to bed. I checked my phone and found I had three missed calls from an unknown number, and one missed call from a long foreign number, no voicemails. I Googled the long foreign number. Ed must be in Hong Kong.

5.24.2013

Wendy was home all day alone, thoughts just running circles in her brain. I feel bad for her and can only console myself by thinking how Ed would handle having to entertain my own mother by himself. Over dinner, Wendy kept asking me about Ed's health, which I guess is understandable, given her own history of epilepsy. She said she's worried that he had another seizure, and then she started crying, and then I started crying. I'm just realizing that I'm worried too. But instead of epilepsy, I'm thinking, What if he's off having an affair? Who is she? Just try and get through this visit and have a good time. Take a puddle jumper to the Big Island. To Kilauea, the volcano, as planned. Once Wendy goes back, reassess things.

6.3.2013

Brought Wendy to the airport, to fly back to MD. She didn't want to go back, but she has work. I took her as far as I could go and hugged her. I didn't want to let go of the hug. Then she got in line for security. Came home to find Ed's Skype status has changed to: "Sorry but it had to be done." I don't know when he changed it. Could've been today, could've been last month. I just checked on Skype and happened to notice it, and I'm crazy enough to think he's sending me a message.

6.7.2013

Woke up to a call from NSA Special Agent Megan Smith asking me to call her back about Ed. Still feeling sick with fever. I had to drop off my car at the autobody shop and Tod gave me a ride back on his Ducati. When we pulled onto the street I saw a white gov vehicle in the driveway and gov agents talking to our neighbors. I've never even met the neighbors. I don't know why but my first instinct was to tell Tod to keep driving. I ducked my head down to pretend to look for something in my purse. We went to Starbucks, where Tod pointed out a newspaper, something about the NSA. I tried to read the headlines but my paranoia just ran wild. Is that why the white SUV was in my driveway? Is that the same SUV in the parking lot outside this Starbucks? Should I even be writing this stuff down? Went home again and the SUV was gone. Took some meds and realized I hadn't eaten. In the middle of lunch, cops showed up at the kitchen window. Through the window, I could hear them radioing that someone was inside the residence. By someone they meant me. I opened the front door to two agents and an HPD* officer. They were frightening. The HPD officer searched through the house as Agent Smith asked me about Ed, who'd

---

* Hawaii Police Department

been due back at work on May 31. The HPD officer said it was suspicious when a workplace reported someone missing before the person's spouse or girlfriend did. He was looking at me like I killed Ed. He was looking around the house for his body. Agent Smith asked if she could see all the computers in the house and that made me angry. I told her she could get a warrant. They left the house but camped out on the corner.

San Diego, 6.8.2013

I got a little afraid that TSA wouldn't let me leave the island. The TVs in the airport were all full of news about the NSA. Once onboard the plane, I emailed Agent Smith and the HPD Missing Persons' detective that my grandma was having open heart surgery, requiring me to be off-island for a few weeks. The surgery isn't scheduled until the end of the month and it's in Florida, not San Diego, but this was the only excuse I could think of for getting to the mainland. It was a better excuse than saying, I just need to be with my best friend Sandra and also it's her bday. When the wheels left the ground I fell into a momentary coma of relief. When I landed, I had a raging fever. Sandra picked me up. I hadn't told her anything because my paranoia was off the charts, but she could tell that something was up, that I wasn't just visiting her for her bday. She asked me if Ed and I had broken up. I answered maybe.

6.9.2013

I got a phone call from Tiffany. She asked how I was doing and said she was worried about me. I didn't understand. She got quiet. Then she asked if I'd seen the news. She told me Ed had made a video and was on the homepage of the Huffington Post. Sandra hooked up her laptop to the flatscreen. I calmly waited for the 12-minute YouTube video to load. And then there he was. Real. Alive. I was shocked. He looked thin, but he sounded like his old self. The old Ed, confident and strong. Like how he was before this last tough year. This was the man I loved, not the cold distant ghost I'd recently been living with. Sandra hugged me and I didn't know what to say. We stood in silence. We drove out to Sandra's bday bbq, at her cousins' house on this pretty hill south of the city, right on the Mexican border. Gorgeous place and I could barely see any of it. I was shutting down. Not knowing how to even begin to parse the situation. We arrived to friendly faces that had no clue what I was going through on the inside. Ed, what have you done? How can you come back from this? I was barely present for all the party small talk. My phone was blowing up with calls and texts. Dad. Mom. Wendy. Driving back up to San Diego from the bbq I drove Sandra's cousin's Durango, which Sandra needs this week to move. As we drove, a black gov SUV followed us and a police car pulled Sandra's car over, which was the car I'd come in. I just kept driving the Durango, hoping I knew where I was going because my phone was already dead from all the calls.

6.10.2013

I knew Eileen* was important in local politics, but I didn't know she was also a fucking gangster. She's been taking care of everything. While we were waiting for her contacts to recommend a lawyer, I got a call from the FBI. An agent named Chuck Landowski, who asked me what I was doing in San Diego. Eileen told me to hang up. The agent called back and I picked up, even though Eileen said I shouldn't. Agent Chuck said he didn't want to show up at the house unannounced, so he was just calling "out of courtesy" to tell us that agents were coming. This

---

* Sandra's mother

sent Eileen into overdrive. She's so goddamned tough, it's amazing. She had me leave my phone at the house and we took her car and drove around to think. Eileen got a text from a friend of hers recommending a lawyer, a guy named Jerry Farber, and she handed me her phone and had me call him. A secretary picked up and I told her that my name was Lindsay Mills and I was the girlfriend of Edward Snowden and needed representation. The secretary said, "Oh, let me put you right through." It was funny to hear the recognition in her voice.

Jerry picked up the phone and asked how he could help. I told him about the FBI calls and he asked for the agent's name, so he could talk to the feds. While we waited to hear back from Jerry, Eileen suggested we go get burner phones, one to use with family and friends, one to use with Jerry. After the phones, Eileen asked which bank I kept my money at. We drove to the nearest branch and she had me withdraw all of my money immediately in case the feds froze my accounts. I went and took out all my life savings, split between cashier's checks and cash. Eileen insisted I split the money like that and I just followed her instructions. The bank manager asked me what I needed all that cash for and I said, "Life." I really wanted to say STFU, but I decided if I was polite I'd be forgettable. I was concerned that people were going to recognize me since they were showing my face alongside Ed's on the news. When we got out of the bank I asked Eileen how she'd become such an expert at what to do when you're in trouble. She told me, very chill, "You get to know these things, as a woman. Like, you always take the money out of the bank, when you're getting a divorce." We got some Vietnamese takeout and took it back to Eileen's house and ate it on the floor in the upstairs hallway. Eileen and Sandra plugged in their hairdryers and kept them blowing to make noise, as we whispered to each other, just in case they were listening in on us.

Lawyer Jerry called and said we had to meet with the FBI today. Eileen drove us to his office, and on the way she noticed we were being followed. It made no sense. We were going to a meeting to talk to the feds but also the feds were behind us, two SUVs and a Honda Accord without plates. Eileen got the idea that maybe they weren't the FBI. She thought that maybe they were some other agency or even a foreign government, trying to kidnap me. She started driving fast and erratically, trying to lose them, but every traffic light was turning red just when we approached it. I told her that she was being crazy, she had to slow down. There was a plainclothes agent by the door of Jerry's building, he had gov written all over his face. We went up in the elevator and when the door opened, three men were waiting: two of them were agents, one of them was Jerry. He was the only man who shook hands with me. Jerry told Eileen that she couldn't come with us to the conference room. He'd call her when we were finished. Eileen insisted that she'd wait. She sat in the lobby with an expression on her face like she was ready to wait for a million years. On the way to the conference room Jerry took me aside and said he'd negotiated "limited immunity," which I said was pretty meaningless, and he didn't disagree. He told me never to lie, and that when I didn't know what to say, I should say IDK and let him talk. Agent Mike had a grin that was a bit too kind, while Agent Leland kept looking at me like I was an experiment and he was studying my reactions. Both of them creeped me out. They started with questions about me that were so basic, it was like they were just trying to show me that they already knew everything about me. Of course they did. That was Ed's point. The gov always knows everything. They had me talk about the last two months, twice, and then when I was finished with the "timeline," Agent Mike asked me to start all over again from the beginning. I said, "The beginning of what?" He said, "Tell me how you met."

6.11.2013

Coming out of the interrogation exhausted, late at night, with days of interrogations ahead of me. They wouldn't tell me how many exactly. Eileen drove us to meet Sandra for dinner at some diner, and as we left Downtown we noticed we still had our tails. Eileen tried to lose them by speeding and making illegal U-turns again, and I begged her to stop. I thought her driving like that just made me look worse. It made me look suspicious. But Eileen is a stubborn mama bear. In the parking lot of the diner, Eileen banged on the windows of the surveillance vehicles and yelled that I was cooperating, so there was no reason for them to be following. It was a little embarrassing, like when your mother sticks up for you in school, but mostly I was just in awe. The nerve to go up to a vehicle with federal agents and tell them off. Sandra was at a table in the back and we ordered and talked about "media exposure." I was all over the news.

Halfway through dinner, two men walked up to our table. One tall guy in a baseball hat, who had braces, and his partner who was dressed like a guy going clubbing. The tall guy identified himself as Agent Chuck, the agent who'd called me before. He asked to speak with me about "the driving behavior" once we'd finished eating. The moment he said that we decided we were finished. The agents were out in front of the diner. Agent Chuck showed his badge and told me that his main goal was my protection. He said there could be threats against my life. He tapped his jacket and said if there was any danger he would take care of it, because he was on "the armed team." It was all such macho posturing or an attempt to get me to trust him, by putting me in a vulnerable position. He went on to say I was going to be surveilled/followed by the FBI 24/7, for the foreseeable future, and the reckless driving Eileen was doing would not be tolerated. He said agents are never supposed to talk to their assignments but he felt that, given the circumstances, he had to "take the team in this direction for everyone's safety."

He handed me a business card with his contact info and said he'd be parked just outside Eileen's house all night, and I should call him if I needed him, or needed anything, for any reason. He told me I was free to go anywhere (you're damn right, I thought), but that whenever I planned to go anywhere, I should text him. He said, "Open communication will make everything easier." He said, "If you give us a heads-up, you'll be that much safer, I promise."

6.16.2013–6.18.2013

Haven't written for days. I'm so angry that I have to take a deep breath and figure out who and what exactly I'm angry at, because it all just blurs together. Fucking Feds! Exhausting interrogations where they treat me like I'm guilty and follow me everywhere, but what's worse is that they've broken my routine. Usually I'd tear off into the woods and shoot or write, but now I have a surveillance team audience wherever I go. It's like by taking away my energy and time and desire to write, they took away the last little bit of privacy I had. I need to remember everything that's happened. First they had me bring in my laptop and copied the hard drive. They probably put a bunch of bugs on it, too. Then they had copies of all my emails and chats printed out, and they were reading me things I wrote to Ed and things Ed wrote to me and demanding I explain them. The FBI thinks that everything's a code. And sure, in a vacuum anyone's messages look strange. But this is just how people who've been together for eight years communicate! They act like they've never been in a relationship! They were asking questions to try to emotionally exhaust me so that when we returned to "the timeline," my answers would change. They won't accept I know nothing. But still, we keep returning to "the timeline," now with transcripts of all my emails and chats and my online calendar printed out in front of us.

I would expect that gov guys would understand that Ed was always secretive about his work and I had to accept this secrecy to be with him, but they don't. They refuse to. After a while, I just broke down in tears, so the session ended early. Agent Mike and Agent Leland offered to give me a ride back to Eileen's, and before I left, Jerry took me aside and said that the FBI seemed sympathetic. "They seem to have taken a liking to you, especially Mike." He told me to be careful, though, about being too casual on the ride home. "Don't answer any of their questions." The moment we drove away Mike chimed in with, "I'm sure Jerry said not to answer any questions, but I only have a couple." Once Mike got talking, he told me that the FBI office in San Diego had a bet. Apparently, the agents had a pool going to bet how long it would be before the media figured out my location. The winner would get a free martini. Later, Sandra said she had her doubts. "Knowing men," she said, "the bet's about something else."

6.19.2013–6.20.2013

While the rest of the country is coming to grips with the fact that their privacy is being violated, mine's being stripped from me on a whole new level. Both things thanks to Ed. I hate sending Chuck "departure updates," and then I hate myself that I don't have the nerve not to send them. The worst was this one night sending a "departure update" that I'm leaving to meet Sandra and then getting lost on the way but not wanting to stop and ask the agents following me for help, so I was just leading them around in circles. I got to thinking maybe they'd bugged Eileen's car, so I began talking aloud in the car, thinking maybe they could hear me. I wasn't talking, I was cursing them out. I had to pay Jerry, and after I did all I could think about was all the tax money being wasted on just following me to my lawyer's office and the gym. After the first two days of meetings I'd already run out of the only decent clothes I had, so I went to Macy's. Agents followed me around the women's department. I wondered if they'd come into the fitting room, too, and tell me that looks good, that doesn't, green's not your color. At the fitting room's entrance was a TV blaring the news and I froze when the announcer said "Edward Snowden's girlfriend." I fled the stall, and stood in front of the screen. Watching as my photos flicked by. I whipped out my phone and made the mistake of Googling myself. So many comments labeling me a stripper or whore. None of this is me. Just like the feds, they had already decided who I was.

6.22.2013–6.24.2013

Interrogations over, for now. But a tail still following. I left the house, happy to get back in the air at this local aerial silks studio. Made it to the studio and couldn't find street parking, but my tail did. He had to leave his spot when I drove out of range, so I doubled back and stole his spot. Had a phone call with Wendy, where we both said that however badly Ed hurt us, he did the right thing by trying to ensure that when he was gone, Wendy and I were together. That's why he'd invited her and been so insistent about her coming. He'd wanted us to be together in Hawaii when he went public, so that we could keep each other company and give each other strength and comfort. It's so hard to be angry at someone you love. And even harder to be angry at someone you love and respect for doing the right thing. Wendy and I were both in tears and then we both went quiet. I think we had the same thought, at the same time. How can we talk like normal people when they're eavesdropping on all our calls?

6.25.2013

LAX to HNL. Wore the copper-colored wig to the airport, through security, and throughout the flight. Sandra came with. We grabbed a gross preflight lunch in the food court. More TVs tuned to CNN, still showing Ed, and still surreal, which is the new real for everyone, I think. Got a text from Agent Mike, telling me and Sandra to come see him at Gate 73. Really? He came up to LA from San Diego? Gate 73 was roped off and empty. Mike was sitting waiting for us on a row of chairs. He crossed his legs and showed us he was wearing an ankle pistol. More macho bullshit intimidation. He had paperwork for me to sign in order for the FBI to release Ed's car keys to me in Hawaii. He said two agents would be waiting for us in Honolulu with the key. Other agents would be with us on the flight. He apologized that he wasn't coming personally. Ugh.

6.29.2013

Been packing the house for days now with only minor interruptions from the FBI, coming by with more forms to sign. It's torture, going through everything. Finding all these little things that remind me of him. I'm like a crazy woman, cleaning up, and then just gazing at his side of the bed. More often, though, I find what's missing. What the FBI took. Technology, yes, but also books. What they left behind were footprints, scuff marks on the walls, and dust.

6.30.2013

Waipahu yard sale. Three men responded to Sandra's "take it all, best offer" Craigslisting. They showed up to rummage through Ed's life, his piano, guitar, and weight set. Anything

I couldn't bear to live with or afford to ship to the mainland. The men filled their pickup with as much as they could, and then came back for a second load. To my surprise, and I think to Sandra's, too, I wasn't too bothered by their scavenging. But the moment they were gone, the second time, I lost it.

7.2.2013

Everything got shipped today, except the futons and couch, which I'm just ditching. All that was left of Ed's stuff after the FBI raided the house fit into one small cardboard box. Some photos and his clothes, lots of mismatched socks. Nothing that could be used as evidence in court, just evidence of our life together. Sandra brought some lighter fluid and brought the metal trash can back around to the lanai. I dumped all of Ed's stuff, the photos and clothes, inside, and lit a book of matches on fire and tossed it in. Sandra and I sat around while it burned and the smoke rose into the sky. The glow and the smoke reminded me of the trip I took with Wendy to Kilauea, the volcano on the Big Island. That was just over a month ago, but it feels like years in the past. How could we have known that our own lives were about to erupt? That Volcano Ed was going to destroy everything? But I remember the guide at Kilauea saying that volcanoes are only destructive in the short term. In the long term, they move the world. They create islands, cool the planet, and enrich the soil. Their lava flows uncontrolled and then cools and hardens. The ash they shoot into the air sprinkles down as minerals, which fertilize the earth and make new life grow.

29

Love and Exile

If at any point during your journey through this book you paused for a moment over a term you wanted to clarify or investigate further and typed it into a search engine—and if that term happened to be in some way suspicious, a term like XKEYSCORE, for example—then congrats: you're in the system, a victim of your own curiosity.

But even if you didn't search for anything online, it wouldn't take much for an interested government to find out that you've been reading this book. At the very least, it wouldn't take much to find out that you have it, whether you downloaded it illegally or bought a hard copy online or purchased it at a brick-and-mortar store with a credit card.

All you wanted to do was to read—to take part in that most intensely intimate human act, the joining of minds through language. But that was more than enough. Your natural desire to connect with the world was all the world needed to connect your living, breathing self to a series of globally unique identifiers, such as your email, your phone, and the IP address of your computer. By creating a world-spanning system that tracked these identifiers across every available channel of electronic communications, the American Intelligence Community gave itself the power to record and store for perpetuity the data of your life.

And that was only the beginning. Because once America's spy agencies had proven to themselves that it was possible to passively collect all of your communications, they started actively tampering with them, too. By poisoning the messages that were headed your way with snippets of attack code, or "exploits," they developed the ability to gain possession of more than just your words. Now they were capable of winning total control of your whole device, including its camera and microphone. Which means that if you're reading this now—this sentence—on any sort of modern machine, like a smartphone or tablet, they can follow along and *read you*. They can tell how quickly or slowly you turn the pages and whether you read the chapters consecutively or skip around. And they'll gladly endure looking up your nostrils and watching you move your lips as you read, so long as it gets them the data they want and lets them positively identify you.

This is the result of two decades of unchecked innovation—the final product of a political and professional class that dreams itself your master. No matter the place, no matter the time, and no matter what you do, your life has now become an open book.

IF MASS SURVEILLANCE was, by definition, a constant presence in daily life, then I wanted the dangers it posed, and the damage it had already done, to be a constant presence too. Through my disclosures to the press, I wanted to make this system known, its existence a fact that my country, and the world, could not ignore. In the years since 2013, awareness has grown, both in scope and subtlety. But in this social media age, we have always to remind ourselves: awareness alone is not enough.

In America, the initial press reports on the disclosures started a "national conversation," as President Obama himself conceded. While I appreciated the sentiment, I remember wishing that he had noted that what made it "national," what made it a "conversation," was that for the first time the American public was informed enough to have a voice.

The revelations of 2013 particularly roused Congress, both houses of which launched multiple investigations into NSA abuses. Those investigations concluded that the agency had repeatedly lied regarding the nature and efficacy of its mass surveillance programs, even to the most highly cleared Intelligence Committee legislators.

In 2015, a federal court of appeals ruled in the matter of *ACLU v. Clapper*, a suit challenging the legality of the NSA's phone records collection program. The court ruled that the NSA's program had violated even the loose standards of the Patriot Act and, moreover, was most probably unconstitutional. The ruling focused on the NSA's interpretation of Section 215 of the Patriot Act, which allowed the government to demand from third parties "any tangible thing" that it deemed "relevant" to foreign intelligence and terror investigations. In the court's opinion, the government's definition of "relevant" was so expansive as to be virtually meaningless. To call some collected data "relevant" merely because it might become relevant at some amorphous point in the future was "unprecedented and unwarranted." The court's refusal to accept the government's definition caused not a few legal scholars to interpret the ruling as casting doubt on the legitimacy of all government bulk-collection programs predicated on this doctrine of future relevance. In the wake of this opinion, Congress passed the USA Freedom Act, which amended Section 215 to explicitly prohibit the bulk collection of Americans' phone records. Going forward, those records would remain where they originally had been, in the private control of the telecoms, and the government would have to formally request specific ones with a FISC warrant in hand if it wanted to access them.

ACLU v. Clapper was a notable victory, to be sure. A crucial precedent was set. The court declared that the American public had standing: American citizens had the right to stand in a court of law and challenge the government's officially secret system of mass surveillance. But as the numerous other cases that resulted from the disclosures continue to wend their slow and deliberate ways through the courts, it becomes ever clearer to me that the American legal resistance to mass surveillance was just the beta phase of what has to be an international opposition movement, fully implemented across both governments and private sector.

The reaction of technocapitalists to the disclosures was immediate and forceful, proving once again that with extreme hazards come unlikely allies. The documents revealed an NSA so determined to pursue any and all information it perceived as being deliberately kept from it that it had undermined the basic encryption protocols of the Internet—making citizens' financial and medical records, for example, more vulnerable, and in the process harming businesses that relied on their customers entrusting them with such sensitive data. In response, Apple adopted strong default encryption for its iPhones and iPads, and Google followed suit for its Android products and Chromebooks. But perhaps the most important private-sector change occurred when businesses throughout the world set about switching their website platforms, replacing http (Hypertext Transfer Protocol) with the encrypted https (the S signifies security), which helps prevent third-party interception of Web traffic. The year 2016 was a landmark in tech history, the first year since the invention of the Internet that more Web traffic was encrypted than unencrypted.

The Internet is certainly more secure now than it was in 2013, especially given the sudden global recognition of the need for encrypted tools and apps. I've been involved with the design and creation of a few of these myself, through my work heading the Freedom of the Press Foundation, a nonprofit organization dedicated to protecting and empowering public-interest journalism in the new millennium. A major part of the organization's brief is to preserve and strengthen First and Fourth Amendment rights through the development of encryption technologies. To that end, the FPF financially supports Signal, an encrypted texting and calling platform created by Open Whisper Systems, and develops SecureDrop (originally coded by the late Aaron Swartz), an open-source submission system that allows media organizations to securely accept documents from anonymous whistleblowers and other sources. Today, SecureDrop is available in ten languages and used by more than seventy media organizations around the world, including the *New York Times*, the *Washington Post*, the *Guardian*, and the *New Yorker*.

In a perfect world, which is to say in a world that doesn't exist, just laws would make these tools obsolete. But in the only world we have, they have never been more necessary. A change in the law is infinitely more difficult to achieve than a change in a technological standard, and as long as legal innovation lags behind technological innovation institutions will seek to abuse that disparity in the furtherance of their interests. It falls to independent, open-source hardware and software developers to close that gap by providing the vital civil liberties protections that the law may be unable, or unwilling, to guarantee.

In my current situation, I'm constantly reminded of the fact that the law is country-specific, whereas technology is not. Every nation has its own legal code but the same computer code. Technology crosses borders and carries almost every passport. As the years go by, it has become increasingly apparent to me that legislatively reforming the surveillance regime of the country of my birth won't necessarily help a journalist or dissident in the country of my exile, but an encrypted smartphone might.

INTERNATIONALLY, THE DISCLOSURES helped to revive debates about surveillance in places with long histories of abuses. The countries whose citizenries were most opposed to American mass surveillance were those whose governments had most cooperated with it, from the Five Eyes nations (especially the UK, whose GCHQ remains the NSA's primary partner) to nations of the European Union. Germany, which has done much to reckon with its

Nazi and Communist past, provides the primary example of this disjunction. Its citizens and legislators were appalled to learn that the NSA was surveilling German communications and had even targeted Chancellor Angela Merkel's smartphone. At the same time, the BND, Germany's premier intelligence agency, had collaborated with the NSA in numerous operations, even carrying out certain proxy surveillance initiatives that the NSA was unable or unwilling to undertake on its own.

Nearly every country in the world found itself in a similar bind: its citizens outraged, its government complicit. Any elected government that relies on surveillance to maintain control of a citizenry that regards surveillance as anathema to democracy has effectively ceased to be a democracy. Such cognitive dissonance on a geopolitical scale has helped to bring individual privacy concerns back into the international dialogue within the context of human rights.

For the first time since the end of World War II, liberal democratic governments throughout the world were discussing privacy as the natural, inborn right of every man, woman, and child. In doing so they were harking back to the 1948 UN Universal Declaration of Human Rights, whose Article 12 states: "No one shall be subjected to arbitrary interference with his privacy, family, home or correspondence, nor to attacks upon his honor and reputation. Everyone has the right to the protection of the law against such interference or attacks." Like all UN declarations, this aspirational document was never enforceable, but it had been intended to inculcate a new basis for transnational civil liberties in a world that had just survived nuclear atrocities and attempted genocides and was facing an unprecedented surfeit of refugees and the stateless.

The EU, still under the sway of this postwar universalist idealism, now became the first transnational body to put these principles into practice, establishing a new directive that seeks to standardize whistleblower protections across its member states, along with a standardized legal framework for privacy protection. In 2016, the EU Parliament passed the General Data Protection Regulation (GDPR), the most significant effort yet made to forestall the incursions of technological hegemony—which the EU tends to regard, not unfairly, as an extension of American hegemony.

The GDPR treats the citizens of the European Union, whom it calls "natural persons," as also being "data subjects"—that is, people who generate personally identifiable data. In the US, data is usually regarded as the property of whoever collects it. But the EU posits data as the property of the person it represents, which allows it to treat our data subjecthood as deserving of civil liberties protections.

The GDPR is undoubtedly a major legal advance, but even its transnationalism is too parochial: the Internet is global. Our natural personhood will never be legally synonymous with our data subjecthood, not least because the former lives in one place at a time while the latter lives in many places simultaneously.

Today, no matter who you are, or where you are, bodily, physically, you are also elsewhere, abroad—multiple selves wandering along the signal paths, with no country to call your own, and yet beholden to the laws of every country through which you pass. The records of a life lived in Geneva dwell in the Beltway. The photos of a wedding in Tokyo are on a honeymoon in Sydney. The videos of a funeral in Varanasi are up on Apple's iCloud, which is partially located in my home state of North Carolina and partially scattered across the partner servers of Amazon, Google, Microsoft, and Oracle, throughout the EU, UK, South Korea, Singapore, Taiwan, and China.

Our data wanders far and wide. Our data wanders endlessly.

We start generating this data before we are born, when technologies detect us in utero, and our data will continue to proliferate even after we die. Of course, our consciously created memories, the records that we choose to keep, comprise just a sliver of the information that has been wrung out of our lives—most of it unconsciously, or without our consent—by business and government surveillance. We are the first people in the history of the planet for whom this is true, the first people to be burdened with data immortality, the fact that our collected records might have an eternal existence. This is why we have a special duty. We must ensure that these records of our pasts can't be turned against us, or turned against our children.

Today, the liberty that we call privacy is being championed by a new generation. Not yet born on 9/11, they have spent their entire lives under the omnipresent specter of this surveillance. These young people who have known no other world have dedicated themselves to imagining one, and it's their political creativity and technological ingenuity that give me hope.

Still, if we don't act to reclaim our data now, our children might not be able to do so. Then they, and their children, will be trapped too—each successive generation forced to live under the data specter of the previous one, subject to a mass aggregation of information whose potential for societal control and human manipulation exceeds not just the restraints of the law but the limits of the imagination.

Who among us can predict the future? Who would dare to? The answer to the first question is no one, really, and the answer to the second is everyone, especially every government and business on the planet. This is what that data of ours is used for. Algorithms analyze it for patterns of established behavior in order to extrapolate behaviors to come, a type of digital prophecy that's only slightly more accurate than analog methods like palm reading. Once you go digging into the actual technical mechanisms by which predictability is calculated, you come to understand that its science is, in fact, anti-scientific, and fatally misnamed: predictability is actually manipulation. A website that tells you that because you liked this book you might also like books by James Clapper or Michael Hayden isn't offering an educated guess as much as a mechanism of subtle coercion.

We can't allow ourselves to be used in this way, to be used against the future. We can't permit our data to be used to sell us the very things that must not be sold, such as journalism. If we do, the journalism we get will be merely the journalism we want, or the journalism that the powerful want us to have, not the honest collective conversation that's necessary. We can't let the god-like surveillance we're under be used to "calculate" our citizenship scores, or to "predict" our criminal activity; to tell us what kind of education we can have, or what kind of job we can have, or whether we can have an education or a job at all; to discriminate against us based on our financial, legal, and medical histories, not to mention our ethnicity or race, which are constructs that data often assumes or imposes. And as for our most intimate data, our genetic information: if we allow it to be used to identify us, then it will be used to victimize us, even to modify us—to remake the very essence of our humanity in the image of the technology that seeks its control.

Of course, all of the above has already happened.

EXILE: NOT A day has passed since August 1, 2013, in which I don't recall that "exile" was what my teenage self used to call getting booted off-line. The Wi-Fi died? Exile. I'm out of signal range? Exile. The self who used to say that now seems so young to me. He seems so distant.

When people ask me what my life is like now, I tend to answer that it's a lot like theirs in that I spend a lot of time in front of the computer—reading, writing, interacting. From what the press likes to describe as an "undisclosed location"—which is really just whatever two-bedroom apartment in Moscow I happen to be renting—I beam myself onto stages around the world, speaking about the protection of civil liberties in the digital age to audiences of students, scholars, lawmakers, and technologists.

Some days I take virtual meetings with my fellow board members at the Freedom of the Press Foundation, or talk with my European legal team, led by Wolfgang Kaleck, at the European Center for Constitutional and Human Rights. Other days, I just pick up some Burger King—I know where my loyalties lie—and play games I have to pirate because I can no longer use credit cards. One fixture of my existence is my daily check-in with my

American lawyer, confidant, and all-around consigliere Ben Wizner at the ACLU, who has been my guide to the world as it is and puts up with my musings about the world as it should be.

That's my life. It got significantly brighter during the freezing winter of 2014, when Lindsay came to visit—the first time I'd seen her since Hawaii. I tried not to expect too much, because I knew I didn't deserve the chance; the only thing I deserved was a slap in the face. But when I opened the door, she placed her hand on my cheek and I told her I loved her.

"Hush," she said, "I know."

We held each other in silence, each breath like a pledge to make up for lost time.

From that moment, my world was hers. Previously, I'd been content to hang around indoors—indeed, that was my preference before I was in Russia—but Lindsay was insistent: she'd never been to Russia and now we were going to be tourists together.

My Russian lawyer, Anatoly Kucherena, who helped me get asylum in the country—he was the only lawyer who had the foresight to show up at the airport with a translator—is a cultured and resourceful man, and he proved as adept at obtaining last-minute tickets to the opera as he is at navigating my legal issues. He helped arrange two box seats at the Bolshoi Theater, so Lindsay and I got dressed and went, though I have to admit I was wary. There were so many people, all packed so tightly into a hall. Lindsay could sense my growing unease. As the lights dimmed and the curtain rose, she leaned over, nudged me in the ribs, and whispered, "None of these people are here for you. They're here for this."

Lindsay and I also spent time at some of Moscow's museums. The Tretyakov Gallery contains one of the world's richest collection of Russian Orthodox icon paintings. The artists who made these paintings for the Church were essentially contractors, I thought, and so were typically not allowed to sign their names to their handiwork, or preferred not to. The time and tradition that fostered these works was not given much to recognizing individual achievement. As Lindsay and I stood in front of one of the icons, a young tourist, a teenage girl, suddenly stepped between us. This wasn't the first time I was recognized in public, but given Lindsay's presence, it certainly threatened to be the most headline-worthy. In German-accented English, the girl asked whether she could take a selfie with us. I'm not sure what explains my reaction—maybe it was this German girl's shy and polite way of asking, or maybe it was Lindsay's always mood-improving, live-and-let-live presence—but without hesitation, for once, I agreed. Lindsay smiled as the girl posed between us and took a photo. Then, after a few sweet words of support, she departed.

I dragged Lindsay out of the museum a moment later. I was afraid that if the girl posted the photo to social media we could be just minutes away from unwanted attention. I feel foolish now for thinking that. I kept nervously checking online, but the photo didn't appear. Not that day, and not the day after. As far as I can tell, it was never shared—just kept as a private memory of a personal moment.

WHENEVER I GO outside, I try to change my appearance a bit. Maybe I get rid of my beard, maybe I wear different glasses. I never liked the cold until I realized that a hat and scarf provide the world's most convenient and inconspicuous anonymity. I change the rhythm and pace of my walk, and, contrary to the sage advice of my mother, I look away from traffic when crossing the street, which is why I've never been caught on any of the car dashcams that are ubiquitous here. Passing buildings equipped with CCTV I keep my head down, so that no one will see me as I'm usually seen online—head-on. I used to worry about the bus and metro, but nowadays everybody's too busy staring at their phones to give me a second glance. If I take a cab, I'll have it pick me up at a bus or metro stop a few blocks away from where I live and drop me off at an address a few blocks away from where I'm going.

Today, I'm taking the long way around this vast strange city, trying to find some roses. Red roses, white roses, even blue violets.

Any flowers I can find. I don't know the Russian names of any of them. I just grunt and point.

Lindsay's Russian is better than mine. She also laughs more easily and is more patient and generous and kind.

Tonight, we're celebrating our anniversary. Lindsay moved out here three years ago, and two years ago today, we married.

ACKNOWLEDGMENTS

In May 2013, as I sat in that hotel room in Hong Kong wondering whether any journalists would show up to meet me, I'd never felt more alone. Six years later, I find myself in quite the opposite situation, having been welcomed into an extraordinary and ever-expanding global tribe of journalists, lawyers, technologists, and human rights advocates to whom I owe an incalculable debt. At the conclusion of a book, it's traditional for an author to thank the people who helped make the book possible, and I certainly intend to do that here, but given the circumstances I'd be remiss if I didn't also thank the people who have helped make my life possible—by advocating for my freedom and, especially, by working ceaselessly and selflessly to protect our open societies as well as the technologies that have brought us, and that bring everyone, together.

Over the last nine months, Joshua Cohen has taken me to writing school, helping to transform my rambling reminiscences and capsule manifestos into a book that I hope he can be proud of.

Chris Parris-Lamb proved himself a shrewd and patient agent, while Sam Nicholson provided astute and clarifying edits and support, as did the entire team at Metropolitan, from Gillian Blake to Sara Bershtel, Riva Hocherman, and Grigory Tovbis.

The success of this team is a testament to its members' talents, and to the talents of the man who assembled it—Ben Wizner, my lawyer, and, I am honored to say, my friend.

In the same vein, I'd like to thank my international team of lawyers who have worked tirelessly to keep me free. I would also like to thank Anthony Romero, the ACLU's director, who embraced my cause at a time of considerable political risk for the organization, along with the other ACLU staff who have helped me throughout the years, including Bennett Stein, Nicola Morrow, Noa Yachot, and Daniel Kahn Gillmor.

Additionally, I'd like to acknowledge the work of Bob Walker, Jan Tavitian, and their team at the American Program Bureau, who have allowed me to make a living by spreading my message to new audiences around the world.

Trevor Timm and my fellow board members at the Freedom of the Press Foundation have provided the space and resources for me to return to my true passion, engineering for social good. I am especially grateful to our CTO Micah Lee, former FPF operations manager Emmanuel Morales, and current FPF board member Daniel Ellsberg, who has given the world the model of his rectitude, and given me the warmth and candor of his friendship.

This book was written using free and open-source software. I would like to thank the Qubes Project, the Tor Project, and the Free Software Foundation.

My earliest intimations of what it was like to write against deadline came from the masters, Glenn Greenwald, Laura Poitras, Ewen Macaskill, and Bart Gellman, whose professionalism is informed by a passionate integrity. Having been edited now myself, I have gained a new appreciation of their editors, who refused to be intimidated and took the risks that gave meaning to their principles.

My deepest gratitude is reserved for Sarah Harrison.

And my heart belongs to my family, extended and immediate—to my father, Lon, to my mother, Wendy, and to my brilliant sister, Jessica.

The only way I can end this book is the way I began it: with a dedication to Lindsay, whose love makes life out of exile.